WAVE MAKING

Inspired By Impact

Copyright © 2024 David Evans Shaw

All rights reserved. No part of this publication may be reproduced, distributed, or transmitted in any form or by any means without the prior written permission of the author.

To wavemakers, disruptors, visionaries, explorers, champions of change, and high-impact leaders of all kinds, including family, friends and colleagues. With deep gratitude for those who have inspired me, and with hope that this book will bolster conviction for seeking fulfillment through spiritually inspired work that contributes to a better world.

– David Shaw

Author, David Evans Shaw

All Photos and Images provided by David Evans Shaw

Wave Images on Part I, II, & III created using DALL-E

Design by G. Blake Jones

Watch Dozens of Short Films Relevant to Wave Making

To YouTube

To Website

About the Author:
David Evans Shaw

A prominent American business and social entrepreneur with extensive global leadership experience in science-based companies, investment management and social impact NGOs, David Shaw has helped build more than a dozen successful technology companies as a CEO, board member or investor. These companies, harness modern science to address important needs in healthcare and other markets.

Shaw's career has included extensive public service in science, arts, conservation and public policy. His public and private advocacy has included leadership roles with The Jackson Laboratory, the American Association for the Advancement of Science, the National Park Foundation, Young Presidents Organization (YPO), Harvard's John F. Kennedy School of Government, the MIT Media Lab, Nautilus Media, Waterbear Media, National Geographic Impact Story Lab, the US Olympic and Paralympic Museum, the Sargasso Sea Alliance and Aspen High Seas Initiative, the International Union for the Conservation of Nature, the San Diego Zoo and Wildlife Alliance, Ocean Elders, Shaw Innovation Fellows, Second Century Stewardship, Maine Medical Center, Discoveråy Communications and Curiosity Stream, The Explorers Club, the Council on Foreign Relations, the Service Year Alliance, Venrock Associates, Arctaris Impact Fund, Just Capital, Polaris Venture Partners, Sustainable Harvest International, the Telluride Science and Research Center, Saildrone, Modern Meadow, Mind Up, and others.

Shaw has been awarded six honorary degrees, and is the recipient of other honors including induction into the Teddy Roosevelt Society, International SeaKeeper of Year, Blue Ocean Festival Wavemaker, Life Science Foundation Biotech Hall of Fame, honoree New York Restoration Project, & UNH Entrepreneurship Hall of Fame.

He supports his advocacy interests with the production of documentary films and is a resident of the State of Maine along with his children and 12 grandchildren.

*"Catch the trade winds in your sails.
Explore. Dream. Discover."*
– Attributed to Mark Twain

Preface

In this age of extraordinary new knowledge creation and opportunity, amidst vast oceans of media and cyclones of change, it can be challenging to stay focused on issues that matter and navigate to a sense of clarity and meaning. For those of us who grew up in a world with rotary dial telephones, decades before the first personal computer, the journey borders on science fiction.

Our individual and collective quests for happiness, purpose, and significance can be confounded by unprecedented complexity, like untangling a slinky in the dark. Yet we all have the potential to lead purposeful, fulfilling, and impactful lives. Evolution has endowed humans with brains that reward us with positive emotions from our choices that yield achievement, belonging, greater purpose, and a positive impact on the world. We can hold the reins of our adventurous journeys to make a dent in the universe. This requires the capacity to transform struggles into opportunity, turning life's lemons into celebratory lemonade, and transforming stormy seas into worthy surfing opportunities.

I invite you to view life experiences chronicled in this book as a humble attempt to share inspirations from my life, just as others have shared their wisdom and experiences with me. The intention of these writings is more about raising thought-provoking questions for lively debate, than providing answers or suggesting ways of thinking. As we all search for personally meaningful purpose and significant impact, I will have succeeded in my goal with this book if it helps others deal with these issues more wisely than I have.

David Evans Shaw

Table of Contents

Introduction...Pages i - xviii

PART ONE
CHALLENGE CONVENTION

Chapter One..Pages 1 - 18
Embrace the Benefits of Struggles

Chapter Two...Pages 19 - 32
Challenge the Status Quo

Chapter Three..Pages 33 - 50
Forge Your Own Path

Chapter Four ....Pages 51 - 65
Cultivate Curiosity

Photo Reference Section............................. Pages 66 - 71

PART TWO
LIVE WITH INTENTION

Chapter Five...Pages 75 - 90
Build a High-Performance Tribe

Chapter Six ....Pages 91 - 104
Capitalize on Critical Thinking and Constructive Debate

Table of Contents

Chapter Seven... Pages 105 - 118
Nurture Resilience and Courage

Chapter Eight.. Pages 119 - 134
De-Risk Through Superb Planning

Chapter Nine .... Pages 135 - 142
Deliver on Promises

Chapter Ten... Pages 143 - 166
Keep the Mission and Vision Fresh

PART THREE
DO GOOD & PURSUE ADVENTURE

Chapter Eleven.. Pages 169 - 194
Be Bold

Chapter Twelve .... Pages 195 - 212
Harness the Power of Partnerships

Chapter Thirteen .... Pages 213 - 220
Seize and Savor Serendipity

Chapter Fourteen .... Pages 221 - 238
Be a Purpose-Driven Force for Good

Chapter Fifteen.. Pages 239 - 248
Never Abandon Optimism

Introduction

"Dare to begin."
– Attributed to W.E.B. Du Bois

The morning sun illuminated a spectacular landscape of volcanic peaks looming above us. Lush green mountains wreathed by puffy cumulus clouds punctuated a deep blue sky. In the company of armed guides, our group of seven hiked quietly in a single file tracing a narrow path through the dense jungle, slowly making our way to a destination high on the mountainside. After hours of arduous trekking, sometimes cutting a path through tangled vines with machetes, we reached an elevation of six thousand feet. I wondered if our efforts would be rewarded when we were startled by rustling sounds in the underbrush next to the trail. Suddenly, the massive head of a silverback gorilla emerged. We were being watched.

It was 2018, and I had journeyed from my seaside home on the coast of Maine to northern Rwanda to fulfill an enduring dream of observing mountain gorillas in the wild. These great apes are Earth's largest primates and one of humans' closest relatives, with whom we share 98 percent of our DNA. They are some of our planet's most celebrated, magnificent, and critically endangered creatures. Roughly a thousand remain in the wild. This represents a very encouraging recovery from a near-extinction low level of just several hundred gorillas in the 1980s. At a time of immense global challenges to our natural world, I have engaged in high-impact conservation globally and was eager to explore opportunities for activism here.

Even after imagining this moment many times, I was still not prepared for the thrill of the silverback's imposing presence. His expressive, obsidian face, with its intelligent eyes, gleamed a mixture of curiosity, wariness, and inner wisdom. These human-like features created a sense of kinship, and it was tempting to try to establish a rapport with this magnificent creature. But I was wary of too much eye contact, knowing that some animals perceive staring as a threat.

This dominant male, weighing north of 350 pounds, radiated immense power and quiet dignity. Named Santo by the guides, he seemed the master of his domain as he munched on wild celery and delicate bamboo shoots. We continued our trek and soon came upon a large gorilla family, including a mother lazing on her back in the sun, and gently cuddling two bright-eyed mischievous youngsters. The tenderness of this scene, juxtaposed with the powerful presence of these creatures and the dramatic setting, was striking. Our long journey had been richly rewarded.

It was an extraordinary privilege to enter the private world of these great apes. A lifetime of adventure, exploration, and stewardship of the natural world has taken me from Antarctica to the Arctic, from the Earth's highest peaks to the depths of the ocean floor. Yet this afternoon ranks as one of the most affecting experiences of my life.

Introduction

And there was more to come.

As shadows lengthened and our Jeeps pulled up to picturesque Virunga Lodge, security gates opened, and a lively group of drummers greeted us with a symphony of vibrant beats and rhythms. "Mister Shaw," someone called out to me, "Doctor Mike wants to see you!"

"Who is Dr. Mike? And what is this about?" I asked, perplexed.

"Please come, he will explain."

"The sound of drums faded as he led me through the lodge into a charming lounge. The moment we entered the room, a middle-aged man with a beard and mustache jumped to his feet and walked toward us, his hand outstretched. "This is a special occasion for me," he said with an American accent, smiling broadly. "My name is Michael Cranfield. I am the chief veterinarian with Gorilla Doctors in Africa. It's an honor to host you here." Appreciative, but puzzled, I asked if we knew each other.

with Mike Cranfield

"Our group is affiliated with the School of Veterinary Medicine at the University of California in Davis, and I've attended your lectures there" he explained. "Here in Rwanda, we provide medical care for the gorillas and your diagnostic products play a critical role in that care. We go up to the mountains, take blood samples, and test them with your equipment. This helps us quickly and accurately identify health issues such as respiratory infections that we can treat with antibiotics. The gorillas benefit greatly from this."

Suddenly the connection was clear to me, and this indeed was a special occasion. We ordered cocktails and were soon engaged in deep conversation, like old friends.

It seemed barely possible to be almost 7,000 miles from home, connecting with an internationally renowned gorilla expert about the animal health company I had founded thirty-five years earlier. It was deeply gratifying. My original headquarters consisted of me, a rotary dial phone, and a desk on the top floor of my house in Portland, Maine. Today IDEXX, a publicly traded company, employs more than ten thousand people and is the world leader in veterinary diagnostics, with customers in more than 175 countries. Gorillas are just a handful of the multitudes whom IDEXX helps every day. This and other impact work in the stewardship of nature is a source of great fulfillment for me and my colleagues.

After several more days of magnificent hiking and wildlife experiences, including immersive time with a troupe of golden monkeys, it was time to depart Rwanda and return home.

To support Dr. Mike and the Gorilla Doctors, I made a short film of our expedition. In June 2019, he joined me on stage at The Explorers Club headquarters in New York City to highlight this remarkable success story in wildlife conservation. Events of this kind can serve as impactful inspiration for club members, who number more than 3,500 globally and include many of the world's

Introduction

leading explorers … ranging from astronauts and mountaineers to marine scientists and others. As a National Fellow of The Explorers Club, I've been very active in our programs including a leadership role in presentations for United Nations World Wildlife Day and UN World Oceans Day. For our 2017 Explorers Club Annual Dinner on Ellis Island in New York Harbor, I engaged my friend Robert DeNiro to be a keynote speaker. He shared his views about the importance of exploration including its impact on personal growth saying, among other things: "I think that all of us are looking for the balance between who we are and who we could be."

That same evening, famed explorer Ranulph Fiennes also made remarks about his extraordinary adventures that led the Guinness Book of World Records to name him "the world's greatest living explorer." It was a treat to be reunited with Ran years after a memorable visit with him at the famous Ngorongoro Crater World Heritage Site in Tanzania, Africa.

with Robert DeNiro and Ranulph Fiennes

Wave Making : Inspired By Impact

***

Growing up in the mill town of Nashua, New Hampshire, in the crucible of the 1960s, the prospect of becoming a prominent entrepreneur and explorer seemed implausible, much less starting a global enterprise such as IDEXX that would give me an instant connection to a place as remote as the mountains of East Africa. However, my decision to devote myself over five decades to harnessing the power of science and new technology to benefit the world has led to many such serendipitous situations.

Besides producing new generations of veterinary and human diagnostic systems, my business colleagues and I have commercialized lifesaving and life-changing biopharmaceutical products, novel medical devices, tests for rapid detection of water contamination, bio-based substitutes for high-end leather, and versatile new biopolymers. I have supported carbon capture systems and wind-powered drones that map the oceans, including shifting weather patterns, in real-time. I have helped build impact media companies, diagnostic and biopharmaceutical businesses, and material science innovators, as well as sustainable agriculture. These ventures and others reflect my belief in science not just as a body of knowledge, but also, more importantly, as an evidence-based approach to seeking truth and understanding.

Great teamwork and inspired collaboration have been important success factors. It's been remarkably fulfilling to work successfully on high-impact teams with shared values and collective purpose in a wide range of exhilarating endeavors. I have been fortunate to be involved in some of the most consequential issues of our times, such as collaborating on ocean health and stewardship projects with marine scientist Sylvia Earle, Prince Albert II of Monaco, Queen Noor of Jordan, Jean-Michel Cousteau, and others.

At a time when modern science plays a transformational

Introduction

role in society via unprecedented overlapping revolutions in the atom, the byte, and the gene, it's been an honor to play leadership roles in outstanding science and technology institutions.

As chair of The Jackson Laboratory working with fellow trustees such as Princeton University President Emerita Shirley Tilghman and MIT Broad Institute Founding Director Eric Lander, I've had a front-row seat in modern genetic science, one of the great technological revolutions in history.

As a Patron of Nature at the International Union for Conservation of Nature (IUCN), working with friends and fellow Patrons such as Jane Goodall, Gregory Carr, Prince Carl Philip of Sweden, Frank Mars, and Japanese conservationists Soichiro and Reiko Fukutake, it has been a privilege to contribute to our mission as the leading global authority on the status of the natural world and the measures needed to safeguard it. My work in wildlife conservation has continued via my advisory role with the San Diego Zoo and Wildlife Alliance, my role as an Ocean Elder, and advisor to the Impact Story Lab at the National Geographic Society. As a presidentially appointed trustee of the National Park Foundation, it was a great honor to play a leadership role in the 2016 US National Park Centennial, to be inducted into the Teddy Roosevelt Society, and to launch science programs to improve park stewardship. A centennial campaign that I helped design got billions of media impressions as people shared their park experiences with each other on social media using the hashtag phrase: #findyourpark.

From my experience as Treasurer of the American Association for the Advancement of Science (AAAS), the world's largest general science society, it has been exhilarating to work with brilliant people including AAAS president Alan Leshner and former MIT president Susan Hockfield, on consequential scientific issues ranging from public policy, research priorities and funding, to communication, and education. One example of

AAAS accomplishments occurred in 2014 when a mission with our scientific counterparts in Cuba contributed to the historic reopening of diplomatic relations between the United States and Cuba in 2015.

Because IDEXX is a leading global animal health company, it's common for people to assume that the company was founded based on special knowledge of veterinary medicine or animals. A more accurate story is that it was founded due to my fascination with the world of science-based entrepreneurship. This inspired me to create a highly compelling venture that embraced some of the distinctive cultural values that characterized my formative years in the 1960s. It was a time of adventurousness and exploration including the Apollo 11 moon landing, and an expedition led by Navy Lt. Don Walsh to the deepest depths of the oceans, the Challenger Deep in the Mariana Trench. The 1960s were also a time of rebellion, counterculture, new media, and civic activism for civil rights, peace, women's liberation, the environment, and other causes.

The sixties gave many in my generation a sense of open-ended possibility. I created IDEXX to be spiritually inspired by my work, to build an enduring great organization, and to demonstrate that world-class modern science-based businesses could thrive in Maine. I realized that becoming an entrepreneur would give me an opportunity to work with a tribe of like-minded mission-driven team members. We would share the purpose of expressing "what great looks like" in our work, disrupting the status quo, and challenging conventional thinking to unlock exceptional long-term value. We would share the belief that "good" is often the enemy of "great". Looking back, it's clear that many achievements came from the decision to embrace the identity of an impact-seeking wavemaker. A top priority was to harness the energy and the superpowers of a highly talented, purpose-driven team to have a significant and positive impact on the world. Productive change

Introduction

often involves "rocking the boat", so we embraced courage and the capability to create waves as powerful determinants for success.

**

In the early 1980s, the immense power of modern science began to fascinate me; it was and is the most powerful transformative force of our times. I was inspired by the idea of putting this power to work to benefit the world and to build great organizations inspired by that vision. John Naisbitt's pathfinding book, *Megatrends*, which predicted a bright economic future at the dawn of the Information Age, seemed permanently parked at the top of the bestseller list. His perspective that knowledge of underlying megatrends could improve important life decisions was captivating. Thanks to the work performed for my clients, I also had a front-row seat to observe seismic changes that were shifting the tectonic plates of the world as we knew it. These included advances occurring in molecular biology, computers, software, medical devices, biotech, genetics, and microelectronics. It seemed clear that there were highly attractive opportunities to harness combinations of these revolutionary technologies to create gamechanging impacts in the medical technology world. There were great waves to be surfed. The Beach Boys captured this spirit in their hit song: "Catch a Wave and You're Sitting on Top of the World".

Armed with my first "laptop" computer, the size of a sewing machine, and using skills developed as a strategy consultant, I began to explore a broad landscape of potential ventures that might meet my criteria for attractiveness and competitiveness. An important starting point was the development of a comprehensive list of prospective fields, ranging from plant and animal genetics to human and veterinary pharmaceuticals, medical devices, nutritional products, and others. Then each opportunity area was evaluated. Where were the greatest unmet customer needs? What were the most attractive target markets in terms of size, growth, and other factors? How could a startup venture develop the competitive advantages to win as an insurgent battling established incumbents? In other words, what factors would influence our ability to be competitive and to become a global market leader? How could we assemble a world-class team and develop an innovative, high-performance culture to support our audacious goals?

I envisioned a company that could be the best in the world at its business, initially building a strategically important beachhead in niche markets and then expanding its scope globally. Even early in my career, it was apparent that there were very significant business and cultural advantages of being the best, of seizing the winner's circle. Vince Lombardi expressed the importance of winning this way: "Winning is not a sometime thing; it's an all-the-time thing. You don't win once in a while; you don't do things right once in a while; you do them right all of the time. Winning is a habit." And he added: "Winning isn't everything, it's the only thing." I was well aware of competitive advantages associated with market share leadership including economies of scale in research and development, manufacturing, marketing, and sales.

It would also be advantageous for the company to get to market quickly with initial products so that we could rapidly gain real-world experience and master a full range of business functions. This caused me to eliminate capital-intensive opportunities that required many years of expensive research and development to launch initial products. Another important success factor was to create a business model with high recurring revenues like subscription services. Gillette was an early role model for this by deriving far more revenue from razor blades than from the sale of razors.

Also on my manifesto: the company would be based in my home community of Portland, Maine rather than well-known high-density tech centers such as Boston or Silicon Valley.

Introduction

After graduating from college, I worked for the administration of Maine Governor James Longley and witnessed the decline of some traditional Maine industries including pulp and paper. There was considerable skepticism that Maine could be a home for an attractive new generation of tech companies, and I saw an opportunity to challenge that thinking with a successful venture and important lifestyle advantages.

As my matrix of prospective opportunities was analyzed and reanalyzed, one answer stood out: animal diagnostics. These are the tests performed on animals to detect diseases and monitor health in ways often similar to human diagnostics. In some cases the patients are companion animals such as dogs, cats and horses. In other cases, they are animals such as livestock and poultry raised for food.

My previous work had shown that this was a multibillion-dollar market, and existing diagnostics were often cumbersome, slow, and unreliable. For pets, it was rare for veterinary clinics to have the kind of in-house diagnostic capabilities of many human medical offices, so samples were routinely sent out to diagnostic labs, impacting optimal patient care. For foodproducing animals, there was a similar need for higher accuracy and convenience. A false positive could result in the unnecessary destruction of a healthy herd or flock, or cause a pet to undergo needless treatment. A false negative could put a pet's health at risk, or allow disease to spread and potentially touch off a public health crisis in the global food chain.

We envisioned that a new generation of fast, accurate, and easy-to-use tests could create outstanding value in the world and be the basis for building an enduring, great enterprise.

Already, advances in biotechnology and medical device technology had begun to revolutionize human diagnostics. With the launch of the home pregnancy test in the late 1970s, for instance, women could learn whether they were pregnant in a couple of hours. Today, of course, it is a matter of minutes. Similar advances had transformed the ability to detect infectious diseases and monitor health issues of many kinds.

Veterinary diagnostics, considered a backwater compared to human diagnostics, was an overlooked and underserved market. This created an opportunity for disruptive thinking, with better insights and knowledge to transcend conventional beliefs.

So, I resolved to build a company that would revolutionize veterinary diagnostics, often employing technology that had already been shown to be effective in human medicine. We would be operating in a field where there was little of the kind of insurance reimbursement that pays for human health procedures, so the value proposition to customers would have to take that into account. We would also have lower regulatory complexity and fewer concerns about patient privacy issues. Most of our products in the United States would be regulated by the US Department of Agriculture rather than the Food and Drug Administration.

The name IDEXX was derived from the term: immunodiagnostics. "Immuno" refers to the immunochemistry technology frequently used in diagnostic tests. It is based on the specific recognition and binding capability of immune system proteins called antibodies. "DX" is a common abbreviation for "diagnostic" just as "RX" is an abbreviation for "prescription". The double XXs signified our intention to be at least twice as successful as our closest competitors. A business plan was taking shape. Now financing was needed to help fan this spark into a flame ... to transform a dream into reality.

***

Introduction

This is a book about what inspired me to seek an adventurous life of meaning and purpose including my experience with IDEXX and more than a dozen other highly fulfilling ventures in business and social entrepreneurship. The book is also a wholehearted tribute to the amazing people I've worked with on these ventures. I have been a fortunate beneficiary of inspiration via experiences shared with me by others. My intention here is to reciprocate that sharing with the hope that others will benefit via encouragement and guidance on their personal quests for impact, fulfillment, and greater purpose.

Wave Making has been built around a set of personal principles that have served me well: understand the value of challenging convention and always asking "what does great look like"; live with intention; pursue adventure; and be a force for good. By the latter, I mean measuring success by your own inner scorecard and metrics of significance, not just by simply accepting traditional societal conventions and scorecards, such as financial gain, that can captivate us. Play the great game of happiness according to rules, rewards, and metrics that spiritually inspire you. Be fulfilled by the good you do: by "doing well by doing good." Modern neuroscience has helped us understand the biology of happiness associated with "doing good", showing that it is a powerful pathway for health and happiness. We all have the ability to achieve a "helper's high" via boosts in brain chemicals including oxytocin, dopamine, and serotonin.

To help illuminate my journey of innovative activism, each chapter centers around a different theme–cultivating the vision to spot opportunities, lowering risk by deconstructing it, tailoring your leadership style to best serve circumstances, recognizing the enduring value of struggle, building a purpose-driven tribe, and delivering on promises –to name a few.

An important motivation for me, like some of my most

admired role models, is to benefit from a life of adventurous exploration and discovery. Throughout human history, this desire has been celebrated as an admirable and essential element of the human spirit, supported by our brain's neurochemical reward system. Ancient Greek societies urged victorious Olympic athletes never to rest on their laurels. Apollo 8 Commander Frank Borman called exploration "the essence of the human spirit". My friend and remarkable explorer Kathryn Sullivan, former Administrator of NOAA, is the only woman to have walked in space and descended to the lowest depths of Earth's oceans. She has said this about exploration: "I'm an explorer, and that doesn't always have to involve going to some remote or exotic place. It simply requires a commitment to put curiosity into action."

with Kathryn Sullivan

Curiosity and necessity have caused humans to explore our world geographically, scientifically, spiritually, and culturally. I admire people who constantly seek out what is great in other individuals and organizations, placing high value on integrity, authenticity, mastery, empathy, purpose, teamwork, or other admirable traits. With a belief that every life experience can be a

Introduction

launch pad for new and even better opportunities, I seek to stay on guard against complacency, with the belief that this is antithetical to wave-making, to living life to the fullest, and to achieving your full potential.

Another motivation for sharing my experiences is the prospect of benefiting young people who, early in life, often seek to understand and challenge the conventional metrics for success and achievement in the world that they are growing into. It was clear early in life that I wasn't destined to be a top student measured by grade point average and test scores. Reflecting the spirit of the 1960s, it was inspirational to find heroes and role models who disdained and transcended established conventions, and who sought and achieved success measured in other less conformist and more personally fulfilling ways. For those adventurous souls, innovation, spiritual inspiration, persistence, and toughness can drive success and a big, fulfilling life … more powerfully for them than standardized, industrial age scorecards such as good grades and top test scores. This led to admiration for people who don't allow one-size-fits-all societal expectations to define their roadmaps in life. My own unorthodox personal journey is not something that my teachers would have envisioned. Yet it better reflects our current age of entrepreneurship and personalization, rather than the age of industrialization and standardization that began in the 19th century.

Human history is full of stories that demonstrate the importance of developing the personal fortitude and mindset to benefit from whatever life throws at you. Success often springs from doing things you love, and from growing a resilient and indomitable spirit that enables the conversion of struggles and disappointments to opportunities. And, the conversion of losses into lessons. For audacious entrepreneurial ventures, doubt and fear of failure are often a constant companion in a world of daunting challenges and extraordinarily high failure rates. Very visible success stories can lead to a different impression, but the reality of entrepreneurship is that great success is extraordinarily rare, and the path to success is full of epic challenges.

The audacity and adventurousness of entrepreneurship are both a source of high risk and extraordinary rewards – including the fulfillment of great achievement. High achievement can be attributed to many factors including hard work, persistence, personality, and human biology. The neuroscience of high achievement and successful attainment of goals is closely associated with the production and continued flow of the brain neurotransmitter dopamine. As a first-time entrepreneur at IDEXX, I was highly focused on building a world-class team to support our big ambitions. We all realized that this kind of high-performance team would best thrive in an environment that supported great business practices, personal growth, appreciation, teamwork, collaboration, emotional intelligence, mastery, innovation, playfulness... and FUN. From observing other successful organizations, and from my days of factory work, I knew that we would all benefit from shaping a culture with a mindset of discovery, that blurred the distinction between work and play. We would best achieve our full potential and unlock higher levels of success if we were very substantively doing what we loved, versus simply thinking of IDEXX as a source of employment. This mindset was captured by Mark Twain when he reportedly said: "work and play are words used to describe the same thing under differing conditions". The creation of those conditions is largely a matter of choice. Twain added: "I don't like work even when someone else is doing it."

From the start, our mission statement declared that we would make IDEXX a great company for employees, customers, and other stakeholders. In fact, we largely replaced the word "employee" with the term "IDEXXer" to reflect a sense of belonging to a tribe versus "working for the man". We were "making waves" not just about WHAT we did, but also about WHO we were…, viewing "work" through a new lens, confronting the opportunity to leave behind some old beliefs about the traditional concept of work and hierarchical employment. The result for many was a sense of flow, a calling, working from the heart, belonging to a tribe, working in a high-trust collaborative community, and embracing the gratification of fulfilling avocation. We operated with the belief that the sense of belonging is a powerful human need, contributing significantly to health, well-being, and performance. Production levels of the neurochemical oxytocin are triggered by "belongingness" with resulting mood and health benefits.

Ventures of this kind can become an "all-in" experience with full absorption and intensity that results in long workdays, long workweeks, and immersive fulfillment. Hardworking actor and comedian Bill Murray showed appreciation for this level of commitment when he is credited with saying: "Whatever you do, always give 100%. Unless you're donating blood."

As we crafted the corporate culture around these themes, we conceived of strategies to ensure that individuals and teams felt the social electricity of our collective mission, and took adequate time from work for the kind of restorative and regenerative breaks that support personal well-being and high performance. These included whitewater rafting trips, hiking in nearby mountains, epic parties and celebrations, Outward Bound programs, and extended "personal growth leaves."

An important source of renewal for me is being in nature and being physically challenged. The outdoors has been nourishment for my soul and well-being since my earliest childhood when we lived in a rural area on the outskirts of Nashua, New Hampshire. My siblings and I attended a nearby YMCA summer camp that offered many outdoor experiences and the independence of being away from home. Around our house, we spent our childhoods riding our bikes, climbing trees, and roaming free. Our parents had little need to be concerned for our whereabouts until we came in through the kitchen door at dinner time. We joined neighborhood sports and sometimes snuck under a chain-link fence into a gorgeous spot whose purpose was to supply the water for the region. But to us, it was the best private water park, where we splashed in the springs, went through the waterfalls in inner tubes, and dared one another to cross the huge ravines walking on slippery log bridges. This watery paradise yielded many happy memories of independence, discovery and free play in my childhood.

As an adult, adventures in remote seascapes and landscapes have offered the added advantage of unplugging from technology. When hiking or sailing, and disconnected from the digital world, my brain is often not consciously focused on work although these can be moments when important new ideas emerge. Modern neuroscience has demonstrated the benefit of unplugging and getting off the grid, and we should all keep this in mind for our well-being.

This book shares the habits and attitudes that have shaped my life, with the intention of benefitting people who seek adventurous lives, set audacious goals, open the aperture of opportunity, stretch themselves, and seek significant impact. For those of us who purposely seek new experiences, who hear different drummers, and who sometimes zig when others zag, it can be deeply gratifying to regularly start new chapters, and continuously expand the scope of our experiences.

Part One
I
CHALLENGE CONVENTION

Chapter One
Embrace the Benefits of Struggles

"A smooth sea never made a skilled sailor."
– Attributed to Franklin D. Roosevelt

As a young boy, I loved reading biographies about adventurous scientists, explorers, and athletes. No matter whose story was being told, the theme was usually the same: transforming adversity into opportunity and impact. French chemist and microbiologist Louis Pasteur was criticized because he disproved the idea of spontaneous generation–the long-held and widely accepted theory that living organisms could grow out of nonliving matter. Refusing to bow to his critics, he went on to become known as the father of bacteriology and the inventor of pasteurization, the process of using heat to destroy pathogenic microorganisms in food and beverages like milk.

Similarly, Nobel Prize laureate Marie Curie's relentless resolve and insatiable curiosity made her an icon in the world of science. She transformed our understanding of radioactivity and championed the use of radiation in medicine. Her inspirational mindset is reflected in this quote: "We must believe that we are gifted for something, and that this thing must be attained." And: "Nothing in life is to be feared; it is only to be understood."

After Antarctic explorer Sir Ernest Shackleton's ship, the *HMS Endurance*, was crushed by ice and sank on its ill-fated 1914 expedition, he and his men survived on penguins and dog meat from their own pack before Shackleton and six men mounted a daring journey across the famously tempestuous Southern Ocean in a twenty-three-foot open boat to find help. The seventeen-day ordeal of navigating through icy waters and massive waves is considered one of the greatest survival stories in human history. Twenty grueling months after first setting sail from South Georgia Island, Shackleton astounded the world by returning all twenty-seven of his men to safety. In 2022 my friend and renowned marine archeologist Mensun Bound led a team that found Shackleton's vessel Endurance 3000 meters deep in Antarctica's Weddell Sea. Two years earlier, I had spent several weeks in the Antarctic celebrating the bicentennial of its discovery. I am now supporting a program with Mensun and others to inspire young explorers with the Shackleton story, to help them "channel their inner Shackleton" consistent with his well-known saying: "by endurance we conquer."

Sir Ernest Shackleton and HMS Endurance

Closer to home, the story of Jim Thorpe, a great native American athlete, fascinated me. He won the decathlon and pentathlon medals at the 1912 Olympic Games in Stockholm, Sweden, although he was stripped of them the year after when it was revealed that he had earlier played semi-pro baseball. (His Olympic record was reinstated in 2022.) He went on to play professional baseball and football. He was also a standout as a boxer, swimmer, lacrosse, and basketball player. A member of the Sac and Fox nation who was born in what would become the state of Oklahoma, Thorpe faced prejudice as a Native American and later in his life contended with alcohol and financial issues, getting work as a security guard, a Hollywood bit player, and a ditch digger to make ends meet for his eight children. But he never gave up.

Chapter One - Embrace the Benefits of Struggles

George Washington's life provides another example of the transformative power of struggles and rebellion. As an awkward teenager, he chose to pursue a life in the military to propel his career. In his twenties, he served as a colonial militia leader and was involved in several instances of controversial leadership. One of these was a skirmish with French soldiers that contributed to the French & Indian War in the 1760s. Years later, when the Revolutionary War began, struggles had caused Washington, now in his forties, to mature into the remarkable leader who astonishingly defeated the powerful British Empire to gain independence for the United States.

Those stories illustrate the multidimensional character of struggles. They can be physical, financial, psychological, or intellectual. In my career, including the creation of IDEXX, I've contended with all of these, and have benefitted from transforming struggles into opportunity, knowledge, and wisdom.

***

I have a vivid memory of standing in front of the thirty-thousand-square-foot, long-vacant, pre-Civil War brick building just rented inexpensively on the Portland waterfront for my new company, AgriTech–later renamed IDEXX. It was May 1984, six months into singlehandedly managing complex and intense activities associated with all aspects of an ambitious startup. Five inspectors had arrived from the city's Department of Public Works to make sure the plumbing system was working properly, in compliance with local regulations.

A few days earlier, a representative of my new landlord had handed me a plot plan of the property so timeworn that it reminded me of a pirate's map. "We think this is the sewer pipe," he said, pointing to an almost indecipherable creased line in the middle of the paper. "It appears to show that it's connected to the

original headquarters for AgriTech / IDEXX

city waste-water system under the street." "I hope so," I answered, feeling more doubtful than I sounded.

To verify the connection, the inspectors poured green dye down the toilets and into the sinks. Then, they went outside, pried up several manhole covers, turned on their flashlights, and peered into the darkness. "Yup, yup, looks good to go," one said. The inspectors were getting back into their cars when one of them called out, "Hey, wait! Look out there!" A slick of green dye had spread across the white-capped waters of Casco Bay. "That's trouble," the supervisor announced. "Your plumbing connects directly to the ocean. You'll have to fix that to occupy this building."

Years later, when IDEXX was a global, multibillion-dollar public company, this kind of problem would have been a minor annoyance. But in these start-up days, it would be hard to find the ten thousand dollars it would cost to dig up the pavement and fix the plumbing. Full of concern about this disruption in our plans a local plumber came to the rescue. He cobbled together an inexpensive solution that pumped the water through our building up to the wastewater system at street level without having to dig up much pavement.

Our plumbing issue serves as a minor illustration of the

Chapter One - Embrace the Benefits of Struggles

culture of overcoming thousands of obstacles, small and large, that eventually resulted in a powerful company culture of problem-solving. Innovative and productive problem-solving builds successful organizational cultures of mental fortitude and agility. Learning to pivot, improvise and seek creative solutions to unexpected challenges are key success factors in business and life.

Today, reality shows like *Shark Tank* and stories of crowdfunding going viral can create the false impression that successful startups are common and even easy to create. So, it's not surprising that young entrepreneurs and aspiring change-makers sometimes solicit my suggestions for "the easy ways to get funding and create success" My answer often surprises them. "I understand why you're asking that," I tell them. "But that is probably the wrong question. Great things in life are often achieved via great struggles. The struggle is an important part of the success process, helping to reveal potential challenges. You shouldn't seek to avoid the learnings associated with struggles. So don't look for the easy fix. Look for the right way. Subject your plans and thinking to high levels of critical scrutiny from very experienced people. Invite them to stress test your plans and find flaws in your thinking. Then incorporate their suggestions to strengthen your venture."

This perspective about the beneficial role of struggling was reinforced recently by Jensen Huang, co-founder of semiconductor company NVIDIA, when he surprised Stanford University students by telling them "Greatness comes from character, and character isn't formed out of smart people, it's formed out of people who suffered. . . I wish upon you ample doses of pain and suffering." Author Robert Heinlein sent a similar message with this statement: "Don't handicap your children by making their lives easy."

Achieving greatness benefits from seeking candid peer review, and benchmarking your own capabilities against the most threatening competition. Olympic swimmers Katie Ledecky and

Michael Phelps, for example, did not win multiple gold medals by racing against Sunday afternoon swimmers. Instead, they trained intensely every day for *years* and tested themselves against the best athletes in the world.

I sought to employ this strategy in the launching of IDEXX. I envisioned an epic struggle ahead, pouring my heart, soul, and life savings - twenty-five thousand dollars - into my fledgling concept. So, it was important to partner with highly experienced, sophisticated investors who "know what great looks like." That is how discussions started with Venrock Associates, the Rockefeller family's famed venture capital firm.

I went to New York City, to their offices at 30 Rock, and, in these pre-cell-phone days, dialed Venrock headquarters from a pay phone on the street below. "I'm calling at the suggestion of Win Rockefeller to talk with Peter Crisp," I said, having met Win, the governor of Arkansas, in consulting work for his Winrock International organization. A Rockefeller family-owned poultry genetics business called Arbor Acres had also been a client. Although the receptionist told me that Crisp was not available, I decided to take the elevator to the 56th floor of 30 Rock and see if I could make any progress. Peter Crisp, who ran Venrock, is legendary for his remarkable track record, including his prophetic backing of Apple and Intel. However, at this first meeting, I wasn't aware of his reputation or even his exact position at Venrock.

This was years before 9/11. The security guards at the front desk did not demand identification or call upstairs to the office to see if I was expected. On the 56th floor, I was greeted by a wary-looking man at the front desk who seemed prepared to take on the role of bouncer. Years later as a partner at Venrock, with an office on this floor, I found that he was a retired FBI agent. "I'm sorry," he told me in a way that brooked no argument, "but we don't allow people in our offices without an appointment." Still hopeful,

Chapter One - Embrace the Benefits of Struggles

I told him that I had to go to LaGuardia Airport soon but was hoping to make a connection before I left.

After a long wait, the security guard handed me a phone and I was speaking with a slightly exasperated Peter Crisp. After underscoring the importance of making advance appointments he told me that he understood that I was going to LaGuardia Airport. "I'm going there too," he said. "If you'd like to ride with me, we can talk in the car." A few minutes later I climbed into the passenger seat of Peter's Volvo station wagon from a sidewalk beside the skating rink at Rockefeller Center. En route to the airport, I described my plan in what today would be called an elevator pitch.

When we pulled into LaGuardia, Peter turned to me. "Your venture sounds interesting. The next step would be to arrange a meeting with my colleague who handles our biotech investments," he said as he scribbled a name on the back of my airline ticket. At home the next day I called a well-connected friend on Wall Street and asked if he knew someone named Peter Crisp at Venrock. "He's the firm's legendary founder, with Laurence Rockefeller," my friend told me, "outstanding reputation, but nearly impossible to meet." When I explained the ride to LaGuardia, and exclaimed his surprise with this phrase: "bewildered as a bear in a ballet class." I have more to say about "serendipity" later in this book. More than 40 years later Peter Crisp and I are good friends.

with Peter Crisp

Months later Venrock agreed to lead our first investment round. They expressed appreciation for the analytical rigor of our plans, the quality of the proposed team, and the deep sense of conviction we demonstrated. It's important to say that the conviction of the leadership team, and their strong sense of ownership of the plan, plays a key role in venture capital financing and successful entrepreneurship. Ideally, the business plan is not primarily a promotional document to obtain financing. It is a plan developed by and for the team and shared with potential funding sources, that reflects rigorous thinking about how to succeed. This is the reason that a couple of years later, a pioneering Wall Street biotech analyst named Peter Drake was so enthusiastic about our plan. Peter, who went on to become a tremendously successful banker and investor, put his pen down and said he would back me fifteen minutes into my planned hour-long presentation for IDEXX. He described our meeting as the single best and most memorable of the 4,500 pitch meetings he sat through during his impressive career, which spanned two decades.

As soon as Venrock agreed to invest, we communicated this decision to other potential funding sources who we hoped would appreciate the value of participating in a funding syndicate led by a highly admired firm. It's wise in most financing situations to cultivate multiple sources of funding since the reliability of any single funding source isn't certain until closing. To ensure this optionality for the benefit of the first funding round at IDEXX, I was in discussions with multiple sources, only to find that they all knew each other and were discussing this funding round amongst themselves. Eventually, we all met at the Bank of Boston and the various firms negotiated with me as a group to complete the multi-million-dollar equity financing round that launched IDEXX. It was a happy day, with a great group of high value-added investors, but also a time of lessons learned about the world of venture capital finance.

Chapter One - Embrace the Benefits of Struggles

The dynamic circumstances of startups require great resilience, multiplexing, improv, scenario planning, and game time decision-making from senior leaders. Sometimes it feels like a fast game of 3-dimensional chess, that requires thinking multiple moves ahead and solving complex simultaneous equations. You sometimes can't secure funding if you haven't secured a leadership team and office space. Yet you often can't secure those without funding. Like playing a high-risk version of Jenga, if you pull out the wrong block or pull it too soon, the whole project can collapse, and you may say goodbye to your life savings and dreams. There is a lot of late-night fear and anxiety when you are launching a new venture. The prospect of failure of course has personal implications, but the implications become much broader and greater when they impact other team members, customers, and investors.

More than a year before we opened IDEXX's doors, I was sitting in my third-floor office in my house on Deering Street in Portland, my desk obscured by piles of paperwork from my extensive research efforts. This was something I had done countless times before in my previous position as a strategy consultant. The work process for me was always the same: a client deadline was looming, and there was immense pressure to deliver solutions to problems and opportunities being addressed. Being stumped wasn't an option.

My anxiety and insecurity grew as the hours ticked by, swiveling my chair from side to side, trying to uncover more insights, and combing through the data yet again. There were bleak moments when the prospect of failure felt very real due to daunting risks. And there were exhilarating moments when I saw clear prospects for great success.

After you go through this sequence enough times, you begin to understand the different ways of looking at issues and how to reframe questions to find new perspectives. There starts to be a pattern that works for you in terms of reaching the right answer. Like it or not, an inevitable sense of doom was an inescapable part of the process. I had to confront ominous risks and threats to get through to the other side. You accept the process for what it is—that is, you accept that the struggle is a necessary part of the process. When channeled thoughtfully this stress has a very productive purpose ... protecting us from harm. The human brain is a magnificent resource for these moments, helping us to be more resourceful, productive, and action-oriented when faced with danger including the prospect of failure.

Struggling to this intense degree has been compared to the heat and pressure it takes to create a diamond. As uncomfortable as the stress was, it played an essential role. Over time, it rewired my synapses, giving me more mental firepower to anticipate threats and recognize similarities in disparate companies. What I experienced in business was not that different from the demands placed on accomplished athletes and musicians who have to perform over and over in the clutch at the same high level. You start to identify what great looks like, forging strength from challenges and sculpting character from adversity. Ernest Hemmingway recognized the benefit of struggles with this famous statement: "The world breaks everyone, and afterward, some are stronger at the broken part."

This was on my mind, sitting uncomfortably at my desk. But this time it was even tougher. Instead of trying to find answers for a client, the duress was coming from me, working for myself to plan my future company. Having that much skin in the game was exhilarating and also intimidating. Somehow the pressure to produce for my own venture was more overwhelming than anything I had experienced working for others. A source of inspiration to transcend this challenge was the wisdom of so many others who have faced the prospect of failure, including hockey star Wayne Gretzky who expressed his perspective this way "You'll always

Chapter One - Embrace the Benefits of Struggles

miss 100% of the shots you don't take."

***

When IDEXX opened its doors on the Portland waterfront in June 1984, our plumbing situation was just a minor distraction compared to the epic challenges of launching a new business. I often think that if you had a crystal ball to look into the future as you attempt something formidable such as building a company from the ground up, training for the Olympics, or writing a novel–you might not do it. It can be exponentially more difficult than you imagine. A certain amount of naivete can be helpful so that hardships reveal themselves a little bit at a time rather than having full knowledge in advance. And if you have full knowledge as a serial entrepreneur, it's helpful to trick your brain into thinking that it will be different next time.

Looking back, we ultimately benefitted from the failure of our first product at IDEXX. The product was designed to detect the presence of antibiotic contamination in milk. Antibiotics are used to treat bacterial infections including mastitis in dairy cows. However, only very minute levels of antibiotics are allowed in milk destined for the consumer market due to the potential for allergic reactions or the development of antibiotic resistance. So, it is common to test for antibiotic contamination. These tests are primarily performed in laboratories at milk plants versus at farms because of the skill required for the testing. This creates the risk that undetected antibiotics in milk from one cow can contaminate a truckload of milk. IDEXX developed an "animal-side" test that could minimize the potential for co-mingling contaminated milk with antibiotic-free milk. While the test worked well, we overestimated the ability of farmers to perform these tests and also the potential for abuse by diluting contaminated milk to levels below detection limits. The product was still sold but was not a basis for building a meaningful initial foundation of commercial operations.

It's a great credit to the early IDEXX team that we quickly faced the bad news associated with this product line and pivoted to other opportunities. Great organizations learn from their mistakes, turning losses into lessons. Our newly organized team was strengthened by this early exercise in critical thinking and introspection about a mistake that could have been avoided with better teamwork and business processes. Our next focus area, identified in the original business plan, was the creation of diagnostic systems to transform the ability to monitor health in the poultry industry. Briefly, the test called an immunoassay, works by using the immune system's ability to recognize and detect foreign objects, called antigens, such as viruses and bacteria. In the presence of antigens, cells produce antibodies, the immune system's frontline defense, which precisely lock onto specific antigens as part of the body's defense system. It is the binding between antibody and antigen that can be detected and measured. Today, similar technology is used in home tests to determine whether or not we have COVID and a wide variety of other antigens.

Poultry is one of the world's principal sources of protein and therefore one of the world's most valuable and important food industries. However, chickens are susceptible to a variety of diseases such as Avian influenza, bronchitis, and Newcastle disease. In most cases, these diseases are managed via vaccination, and a critical healthcare practice in the poultry industry is to ensure that vaccination levels are effective in preventing disease. This creates a strong demand for effective health monitoring systems in support of the efficient production of eggs and chicken meat.

As a consultant, I had seen how onerous and unreliable the industry's existing testing procedures were. Blood samples from flocks were sent to public or private laboratories for testing. For super producers like Tyson, who might have growers in several

CHAPTER ONE - EMBRACE THE BENEFITS OF STRUGGLES

different states, blood samples often went to a number of different labs. These labs operate in the same manner you would expect at a university or government agency. Technicians perform their artistry at workbenches lined with beakers, petri dishes, sodium chloride, agar, and other materials and equipment to detect the presence of antibodies or antigens. Hours or days later test results are provided to veterinary staff or production managers in the field. Time delays as well as accuracy issues created significant operational challenges, along with the lack of standardized test methodologies and data capture capabilities. -All of these factors could contribute to increased production costs. As an example, if antibody levels in a flock were not protective against viral infection, and disease spreads in a flock, the conversion of grain to meat could suffer, raising the cost per pound of meat produced. In poultry, the conversion rate is less than two pounds of grain per pound of meat. For beef, the conversion rate is close to six pounds of grain per pound of meat.

We saw that new generations of technology, proven in human health applications, could offer vast improvements to this system including test kits that would deliver reproducible and consistent results in multiple labs. We could demonstrate to customers that if a single sample was broken into multiple sub-samples and sent to multiple labs our results would be accurate and consistent. This same process demonstrated that traditional test methodologies could be inconsistent and therefore undermine confidence in decision-making. Diagnostics is in many ways an information business, and the value of the information is based on its accuracy and timeliness. We were able to show that old test methods too often produced information of questionable value and, even worse, that production management effectiveness was jeopardized by flawed information. Soon our new diagnostic systems, complete with laptop computers for data analysis, were getting a lot of attention from major poultry producers around the world. Rather than targeting diagnostic laboratories as the primary customer in a poultry company, we focused our efforts on the more senior production managers where our value proposition was much higher as a production management tool with benefits measured in millions of dollars versus simply cost-per-test in a lab. There can be a perception that pricing in this market would be far lower than in human diagnostics but that isn't necessarily true since a flock's health can be monitored effectively by statistically sampling a small number of animals in a population of hundreds or thousands animals versus testing each individual.

At IDEXX, we created a policy of rigorously preparing for upcoming customer meetings because, as a new company, we couldn't afford to make bad first impressions in the relatively small world of veterinary diagnostics. Every customer and every endorsement counted. So, on our inaugural trip to meet prominent customer prospects in Arkansas, we felt well prepared.

But as we headed south, fortune was not on our side as we encountered trouble beyond our control. Our plane encountered a large storm system, causing us to divert our landing from Fayetteville to somewhere in Alabama. Then the airline company lost our luggage, and we had to drive all night to reach our destination, deep in the Ozark Mountains. Next, during the presentation, the motherboard of our computer blew up, leaving us with no choice but to hand-calculate all of the test results. As we were doing all this, we looked at one another, each thinking the same thing: *There's something weird about this blood sample.* But no one could figure out exactly what was wrong. Despite these obstacles, when we finished our demo, the audience of Arkansans applauded, and their feedback could not have been more enthusiastic.

Then, they put on their jackets, thanked us graciously for coming, and walked out without purchasing so much as a single test kit. It was a bleak moment for IDEXX. As our bank account dwindled and costs escalated, we had hoped for significant sales

Chapter One - Embrace the Benefits of Struggles

from this important gathering of prominent poultry producers. Just a handful of large companies dominate the US poultry market. We needed them and we believed they needed us.

Feeling dejected, we drove back to our hotel and bought a handle of Jack Daniel's whiskey. But before pouring a round we recapped the day in an attempt to find why it wasn't more successful. Soon we agreed to call one of the meeting participants to get some feedback. What followed was an insightful discussion about culture. We were told that there was great enthusiasm in the room and even follow-up discussions among participants about how impressed people were with us and our system. This included our ability to accurately identify and disqualify the "weird sample" that wasn't chicken serum after all. It was a blood sample from a dog that had been added in a lighthearted and unsuccessful effort to trick us.

But we had skipped a step in our visit. As New Englanders we had come as strangers and failed to understand an important aspect of southern culture... we hadn't built a social connection with people in the room. It was suggested that an ideal strategy for creating the missing social connections was to shoot some quail with people who had attended our meeting. We did that. Soon we were dining on quail from a group hunting experience and happily processing orders for IDEXX equipment. The social bonds from that early experience lasted many years, and the experience had a long-lasting impact on our inclination to seek strong social relationships with customers in all of our businesses.

This lesson and others learned in our early ventures, prepared the company well for further success as we navigated our way to leadership in other markets. One of these markets was the application of our technology to diagnostic needs in the livestock industry. Unlike practices in most of human health, with the notable recent exception of COVID, commercial animals such as livestock are frequently tested when they cross geopolitical borders to prevent the spread of certain diseases. IDEXX developed and commercialized tests for a number of these applications including bovine brucellosis, a highly contagious and costly zoonotic disease in livestock and wildlife, that can also infect other animals and humans. For decades, governments have worked to eliminate this disease through testing, quarantine, and eradication. The IDEXX brucellosis test system introduced and approved in the 1990s, offers automation, convenience, and accuracy advantages. This test and others for government regulatory programs are primarily sold to government customers. In total, they are a very significant segment of the veterinary diagnostic market, and private-sector products challenge the long convention of in-house diagnostic procedures performed by government laboratories. Penetrating this market required insightful analysis of total costs associated with testing, since in-house testing can appear to be quite inexpensive. Total costs need to take into consideration labor costs as well as the hidden and sometimes vast cost of test methods that produce false positives or more dangerous false negatives.

Chapter One - Embrace the Benefits of Struggles

Takeaway: The antibiotics-in-milk product failure, along with early poultry and livestock experiences, provide good examples of the importance of turning challenges into opportunities, of reimagining product and market opportunities, and of learning important lessons from mistakes. Experiences of that kind also illustrate the importance of mastering difficult situations. In the world of sailing and boating, the greatest skill development and learnings usually come from turbulent conditions A fair-weather sailor who only sets out when the water is calm, may not master the skills needed to handle a storm. In the adventurous world of entrepreneurship, risk management capabilities are highly valued, including the ability to reduce risk by anticipating challenges based on thoughtful planning and prior experience. I purposely seek a broad range of experiences in life knowing that this builds a deep library of reference knowledge. This library can be called upon when needed for better outcomes in circumstances ranging from navigating a blizzard on a highway to boardroom debates.

Chapter Two
Challenge the Status Quo

"Be the change you want to see in the world"
- Mahatma Gandhi

The head of IDEXX manufacturing called me early one morning. She had agreed to host a cohort of New England high school chemistry teachers at IDEXX. But she wasn't feeling well and asked if I would step in for her.

"Hi everyone," I said. "I'm sorry you're getting the founder and CEO of IDEXX instead of the head of manufacturing, but she's indisposed. I'm going to give you my perspective on the company, what we do, and how we do it, and then I am happy to answer your questions."

I explained that we used immunochemistry to create a whole new generation of high-performance diagnostic products. After I finished, a middle-aged teacher raised her hand.

"What motivated you to do all this?" she asked.

"My high school chemistry teacher motivated me," I said. "I took AP chemistry, and I was president of the chemistry club."

"Where did you go to high school?" she asked.

"Nashua, New Hampshire."

A man standing in the front of the group looked thunderstruck. "Did you say your last name is Shaw? You're not Fred Shaw's brother, are you?" he blurted out.

That's when I recognized him: Mr. Scheer! Marco Scheer had taught my advanced placement chemistry class and served as my advisor when I was president of my high school chemistry club. "Yes," I said, forcing a smile, "I'm his brother." It was a moment of amazing serendipity mixed with some fleeting sadness. I was disappointed that he didn't immediately recall me, and my crowning achievement in his class: experiments to better understand chemiluminescence ... chemical reactions that generate light-emitting excited states. Ironically my high school chemistry had some relevance to our work at IDEXX because test results for immunoassays or other diagnostic methods are frequently determined through optical signals. IDEXX also had tests that generate bioluminescent signals, and I have always been fascinated by bioluminescence in nature including by creatures in dark ocean depths. Our meeting concluded with a happy moment when Mr. Scheer congratulated me on our work, something I wish my parents could have heard.

***

Leaning back in his captain's chair and forming a church steeple with his fingers, the admissions officer at Phillips Exeter looked at me and said, "You don't seem too enthusiastic about coming here." When I said that I wasn't interested a slight crease of confusion appeared between his eyebrows and a touch of irritation showed on his cleanly shaved face. Selling Exeter to reluctant students was not usually part of his job description. He asked me to explain.

"This is not what I want," I said, my snarky thirteen-year-old self on full display. "It was good of my parents to drive me here because they thought an Exeter education would benefit me. But I just don't think that I would thrive here."

My understanding was that the academic environment at Exeter was intense and very competitive – great for many but perhaps not for me. To graduate from Exeter or other elite schools

Chapter Two - Challenge the Status Quo

was to join a powerful alumni network that offered entree to high levels of professional achievement and social status. As a tenth grader immersed in the distinctive culture of the 1960s, I heard a different drummer. Perhaps George Gobel captured a similar sentiment when asking "Did you ever get the feeling the world was a tuxedo and you were a pair of brown shoes?"

***

Early in life it was apparent that I wasn't inspired by, or accomplished at, meeting some important societal measures of success. I wasn't a great student and didn't score high on standard tests like SATs. It was always a welcome relief to find others in those same circumstances, whether they were friends or, better yet, mythical heroes like Mark Twain who famously is believed to have said: "I have never let my schooling interfere with my education." And "education: the path from cocky ignorance to miserable uncertainty." Throughout my life, my inclination has been to push back against the expectations of others that don't serve me well. It's not clear where this refusal to conform came from, but it has been a lifetime pattern. My father had a successful career in the Navy and worked in management at a shoe company, which provided a comfortable life for our family. My younger brother John would follow Fred to Exeter. They attended prestigious private universities and colleges like Columbia and Pomona and graduate school programs like Harvard Business School and Harvard Law School. My sister Martha built a successful career in both marine geology and communications.

In our family, history and ancestral exploits mattered. A portrait of my great, great grandfather Elijah Morrill Shaw hung in the living room of my boyhood home. He had served as a captain in the Tenth Maine Civil War regiment, and later supervised a mill in Nashua. He was a founder of the Nashua YMCA and a benefactor of one of the YMCA summer camps that I attended in

New Hampshire.

The prevailing sentiment about metrics of success and achievement was well known in my childhood, and not in my favor. While New Hampshire might be famous for the "Live Free or Die" state motto on its license plates, it shares a characteristic of many communities around the world as a place where prestige, education, social standing, and the past are woven tightly together. My father was involved in many civic organizations including the YMCA. My mother was a social worker, who played a lead role in the local Head Start program and an Adult Learning Center. And she was the first woman elected to the Nashua public library board. My parents were active gardeners. In the 1950s, after the great depression and World War Two, community involvement and upright citizenship were highly valued. People sought the comfort of respectability and knowing that their offspring were headed for success.

my parents, Muriel and Frederic Shaw

Instead of an elite private institution like Phillips Exeter, my high school years were spent at Nashua High, as a B student.

Chapter Two - Challenge the Status Quo

Rather than studying, my preference was to go white-water kayaking, hiking, camping in the White Mountains, skiing and occasionally playing guitar and French Horn. It was good fortune to have friends who shared my interest in seeking adventurous fun. This included flight lessons, launching hobby rockets, racing motorcycles, and amateur electronic projects like building a Tesla Coil. In my senior year, for instance, a friend and I competed in a demolition derby with a Buick Special station wagon we bought for $10. We were proud to finish second and win $50. My group of friends happily saw ourselves as mavericks and renegades consistent with the famously rebellious anti-establishment culture of the 1960s.

My parents were understandably worried about my future and wondered how I would eventually support myself. But their hopes for me were counterpoised against the swirling social currents of the 1960s. I was a proud child of the Woodstock Generation, deeply influenced by the counterculture's musicians, artists, and activists, who pursued significance and self-expression as nonconformists and pioneers. Rock and roll, with its message of revolution, freedom, and self-creation, shaped my thinking, whetting my appetite for a freer existence. It was inspirational to me that teenagers from England had the internal fire to form bands like The Beatles and The Rolling Stones, landing themselves on the world stage, and setting off a youthquake that was reshaping our culture.

To the soundtrack of The Rolling Stones "(I Can't Get No) Satisfaction", released in 1965, I shared my generation's questioning of authority. To me, being a rebel seemed like a high calling and a courageous decision. Some of the great rock and roll anthems of those times celebrated love and freedom, and others supported activism for civil rights and peace. Popular "summer of love" songs and albums in 1967 included The Beatles extraordinary Sgt. Pepper's Lonely Hearts Club Band album and All You Need is Love, Light My Fire by The Doors, Brown Eyed Girl by Van Morrison, Purple Haze by Jimi Hendrix, and A Whiter Shade of Pale by Procol Harum.

The 1967 Summer of Love gave way to a year of turmoil, tragedy, and change. By 1968 protest songs became more common amidst civil rights activism and the assassination of Martin Luther King Jr., the assassination of Robert Kennedy, a black power demonstration by American medalists John Carlos and Tommie Smith at the Summer Olympics in Mexico City, the trial of the "Chicago Seven" related to the disruption of the 1968 Democratic National Convention, the activities of the Blank Panther Party, the escalation of the Vietnam War including the Tet Offensive, Cold War tensions, and other events. Popular songs during this time period included Revolution by The Beatles, Street Fighting Man and Jumpin' Jack Flash by The Rolling Stones, What's Going On, by Marvin Gaye, Draft Morning by the Byrds, Fortunate Son by Creedence Clearwater Revival, I Don't Want To Go To Vietnam by John Lee Hooker, Abraham Martin and John by Dion, Star Spangled Banner by Jimmy Hendrix, Unknown Soldier by The Doors, Saigon Bride by Joan Baez, White Boots Marching in a Yellow Land by Phil Ochs, and many more.

The tumultuous decade of the 1960s came to an end with more mood changes including inspirational events such as the Apollo moon landing, the Woodstock music festival, the PEACE MORATORIUM and creation of ARPANET.

Immersed in the era's activism and idealism, a vision began to emerge of a life of impact inspired by contemporary leaders and movements such as Martin Luther King Jr. for civil rights activism, John Muir and Rachel Carson for environmental activism, and many others including Muhammad Ali and Albert Einstein for anti-war activism. With friends, I joined in anti-war protests with the belief that our role in Vietnam was tragically wrong-minded and

Chapter Two - Challenge the Status Quo

that our government was undermining its credibility and public trust through misinformation. Rachel Carson's powerful exposé, *Silent Spring*, inspired environmental activism by describing how pesticides were poisoning the natural world. My awareness of pollution increased including concern that the Nashua River turned red or blue depending on the color of the dye being used by companies along its shores.

My desire to swim against the tide continued when it came to choosing a college. Thanks to a family friend the University of Virginia (UVA) scheduled an interview for me, but the visit created an impression of an "establishment" organization, that would also put on display the fact that high academic achievement didn't motivate me.

My decision that institutions like Exeter and UVA weren't right for me meant turning my back on the constructs of what others often celebrated and what I considered to be conventional metrics of success. Despite disappointing my parents, it was important for me to establish the meaning of achievement and success on my own terms, just as it has been inspiring to observe this in others.

Importantly, this isn't something to view as a choice between ambition or passivity. It is a choice between asserting your independence and staking a claim to your own life versus yielding to convention and acceding to the expectations of others. Challenging convention is an essential element of wave-making and change-making.

Great writing and storytelling captivates me, and I have been a voracious reader. In pursuit of this passion, I traveled inexpensively to England the summer of 1969 before college to take literature classes at the University of Exeter in southwest England. The course textbook, now badly tattered, still sits prominently in my office, with its anthology of writings by great authors including

William Butler Yeats, William Blake, Alfred, Lord Tennyson, and others. One of many highlighted passages is this famous line from Tennyson's poem Ulysses: "To strive, to seek, to find, and not to yield." My time that summer at Exeter, London, Paris, and hitchhiking to several other locations in Europe amidst the 1960s culture was transformational. This included a memorable summer solstice event at the ancient Stonehenge monument, which influenced a large-scale bronze sculpture I created decades later, and named Bronze Henge.

Bronze Henge sculpture at my home in Maine

    At UNH, my major was American Literature with a minor in political science. My most admired authors were the experiential ones, writing about what they had seen and felt personally. Among my favorites were: Jack London, a hobo and sailor who headed to the Alaskan Klondike during the Gold Rush and wrote such classics as *White Fang*, *Martin Eden*, and *The Call of the Wild*; Ernest Hemingway, who was seriously wounded as an ambulance driver in Italy during World War I and went on to pen masterpieces like *A Farewell to Arms*, *For Whom the Bell Tolls*, and *The Old Man and the Sea*; and Mark Twain, a distinctive voice for America and author of *Adventures of Huckleberry Finn*, *The Innocents Abroad*, and *Roughing It*,

Chapter Two - Challenge the Status Quo

who did stints as a miner in the American West and as a Mississippi River steamboat pilot. The wisdom that these authors imparted by sharing their experiences inspired me. For example, in his book *Martin Eden,* Jack London wrote: "I won't subordinate my taste to the unanimous judgment of mankind."

My admiration for Mark Twain eventually led me in 1977 to publish an article in Down East magazine about a group of "Maine's holy land colonists" that Twain encountered in his Middle East travels chronicled in *The Innocents Abroad.* Twain was aboard the American excursion steamer, Quaker City on October 1st, 1867 when he found and helped rescue this group of destitute pilgrims from their colony near Jaffa, Syria. He described the incident in a letter to the *New York Tribune* the following day. The story has meaningful historical significance as it relates to both the migration of Mormons to Utah following the US Civil War, and to forerunners in United States relationships with Israel. As a member of the executive committee of the U.S.-Israel Science and Technology Commission many years later, appointed by President Clinton, it was helpful to know this obscure story.

It wasn't just music, literature, and social movements of the 1960s that shaped my early thinking. My concern that conventional thinking shackles us to a life of limitations was also galvanized by the optimism and soaring ambition of the Space Race between the United States and the USSR. In 1961 Alan Shepard, a US Navy test pilot became the first American to go up into space. He was born near my hometown in New Hampshire and our family felt some kinship because my father was a Navy pilot in World War II. As a ten-year-old boy, this personal connection to an astronaut gave me a sense of great possibilities as we watched the ticker tape parade our town held to celebrate Shepard's successful flight.

In the summer prior to my freshman year at UNH, Neil Armstrong climbed down the ladder and took "a giant leap for mankind" onto the moon's powdery surface on July 20, 1969. This momentous event occurred just seven years after President John F. Kennedy implored the nation in his speech at Rice University in Houston, Texas: "We choose to go to the Moon in this decade and do the other things," Kennedy said, "not because they are easy, but because they are hard, because that goal will serve to organize and measure the best of our energies and skills."

Sitting with friends in Nashua, we watched the grainy black and white images of the astronauts bounding along in their puffy suits and planting the American flag. It was awe-inspiring to see that human imagination, adventurousness, and technological capabilities had pulled off this feat. The space program symbolized how a wave-making mindset shared among a group of talented people–scientists, engineers, astronauts, administrators–came together to do great things. It was an historic moment that helped shape my own life and my desire for a greater purpose.. We saw our small blue planet in the immensity of space for the first time, and there was a game-changing realization that we Earthlings are all crew members on spaceship Earth.

Apollo 8's 1968 Christmas Eve photo from the moon of Earth floating in the blackness of space, had previously revealed to us just how exquisite and fragile our blue planet is. The astronaut

Chapter Two - Challenge the Status Quo

who took the shot, Bill Anders, famously said: "We came all this way to explore the Moon, and the most important thing is that we discovered the Earth." Not long after, April 22, 1970, which happened to be my nineteenth birthday, was designated as the first Earth Day. Ever since I have co-celebrated my birthday with Earth Day, and it has been an inspiration for high-impact stewardship of our natural world. Most years this includes production and publishing Earth Day films including one that celebrated the 50th anniversary of Earth Day in 2020.

***

A new dimension of freedom revealed itself to me by challenging the status quo during the summer after my freshman year. Long captivated by the fabled frontier spirit and epic landscapes of the American West, I found a cheap flight to Denver, Colorado as the first leg of an adventure to experience a mythical place that New York Tribune editor Horace Greeley is credited with commending in 1871 with this phrase: "go West." New Hampshire, with its considerable charms, lacked an association with the pioneer-explorer days that we learned about through books and television. Yes, we had the nineteenth-century orator, lawyer, and politician Daniel Webster with his famous and prescient 1830 plea against states seceding from the Union, "Liberty and Union, now and forever, one and inseparable!" but there was no equivalent to Lewis and Clark crossing the continent with their Corps of Discovery, and young Sacagawea, a baby clasped in her arms, guiding and interpreting for them.

After landing in Denver with my friend John Burns, we hitchhiked more than three hundred miles to Telluride, then a tiny ghost town high in the remote San Juan Mountains, where the real Butch Cassidy robbed his first bank in 1889. Parts of the 1969 film Butch Cassidy and the Sundance Kid had been filmed here, and years later I would ski with "Sundance Kid" Robert Redford at his Sundance Resort, and host him in Maine including a visit to Acadia National Park. He inscribed his book *The Outlaw Trail* to me with the words "from an outlaw at heart."

Along with a wonderful free spirit named Hattie Billings, we spent the summer helping to run a three-table restaurant housed in a former turn-of-the-century bordello called The Good Times Society. We honed my skills for making breads, soups, and other items on our limited menu. We hiked and occasionally rode horses high in the mountains amidst abandoned silver and gold mines, including a once-thriving mining village called Tomboy. And we got well acquainted with fascinating local personalities, including sheep ranchers and hippies, distinctively different from New England.

Telluride in the 1890s

Good Times Society 1890s (Left) and 1970 as a restaurant (Right)

Chapter Two - Challenge the Status Quo

We were camping on a mountaintop on a cool, clear night in August, a few days before returning East. Rugged black peaks stretched out before me, and an infinite number of stars shimmered in the inky blue firmament. Back then, there was almost no distraction from man-made light because Telluride had a population of several hundred people. This open horizon offered a stark contrast to Nashua, with its mill town history and large brick factories.

Lying in my sleeping bag, the prospect of a life full of boundless spiritually inspiring opportunities took shape and, I resolved to live as adventurously, impactfully, and experientially as my abilities and imagination could sustain. I imagined myself as an explorer or perhaps even an outlaw in these wild west surroundings, hungry for discovery and adventure, both real and metaphorical. Or in the words of Mark Twain's Huckleberry Finn, "to light out for the Territory ahead of the rest."

From this time on, my goal was to be one of those pathfinders, seeking to impact big issues of our time including transformational science, entrepreneurship, capitalism, and stewardship of the natural world including oceans. It's fascinating to me how many people have pivotal experiences like mine in Colorado, and how impactful they can be. For me, this was followed by another inspirational adventure in Colorado one year later when I traveled to Vail and worked evenings as a waiter at Pepi's Restaurant in the Gasthof Gramshammer Hotel. During the day I lived the life of a supremely happy ski bum with pioneering freestyle skier Wayne Wong.

Takeaway: I hope that my story inspires a sense that great things are possible when you believe in yourself, when you seek opportunities aligned with your interests and capabilities, when you do what you love, and love what you do.

Chapter Three
Forge Your Own Path

*"Do not go where the path may lead,
go instead where there is no path and leave a trail."*
– Attributed to Ralph Waldo Emerson

Flying over Penobscot Bay at dusk is to witness the mystical alchemy of picturesque islands, blue water, and fading light as the sun sets over the Atlantic Ocean. The unique beauty of the Maine coast is unforgettable, with its endless fretwork of narrow inlets, small islands, sandy beaches, rocky outposts, and hidden coves.

Long before IDEXX, I was aboard a tiny Aeronca Champion aircraft flying high above the picturesque coast of Maine. First built in the 1940s, the Champ as it is called, was a lightweight, high-wing, two-person, one-engine, bit of metal tubing with a cloth covering. Instead of a wheel, the pilot used a stick and rudder to steer the plane. A friend who lived on Vinalhaven Island in West Penobscot Bay was piloting the Champ as we searched for schools of herring, which appear as dark cloud shadows on the water. My friend then radioed the fishermen below, directing them to the location of the herring, which they caught in a huge net called a purse seine.

It was an exhilarating experience and reminded me of stories by the French writer Antoine de Saint-Exupéry. His writing is poetic and lyrical, imbued with a deep wisdom born of his heroic life of adventure. Best known for his fable *The Little Prince*, Saint-Exupéry was also a pilot whose memoir, *Wind, Sand and Stars*, draws upon his stint delivering mail in North Africa in the 1920s. Those early planes had virtually no instrumentation. Sometimes flipping upside down, he would occasionally plummet in a tailspin, towards the ocean. Once, Saint-Exupéry crashed in the middle of the Libyan desert where Bedouin nomads rescued him. He fought for France during World War II, dying at age forty-four when his plane disappeared into the Mediterranean. He captured an important theme related to the ownership mentality of mission-driven entrepreneurial ventures is attributed to him in this quote: "If you want to build a ship, don't drum up people to collect wood and don't assign them tasks and work, but rather teach them to long for the endless immensity of the sea." Saint-Exupéry's book *Wisdom of the Sands* is full of interesting insights on leadership.

At the time of my herring spotting flight in the Champ, I was working in Maine state government. I had accepted a job in the administration of Governor James Longley, the first gubernatorial candidate in the state to be elected as an independent. Appointed a planning and budgetary aide for marine resources, agriculture, forestry, and conservation, I knew relatively little about these areas. But I saw this as a great opportunity to drink from the firehose, learn about domains of great interest to me, and fulfill a public service commitment that is important for all Americans. I shared the Sixties ethos of activism including aid to underserved people and communities to fulfill their human potential. I supported the Great Society programs to alleviate poverty. My mother, after all, was a Head Start worker–a program created after LBJ declared a "War on Poverty" in 1964 as part of his Great Society initiative. She worked with disadvantaged children in Nashua and later taught English as a Second language to immigrant students.

Chapter Three - Forge Your Own Path

I remembered how I felt when I watched John F. Kennedy's inauguration on January 20, 1961, when the president issued this challenge, "And so, my fellow Americans: ask not what your country can do for you—ask what you can do for your country." I was only nine years old, but JFK's call to public service stayed with me. His administration—often called Camelot—had endowed the idea of working in the public sector with glamor and a sense of duty.

When most outsiders think of Maine, they envision the quaint seaside towns with lobster rolls and blueberry pie. They picture the imaginary Cabot Cove portrayed on the hit TV show *Murder, She Wrote*, starring Angela Lansbury as a mystery writer and amateur detective. Or people think of summer compounds such as Kennebunkport, Boothbay and the Bar Harbor area frequented by wealthy homeowners . But in the 1970s, Maine—the largest of the six New England states—often ranked as the poorest. In fact, it was one of the poorest states in the United States outside the Deep South. While tourist dollars bolstered the coastal areas, Maine's interior remained very much a nineteenth-century subsistence economy based on natural resources like lumber and agriculture. More than four-fifths of the state is forest.

I was determined to collaborate with colleagues to improve opportunities for citizens of my adopted state. As I later wrote in an article published in *The New Englander* magazine in 1977 in support of community development corporations: "For many reasons, Maine's economy has never yielded its people much more than a lean existence. Hard winters, rugged terrain, and geographical isolation from mainstream commercial activity have combined to limit the state's prosperity. Despite years of effort spent attempting to attract outside industry, it now ranks forty-second in per capita income; and given the high cost of living in northern New England, Mainers are really in worse shape than that standing suggests."

From my desks in the Budget Office and another in the

State Planning Office, I was able to observe the inner workings of government. I admired Governor Longley's energy and commitment, and saw the same passion in his commissioners for agriculture, marine resources, and forestry.

It was inspirational for me to see that, despite my junior experience, I was able to contribute meaningfully to some important projects. These included support for the expansion of agricultural cooperatives in Maine, value-added food processing, forest management programs, and other initiatives. As an example of a notable project, forces of gentrification were taking over traditional working waterfronts along the coast. I helped conceive of, and lead, an effort to preserve working waterfront space for use by commercial fishermen, ensuring that they didn't lose the water access they need. We achieved this by issuing state bonds to underwrite fish piers in a number of coastal communities, essentially building roads to the ocean.

Amidst my tenure in Maine state government, the Magnuson-Stevens Fisheries Conservation and Management Act enacted by Congress expanded US jurisdiction from just 12 miles to 200 miles from shore. This dramatic change in ocean stewardship had many consequences including the ability to regulate foreign fishing which often dominated extraction in those waters. The domestic economy got little benefit from this foreign fishing activity and suffered from the adverse consequences of overfishing. Suddenly vast new ocean territories were reserved as protected fisheries zones for domestic fleets. All economies seek to benefit from value-added activities associated with natural resource extraction, and the Maine seafood industry faced this opportunity, and challenge. One example of my involvement was to support a value-added facility in Vinalhaven so that struggling local fishermen would have a better market for their catches. Instead of local fishermen selling the raw fish for the going price at the dock, or fish going to foreign fleets , we used federal funds to build a freezing and processing plant. This opened new markets

Chapter Three - Forge Your Own Path

for exporting frozen fish to northern Europe where herring was very popular among consumers.

I also had the opportunity to support an initiative that protected hundreds of thousands of acres of public lands in the state of Maine. Because of an early nineteenth-century law, the State had "common and undivided ownership interests" in every "unorganized township" in Maine. Created in anticipation of settlement that was preempted by great migrations to the American West, these townships account for nearly half of Maine's total land mass. We determined that the state would benefit from trading those unusual ownership rights for fee-simple ownership of lands for public use. I worked with, and learned from, Richard Barringer, inspirational director of the Bureau of Public Lands, to negotiate their return to public use and management. The outcome was not merely a boon to land conservation efforts in Maine but a shift in the relationship between the state and other landowners in Maine including the pulp and paper industry. My reading in those days included a fascinating book called *The Paper Plantation* by Ralph Nader's study group.

This early lesson in large-scale land and ocean conservation inspired other stewardship efforts later in my career as I came to better understand ominous threats to the natural world from human civilization. From my earliest childhood, I had been attuned to nature. But these experiences gave me a tremendous sense of urgency and agency, a sense of being a wave maker who could impact environmental stewardship through my individual efforts and through government programs that I had come to know.

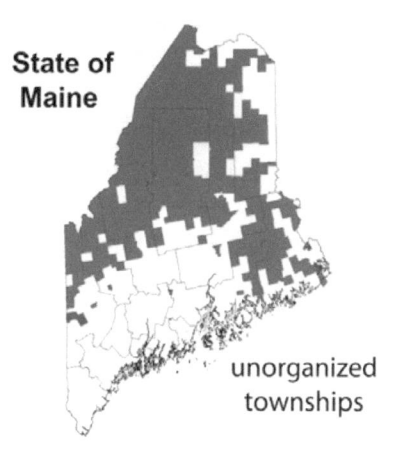

State of Maine

unorganized townships

37

My experience working with Governor Longley deepened my belief in the importance of public service in America, including early career experience. I have continued extensive public service throughout my career including work with General Stanley McChrystal and others in the Service Year Alliance dedicated to our mission of making early career public service a common expectation and opportunity for all young Americans.

"It's not enough to be great. You have to be great together."
—GENERAL STANLEY MCCHRYSTAL (RET.)

Another benefit of this experience was the development of a deeper and more nuanced appreciation of the relative capabilities of the private and public sectors. I realized then, and still believe, that it's easy for all of us to inadequately understand the strengths and weaknesses of both sectors, especially in a world where drama is often amplified by media sources.

After nearly four years of government service, I was ready for a change, and eager for a very different experience in the private sector.

My decision might have surprised the UNH grad who

CHAPTER THREE - FORGE YOUR OWN PATH

skipped graduation and rode off on his motorcycle. Brewed in a 1960s culture, I believed that financial success wasn't the top priority in life, and that "working for the man" in big corporations was a dreary and distasteful prospect. However, I came to understand that my DNA, including my desire for freedom, self-determination, and high-impact activism was more aligned with the culture and success factors of the business world. It was a surprising and life-changing discovery.

The private sector discipline to set goals and achieve results was very attractive to me, along with the sport associated with business competitiveness. To make ends meet, I kept my day job and enrolled in night classes for an MBA to learn about finance, accounting, marketing, and how to put together a business plan. The world of tech entrepreneurship seemed to offer a great opportunity for impact, leveraging the transformational power of modern science.

Although state government did not ultimately align with my vision of how to best create value in the world, it was fulfilling to be in a public service role, and I gained knowledge that would prove crucial later in life. It has been beneficial to have first-hand knowledge about how government works, and about natural resource industries including farming, fishing, forestry, and food production. No amount of reading and research could match the perspective gained from my direct experience and from relationships built with lifelong practitioners that I interacted with. To assimilate knowledge and create value in my work, I developed a skill during my years with Longley that has served me well for decades.

In every industry, in every area of commerce, there are experts who track data and trends, and who enjoy sharing their knowledge with an attentive and appreciative listener. It is human nature to want to show expertise, to be consulted and acknowledged as an authority on a subject. Sometimes, these specialists could be found by knocking on doors inside a department in the Maine government. And sometimes, authorities on relevant subjects could be reached remotely by simply picking up the phone, announcing that I was calling on behalf of Maine state government, and needed advice.

This was how I found a sage who would open the aperture of my worldview for new opportunities.

***

Going to a movie theater in downtown Portland in 1977, I watched the first *Star Wars* movie, *A New Hope*, which starred famed English actor Alec Guinness as Luke Skywalker's wise mentor, the Jedi Master Obi-Wan Kenobi. He utters one of the most transcendent lines in cinematic history: "Use the Force, Luke." Via *Star Wars*, George Lucas illuminated many universal truths about not just the battle between good and evil within the human heart, but also the need we all have to discover the right path—to find our destiny you might say. George might call it "the hero's journey" with a nod to his friend Joseph Campbell. Campbell studied powerful myths in human history and discovered that many mythological narratives frequently share a common structure. In his book, *The Hero with a Thousand Faces*, Campbell presents details of this 12-step structure in the form of the journey of the archetypal hero found in world myths. Campbell's observations about these journeys are inspirational to me, including these quotes often attributed to him:

"It is by going down into the abyss that we recover the treasures of life. Where you stumble, there lies your treasure."

"We must let go of the life we have planned, so as to accept the one that is waiting for us."

"Follow your bliss and the universe will open doors where there were only walls."

When I reflect on the cultural touchstone that is *Star Wars*,

CHAPTER THREE - FORGE YOUR OWN PATH

I realize that I have been blessed with Obi-Wan Kenobi-type relationships including a man I met while I worked for Governor Longley. He wasn't a hermit hiding out on the planet Tatooine but rather a world-famous professor named Ray Goldberg at Harvard Business School in Cambridge, Massachusetts. Ray was and remains today one of the most influential figures in what would become known as agribusiness. In fact, he and another Harvard professor, John H. Davis, literally wrote the book on agribusiness in 1957. This is the process that begins with a farmer buying raw materials—seed or livestock—and ends with food in kitchens around the world. ... the world of "farm to fork."

with Ray Goldberg

Ray had started working at age ten in his father's small feed, grain, and hay operation in Fargo, North Dakota, before earning a PhD in Agricultural Economics. In addition to writing books and teaching, Goldberg, like many Harvard Business School professors, ran a thriving consulting business.

Potatoes were Maine's biggest agricultural product, with poultry running a close second. But both sectors were struggling to compete with the likes of Tyson chicken and Simplot potatoes, which provided

McDonald's with its French fries. To help the farmers, I needed to understand why some Maine agricultural sectors were falling farther and farther behind. While still in Maine state government I sought Ray's advice.

Some agriculture policy officials may rely on collected anecdotal evidence, but Ray's approach was data-driven and systematic. As a result, his advice was sought by agribusiness industry participants around the world. One day, at his Harvard B-School office, we were discussing how the global food and agriculture systems were undergoing a dramatic transformation that had disadvantaged Maine farmers and other small independent producers. To understand the exact nature of those disadvantages Ray suggested that we seek comparative performance information for similar operations in other geographies. He also suggested that we seek the perspective of senior leaders in the food and agribusiness world, including the CEO of agribusiness giant Cargill. Cargill was, and remains, a towering agricultural powerhouse, operating in seventy countries, with 155,000 employees. I remember reading the book *Merchants of Grain* at the time and discovering the largely private world of companies like Cargill, Continental Grain, Bunge, and a few others that dominate the world grain industry. I didn't realize then how well I would later come to know them.

Soon I had the opportunity to meet with industry and policy leaders via the annual Harvard Business School Agribusiness Seminar led by Ray for many years. This opened the door to a bigger world and outstanding expertise that reframed my perspective on issues in Maine. Returning to the state capitol, I felt more empowered to tackle local issues and opportunities, and I was able to listen and interact in a different way. I gained confidence in my capability to contribute in higher impact ways that had not previously been exercised in my government role or encouraged earlier in my life. In contrast to feedback I had often received as a student, Ray demonstrated admiration for my abilities and the prospect that we could achieve

CHAPTER THREE - FORGE YOUR OWN PATH

great things together. During our interactions, I got a glimpse of what "great looks like," including the importance of being inspired and empowered by greater self-confidence.

This is the reason why when Ray said, "Let's work together," I didn't hesitate to join him and other colleagues in an enterprise to engage in strategic consulting assignments for food and agriculture companies, as well as for government agencies, around the world.

Upon joining Ray's company, AgriBusiness Associates, I became immersed in understanding the vast, complex, and critically important world of food and agriculture. The global agriculture industry exceeds $10 trillion and is present in every country, with more than 500 million farmers supplying food for the planet's 8 billion-plus human beings. Working in an industry addressing world food needs quickly became very rewarding on many levels including the industry's important role in addressing human nutrition and wellbeing. Of course, agriculture is an ancient and highly respected vocation. George Washington put it this way: "Agriculture is the most healthful, the most useful, and the most noble employment of man." Daniel Webster called farmers "the founders of human civilization."

It's important to note that Ray's view of the agribusiness world extended beyond traditional boundaries, as captured in this statement: "We're much more than a commodity industry; we're a nutrition industry, we're a health industry, we're an energy industry, we're an economic development industry. . . . Our ultimate customer is society at large."

It was gratifying to have the opportunity to meet with and support the work of independent farmers and food producers, and also to understand opportunities for innovation and novel relationships that impact food cost and quality from farm to table. Soon after our relationship started, Ray provided a memorable answer to my questions about the kinds of things we would be working on. "Well, the newly elected Prime Minister of Jamaica needs to find ways to improve the future of the Jamaican food and agricultural economy," he said in an offhand manner. Excited by this opportunity, I offered to help.

Soon, as winter descended in Maine, I was on a plane to Kingston, Jamaica, to meet with its Prime Minister, Edward Seaga. Seaga's predecessor, Michael Manley had become very friendly with Cuba and its leader Fidel Castro. This was viewed as a risk in the United States regarding the spread of communism and unwanted Russian influence in the western hemisphere – close to American shores. So, a group of us began working with the new Seaga government to support democracy and expand Jamaica's private sector economy. The goal was to benefit Jamaican citizens with a better alternative than Cuba's dictator-led socialist system. Our work ranged from tourism and minerals to agriculture and food systems. One of the initiatives I worked on was to help restructure and expand the now-iconic Jamaican Blue Mountain Coffee brand. When I first met with coffee growers high in the Blue Mountains above Kingston, they tended to compete against each other selling non-branded commodity-priced coffee beans, not grasping that they would benefit far more from cooperation. Eventually, we were able to help them work together in a farmer cooperative structure, similar to the kind that Land O'Lakes dairy farmers and Sunkist citrus growers had used to their benefit. Our group had a great deal of experience with these producer cooperatives. The upshot was a brand that is still recognized by consumers around the world and sells at a premium price today. Years later, as I was building a business in Japan, I happily and regularly paid a premium price for servings of Jamaican Blue Mountain coffee at the Okura Hotel in Tokyo. I now think of these farmers every morning when I stand at my kitchen counter and brew myself a superb cup of Jamaican Blue Mountain coffee.

Our work offered outstanding opportunities to experience distinctive aspects of Jamaican culture including unforgettable reggae

Chapter Three - Forge Your Own Path

concerts by Bob Marley's Wailers, Peter Tosh, and others at the famous Reggae Sunsplash festivals. Marley's musical themes were revolutionary and motivational including "live the life you love." At the famous "One Love Peace Concert" on (Earth Day) April 22, 1978, amidst our work there, Marley demonstrated his ability to be a force for good in Jamaica. He used his celebrity status to enable political rivals Seaga and Manley to join him on stage in an important public symbol of unity after a violent election. He died in 1981 of cancer, but his legacy continues to contribute to the vibrant culture of the country. Despite an unfortunate incident of being held at gunpoint near the Jamaican village of Savanna la Mar during our work there, I have returned often in more peaceful times, sometimes with my extended family, to enjoy the country and its people.

Strategic consulting required constant travel. I worked with powerful multinational corporations such as Japanese soy sauce producer Kikkoman, the large Thai agribusiness conglomerate Charoen Pokphand, Mexico's state-owned petroleum company Pemex, and Wilbur-Ellis a large crop protection company based in San Francisco. I went to Cuban bakeries in Miami to find out how many were using high-gluten flour so I could advise my client Bay State Milling, a Boston flour company, on where to build a new mill. I advised Northeastern dairy cooperatives on broad-ranging collaborative ventures including the acquisition of HP Hood, and I helped the Aalsmeer Flower Auction in Holland expand its presence in America. Client assignments ranged from the California wine business, China's state farm organization, Florida citrus operations, the hops industry, livestock and poultry production, seafood and fisheries, grain for feed and food, crop protection, plant and animal genetics, fuel ethanol production, and assignments with Lazard Freres, Continental Grain, Archer-Daniels-Midland, and others to assess the industry impact of breakthroughs in biotechnology.

My horizons continued to expand via travel, novel experiences, and access to thought leaders. When you are associated with a business guru like Ray Goldberg, one of the preeminent wave makers in his field, the inbound flow of information, insights, and professional relationships creates a powerful firehose. As an example, in my role advising corporate boards on important strategic issues, I consulted with Minneapolis-based food giant General Mills, headed by an executive named E. Robert "Bob" Kinney, about possible acquisitions and partnerships in Mexico. This along with dozens of other assignments provided me with industry expertise but also an extraordinarily helpful framework of "what great looks like" in business. How to identify attractive markets and how to win against competitors.

Being a consultant with a constantly rotating roster of clients led to the accumulation of experiences in a wider variety of circumstances and at a far faster pace than would be common working in just one organization. New assignments every couple of months, caused me to plunge into new information pools about completely different industries. I had to shift my thinking and adjust, continuing to be creative, thoughtful, and aggressive. This demanding work raised my intellectual ceiling. It was also useful to me that Ray had assembled an astute team of more than a dozen strategic consultants as collaborators, many of whom he hired from Harvard Business School. Three associates from those days eventually collaborated with me at IDEXX.

When I wasn't flying around the world, I commuted between our office outside Boston and my home in Portland. It was two hours each way and that was valuable time for contemplating factors that made companies successful, and searching for insightful patterns and practices. I developed a checklist of the elements that influenced the success or failure of businesses.

Working with Ray was ideal for me at that time. Determined to make my mark on the world, I was trying to learn as much as possible about business as it is practiced at the highest levels.

Chapter Three - Forge Your Own Path

One day, First Chicago Bank reached out to me. They were calling in a loan on a large poultry producer in Arkansas and asked me to conduct a fairness valuation on the company—establishing a price for the business that both the buyer and seller could agree upon. I flew down and checked into a hotel. The bank officials had rooms at one end of the hallway, and at the other end were the rooms occupied by the poultry company executives. My room was right in the middle. All night, and for the next two days, I went back and forth, up and down the corridor between various parties to negotiate a price and agree on next steps. In a transaction involving the famous Little Rock-based financial service firm, Stephens Inc., the company was sold to the Bass brothers of Ft Worth, Texas, and later purchased by Tyson Foods.

It was eye-opening for me to learn about this aspect of business. My role was important , and my weekly fees were more than my annual income years earlier working in Maine state government. But I had started to feel like a highly paid fixer, brought in to fix other people's problems. During that trip to Arkansas, I realized I no longer wanted my income to be tied strictly to the number of hours I worked. In other words, it was difficult to scale up as an individual consultant. The work was lucrative and interesting, but I was eager to be a builder rather than an advisor.

Looking down the hallway of my own life during that period, I started to envision a new and more inspirational destination. It was motivational to get to know many entrepreneurs like folksy but shrewd Don Tyson. His father had started the family poultry business by putting chickens in the back of a pickup truck in Arkansas and hauling them to sell in open markets in Kansas City, St. Louis, and Chicago. Don went on to build one of the biggest food companies in the world: Tyson Foods. Many years later, I became aware of claims about practices at the company including shortcomings on environmental and labor matters. My experiences had given me admiration for some of the pioneers in plant genetics and farming equipment, and I was especially impressed with E Robert Kinney whose entrepreneurial career brought him to General Mills, eventually as CEO.

with Bob Kinney

Motivational stories encountered in food and agriculture inspired me to explore a new arena, the world of entrepreneurship. I remember coming across Theodore Roosevelt's famous speech: "It is not the critic who counts: not the man who points out how the strong man stumbles or where the doer of deeds could have done them better. The credit belongs to the man who is actually in the arena, whose face is marred by dust and sweat and blood."

Part of rejecting conventional wisdom is listening to the voice inside that says that it's time to rethink priorities, to explore greater fulfillment through new opportunities. This might take the form of an inchoate sense of needing to find a new direction. Or it might be very specific about a new plan.

I remember precisely the moment of reaching full resolution to create a succession plan for myself at Agribusiness Associates and launch a new venture. It was May 24, 1983, the day my third child,

Chapter Three - Forge Your Own Path

Eliza, was born. There was something about looking down at her newborn face in the hospital bassinet and feeling her tiny hand clutch my finger that made me want to be my best self. The realization came to me with absolute certainty that it was time to put my energy into creating an enduring great company, working for myself and with a tribe of like-minded team members. This timing also coincided with a change in ownership structure at Agribusiness Associates where a client of ours, London and Continental Bankers became the major shareholder.

Highly rewarding experiences as a civil servant and a strategic consultant had helped me gain perspective on ways to create impact and achieve a fulfilling sense of purpose. Forging my own path required an accumulation of experiences in the world–almost layering them on top of one another like a sedimentary rock formation–to grow beyond the limits of my background. These helped me formulate a framework for further thinking about "what great looks like."

Takeaway: Business, entrepreneurship, impact investing, social activism, and public service have been sources of purposefulness, passion and happiness for me. While my path was inspired by the experience of others, it is authentically my own creation, and the role of serving as my own architect creates a great sense of ownership and satisfaction.

If you have not figured out what you want to do yet, don't despair, and don't settle. Take time to travel the winding path of exploration and discovery to find what is beautifully suited to you. Find that mission, that meaning, that reason for being–what the Japanese call *ikigai*–that enables you to live a life of your own authentic design. Hector Garcia, author of a book about *Ikigai*, has this perspective: "It is not what happens to you, but how you react that matters … it is much more important to have a compass . . . than to have a map." Logotherapy created by Western psychologist and Auschwitz survivor Viktor Frankl also focuses on finding happiness by recognizing that we always have the freedom to consciously choose our attitude. And he warns about chasing happiness: "happiness cannot be pursued; it must ensue."

Chapter Four
Cultivate Curiosity

*"Millions saw the apple fall,
but Newton was the one who asked why."*
– Attributed to William Hazlitt

A single word has often given me the mental discipline to challenge conventional wisdom and spurred my growth in diverse directions. Its three letters have served as a gateway to exploration and discovery, to curiosity, to a rich and intellectually nourished life, and to significant professional success.

The word is: why.

As Albert Einstein reportedly noted, "I have no special talent. I am only passionately curious."

As parents and grandparents know, every child is a relentless questioner, and that one word captures their boundless curiosity. Why is the sky blue? Why do zebras have stripes? Why does the ocean have tides? Why are you writing a book?

And then the real world closes in. For many children, inquisitiveness and a mindset of playful discovery is smothered bit by bit as they are marched through the educational system, which can often result in less questioning and more learning of teacher-approved answers. Maybe my failure to become an academic star was not only due to my disinterest in school but also connected to my persistent use of the word why, including: why should I follow the conventional path?

As an adult, the adventurousness associated with curiosity and asking "why" can lead to a life of fulfilling exploration and discovery. It causes persistent questioning of conventional wisdom and peeling the onion in search of special insights. It ignites mental agility, a hunger for learning, and openness to new ideas. We can all travel far along the road of learning and understanding with this one simple word.

Too often, we risk becoming prisoners of our own expertise. "Why" questions allow you to explore not the minutiae of a subject but probe the foundations, the underlying assumptions, the thinking beneath the surface. Confucius conveyed an important truth when he is credited with observing that: "the person who asks a question may be a fool for a minute. But someone who does not ask questions may be a fool for life."

To ask "why" as a leader can be a path to upending the status quo. Some see it as an act of defiance. Russian American novelist Vladimir Nabokov supposedly stated his belief that "curiosity is insubordination." Clayton Christensen, a renowned professor at Harvard Business School, is credited with pointing out, "Management teams aren't good at asking questions. In business school, we train them to be good at giving answers." In other words, MBA students may be trained to speak and then execute, rather than question and then listen. And top leaders such as CEOs may follow a tradition of issuing dictates to be followed by subordinates. But this can fail to engage the brainpower of an organization. In disruptive businesses of the kind I've helped build, the quality of critical thinking and the sense of ownership benefits dramatically by engaging a community of colleagues and teammates via provocative questions and a hunger for novel insights.

To create a world-class organization in support of the great aspirations of IDEXX, I recruited successful executives from companies that had demonstrated exceptional expertise in fields and functions relevant to our intent to create competitive advantages in each area. For research and development, we often recruited top people at Abbott Laboratories because of their stellar performance in human diagnostics. For product marketing, we often turned to legendary marketing organizations such as Proctor & Gamble or

Chapter Four - Cultivate Curiosity

other consumer packaged goods leaders. For sales, we sometimes sought animal health domain expertise from leading veterinary pharmaceutical companies, or, more frequently, capital equipment salespeople from the worlds of medical devices and office equipment. Xerox salespeople and junior military officers were great sources of sales and management talent. For finance, it was tempting to seek talent from finance "academies" such as GE despite our distaste for some aspects of their culture. Manufacturing talent was sometimes sourced from medical device companies such as Becton Dickinson, or from consumer electronics companies that were in those days under great pressure to improve manufacturing systems to meet the threat of competition from Japanese companies such as Sony and Matsushita. The organization benefitted enormously from the sense of "what great looks like" from these accomplished leaders with experience in high-performance companies. All of this experience and expertise then needed to be thoughtfully adapted and harnessed to meet our specific needs and circumstances in a small entrepreneurial environment, far different than that of a large already-successful corporation. The distinctive needs of insurgent versus incumbent organizations are addressed later in this book. The challenge was to incorporate and synthesize relevant best practices and expertise from many sources to create competitive advantages, while avoiding the adoption of practices and processes that weren't relevant to our circumstances. It's not unusual for people to continue using practices from a prior employer beyond their relevance.

In my business experience, a choice by a leadership team to create a culture of curiosity and critical thinking can lead to radically higher impact and better quality meetings. This includes a sense of cultural failure when business outcomes such as product design suitability could have been improved with more rigorous thinking and team interactions during the development process.

But it can be difficult for leaders to break the habit of being authorities on subjects, and to transfer a sense of intellectual ownership deep into an organization. I struggled with this transition as a leader even while knowing that my value as a leader was higher as an "orchestra conductor" versus a musician.

An important influence for me in this leadership style transformation was General Mills CEO Bob Kinney, who became a close friend and mentor. I clearly remember an incident in IDEXX's early days, when I was struggling with a decision and I asked him, "What would you do, Bob, if you were me?" He turned to me with an amused expression, and said "I'm sure you'll figure it out, David."

In an instant, a highly admired Fortune 500 CEO had entrusted a ~30-year-old first-time entrepreneur with full ownership of the decision. I was flattered, but also nervous that I didn't have the benefit of his decades of corporate experience and deep reserves of sagacity. Bob was, after all, a legendary business leader and entrepreneur who had started cooking and canning crab meat in his Bar Harbor, Maine, kitchen during World War II. He went on to head Gorton's Seafood in Gloucester, Massachusetts, where he saw the opportunity to expand the use of frozen fish for post-war households eager for convenience. Gorton's would go on to dominate the market by selling that most iconic staple of many a baby boomer's childhood, the fish stick. And they provided the fish in McDonald's Filet-O-Fish. He eventually took the helm at General Mills, home to Cheerios and Betty Crocker, among many other dominant brands.

When we met, there was an immediate connection. Bob had been born and raised in Maine, attending Bates College in Lewiston. He owned a summer house in Maine where I often visited him. And he maintained close ties with his home state as a civic leader involved with a number of significant nonprofits. One of these nonprofit institutions was The Jackson Laboratory, a world leader in mammalian genetics research. Bob urged me to join the board of trustees at Jackson and this became a very fulfilling long-term relationship for me, including service as chair of the board.

Chapter Four - Cultivate Curiosity

Our friendship provided me with perspective on the inspirational life of a highly accomplished executive, and I enjoyed our long relationship socially and professionally. Our friendship did not mean that Bob would provide me with answers to questions he believed I should learn to answer on my own. With a twinkle in his eyes, he showed trust in my judgement and often repeated, "David, I know that you'll come to the right conclusion." His trust in me was greatly appreciated.

Another mentor in those days was Dr. Mary Good, who served as Acting Secretary of Commerce and Under Secretary of Commerce for Technology in the Clinton administration. She also served as President of AAAS, where I served as a Trustee and Treasurer. Later she served on the IDEXX board of directors. Working with the Clinton White House, Mary recruited me in 1993 to serve on the Executive Committee of the US-Israel Science and Technology Commission to support peace in the Middle East. This followed promising diplomatic meetings at Camp David with President Clinton, Israeli Prime Minister Yitzhak Rabin, and Palestine Liberation Organization Chairman Yasser Arafat. The historic, and courageous, handshake between Rabin and Arafat occurred on September 13, 1993. I appreciated Mary's willingness to empower me in this role, and was honored to contribute to highly consequential negotiations in those times including high-level meetings with public and private Israeli leaders, and the creation of U.S.-sponsored programs to support peace. These programs included incentives for Israeli military-industrial companies to convert more of their capacity to consumer products, and to provide economic opportunity for Palestinians. In 1994 Arafat, Rabin, and his long-time political rival Shimon Peres won the Nobel Peace Prize. From my discussions with Rabin, I know that he was well aware of the risks associated with his advocacy for peace, including proposing Palestinian control of certain West Bank areas, and negotiating a treaty with Jordan in 1994. He was assassinated in 1995 by an Israeli extremist. Opposition leader Benjamin Netanyahu reflected that "it was an error to make peace with the enemy."

Empowerment of others, such as matters entrusted to our US Israel Commission, requires a willingness to take measured risks and understand the power of learning from mistakes and failures. To support this leadership style I sometimes tell colleagues, "I've made more mistakes than anyone here, but those errors are where wisdom comes from." As with children, taking responsibility is a key source of learning and personal growth. As the great Irish novelist and poet James Joyce wisely noted, "Mistakes . . . are the portals of discovery."

My life experience has given great conviction about the importance of building organizations of people who operate every day with the mindset of owners, including the sense of personal commitment, initiative, and responsibility that implies. Others have sometimes characterized this mindset as that of "crew members," implying a sense of teamwork to accomplish a mission. Building organizations of this kind requires supportive recruitment and organization development processes, as well as a willingness to acknowledge that some people won't succeed in that kind of culture. As in high-performance sports teams, there must be a mechanism for supporting those who thrive in a high-performance culture and acknowledging that others ultimately will not be able to contribute at levels necessary for collective success. As a leader in wave-making meritocracies, I've been responsible for cultivating shared beliefs about "what great looks like" and ensuring that processes and practices are in place to support high performance consistent with the organization's goals. These include regular reviews of both WHAT has been accomplished and HOW it was accomplished. It requires both compassion and tough-minded discipline to set a high bar for determining who will grow with the team and who won't.

Curiosity and critical thinking play critical roles in evaluating investment opportunities. Warren Buffett reflected on the importance of this when he said, "Risk comes from not knowing what you're doing." And: "Never invest in a business you cannot understand."

Chapter Four - Cultivate Curiosity

***

Adventurous curiosity and love of exploration are qualities that I greatly admire in friends and colleagues. This same mindset has helped me to expand my intellectual horizons into a variety of private sector domains and far beyond the confines of business. In my role as pro bono Trustee and Treasurer of the American Association for the Advancement of Science (AAAS), the world's foremost science association established in 1848, it was inspirational to participate in discussions with brilliant scientists about strategies to fulfill our mission to: "advance science, engineering, and innovation throughout the world for the benefit of all." Via more than 120,000 members, prestigious journals, scientific meetings, advisory services to Congress and federal agencies, and otherwise AAAS plays a critical role in what I believe is the greatest period of scientific discovery and new knowledge creation of all time. This includes our quest to understand the implications of the three great overlapping revolutions of our times: the atom (physics), the byte (digital electronics), and the gene (biology including genetics).

Science and technology are increasingly embedded in many aspects of modern life with major societal implications for issues ranging from health and wellbeing, to energy resources, transportation, communications, food and agriculture, recreation and entertainment, sustainability and much more. Economic prosperity worldwide is highly influenced by public and private investments in science and technology. Society has benefitted via amazing breakthroughs, vast knowledge expansion, and a vast array of novel goods and services. Yet these breakthroughs can also present undesirable and sometimes unforseen challenges such as environmental impact and social change.

Importantly, society also benefits from science's disciplined, evidence-based way of thinking – that sometimes conflicts with belief-based thinking. Public anti-science sentiment has increased in recent years and this in part reflects a conflict between personal beliefs and science-based evidence regarding evolution, climate change and other matters.

Over several decades the United States federal R&D spending has remained relatively stable at 2.5-3% of GDP while some other nations have increased their spending to higher levels. For example China's R&D spending as a percent of GDP has nearly tripled to 2.6% of GDP over several decades. Relative spending by countries influences the number of researchers, patents issued, science papers published, and discoveries that impact global competitiveness.

In the United States government, the Department of Defense dominates R&D spending with nearly half of the total federal R&D budget of more than $150B. Health and Human Services, including NIH, accounts for roughly one quarter of total federal R&D spending, followed by the department of energy, NASA, the National Science Foundation, Agriculture, the National Oceanic and Atmospheric Administration, and others.

Industry R&D spending is typically twice the federal spending level and highly focused on development versus research. An important factor in private sector R&D spending over several decades has been the vast expansion of entrepreneurial ventures in life sciences, technology and other disciplines. US venture capital investments in entrepreneurial tech ventures exceeded $150B in 2023, down from a high of more than $300B annually.

I am not a scientist, and it can be intimidating to lack deep domain expertise in subjects under discussion. But great value can often be added simply by asking "why", by listening for comprehension, probing, and understanding the logic behind a complex issue. It can be very important to admit a lack of understanding of technical issues and ask for further explanation. Scientists with deep domain expertise can benefit from these conversations by having to explain their work in terms understandable by the general public. Legendary scientist

Chapter Four - Cultivate Curiosity

Albert Einstein reflected this sentiment when he allegedly said: "If you can't explain it simply you don't understand it well enough." Just as when I worked for Governor Longley, I discovered that accomplished scientists often enjoy the opportunity to explain their work to people outside of their field. The two-way benefit of explaining and teaching was captured well by author Robert Heinlein who once said: "When one teaches, two learn."

Through the AAAS, I had many opportunities to experience the power of science to impact the world. One of many examples of this was the opportunity to be a keynote speaker at the 2014 World Semiconductor Summit in Abu Dhabi as participants explored the future of this transformational technology. Another example is the role it played in fostering a diplomatic breakthrough with Cuba. The United States had severed ties with Cuba in 1961 during the Cold War because its leader, Fidel Castro, ardently embraced communism and the USSR.

with Peter Agre in Havana, Cuba

I had become friends with Nobel Prize laureate Peter Agre, a remarkable molecular biologist on the faculty of Johns Hopkins University. With other members of the AAAS board and leadership team, we conceived the idea of organizing a "science diplomacy" mission to Cuba with the Cuban Academy of Sciences. On a previous scientific visit to Cuba Peter had met with Fidel Castro and a number of distinguished scientists. On our mission in 2014, we met with accomplished Cuban scientists, reviewed scientific programs, established a productive dialogue, and signed a cooperation agreement between AAAS and the Cuban Academy of Science. While there, we visited sites associated with the momentous times of the Cuba missile crisis in 1962. In October of that year, the United States and the Soviet Union engaged in a very tense military and political standoff when it was discovered that nuclear-armed missiles had been installed in Cuba, over 100 miles from US shores. During our 2014 visit, I heard for the first time the story of a Soviet submarine carrying a nuclear torpedo that traveled through the US blockade. It was later found that a heroic act by Russian submarine B-59 deputy commander Vasili Arkhipov thwarted the launch of this nuclear weapon, and perhaps averted World War 3, by purportedly swallowing his launch key. Miraculously the nuclear torpedo was never launched. And via diplomatic discussions the world will never forget, Kennedy and Khrushchev avoided war, and perhaps the most dangerous moment in human history.

at 2015 reopening of Cuban embassy with José Ramón Cabañas Rodríguez, first Cuban ambassador to USA in more than 50 years, and Frances Colón, Deputy Science and Technology Adviser to the U.S. Secretary of State

Chapter Four - Cultivate Curiosity

Upon our return to the United States, we shared our experience with Dr. John Holdren, science advisor to President Obama and president emeritus of AAAS. Our mission helped lay the groundwork for the Obama Administration to re-establish diplomatic ties with Cuba the following year. Peter and I were among the guests of honor at the reopening of the Cuban embassy in Washington, DC. In 2016, Obama made an historic trip to Cuba, the first sitting US president to visit the island since Calvin Coolidge in 1928. I was proud to be part of an effort that demonstrated the ability of science to play a role in diplomacy, and it's gratifying to see AAAS continue to play this role globally as needed.

On a personal level, curiosity and willingness to explore new domains have expanded my world, allowing me to build productive relationships with, and learn from, brilliant scientists and academics. As I sought to navigate my way through the world of entrepreneurial wave-making, I'm fortunate to have acquired broad and worldly experience that can add value in these relationships. I find that assuming the role of questioner offers highly valued opportunities for extraordinary people to explain their work, techniques, vision, and theories. And this demonstration of interest, and willingness to learn, can forge important human connections. Most people are happy to share something that's meaningful, whether it's a decision by a neighbor to open a cheese shop down the street, or why my friend, the actress Goldie Hawn chose to become an advocate for children's mindfulness as a way to help them manage stress. I will talk more about our collaborative work later in the book.

***

A desire for growth, adventure, and discovery motivates me to travel the world, including a region so remote and isolated that few Westerners have ever journeyed there. This particular adventure began two decades ago in Shanghai China at a lecture about Buddhism by a noted scholar. The lecture rekindled my curiosity about the appeal of

Buddhism, the world's fourth-largest religion, with its basic premise that suffering is a choice. I meditated on the implications of this belief, pondering the "why" of pain and misery. I've learned to share a Buddhist belief about the importance of cultivating an attitude of non-attachment, i.e., that one must develop the capability to achieve an internal sense of acceptance, peace, and patience. My life experience has taught me that we have far more control over thoughts and our mental outlook than I realized early in life. So, I appreciate the value of these Buddhist teachings and beliefs.

In addition to contemplative practices, my exploration of this spiritual path included talking to friends who were practicing Buddhists and reading relevant books. These included *The Monk and the Philosopher: A Father and Son Discuss the Meaning of Life* by the French intellectual Jean-François Revel and his son Matthieu Ricard, a celebrated monk and former genetics researcher. Abandoning his promising career as a scientist, Matthieu has served for many years as the Dalai Lama's French interpreter and science advisor. His background in Western science as well as Buddhist teachings increased my appreciation of his widely attributed wisdom, such as: "Knowledge does not mean mastering a great quantity of information, but understanding the nature of the mind." Or "Happiness is a skill, emotional balance is a skill, compassion and altruism are skills, and like any skill they need to be developed."

I traveled to Tibet, sometimes called "the roof of the world" to experience its spectacular landscapes and distinctive culture. In two weeks of epic hiking, we trekked to sacred hermitage caves and temples established centuries ago. We observed life in tiny mountain villages, and we visited with monks in their saffron robes. The isolation of these places is striking, and it was clear that our visits were a rare occurrence. We saw that monks in remote monasteries sometimes seek further isolation by retreating from the world to meditate for five or more years.

Chapter Four - Cultivate Curiosity

It was an extraordinary experience in many ways. The natural world on the Tibetan high plateaus is awe-inspiring. The way of life is ancient in a world where this has become increasingly rare. The rutted, narrow roads were barely navigable. The local food was challenging, including "sampa", a sacred favorite made of grains and honey, and formed into balls by hand. While we appreciated the gesture of hospitality when offered sampa, hygienic concerns were often validated with resulting sickness, and I lost more than 25 pounds from sickness combined with long strenuous hiking. But the magnificent, sparsely populated landscape with its towering snow-capped mountain tops, its bucolic valleys, and friendly people left indelible memories. Because I wanted to travel with someone who could share a deep knowledge of Tibet and its culture, we were accompanied by an English-speaking Buddhist monk who walked with us for two weeks along ancient pathways. At one point, we were joined by a reclusive barefoot Lama—a monk who quietly chanted and sometimes spoke to us in Tibetan over his shoulder as we journeyed through the mountains. Watching that Lama, seeing villagers call to him, asking him to come down to their little huts outside of which the Lama and the families knelt and prayed together for a few minutes,

befriended by a Lama, trekking in Tibet

was fascinating. I'm appreciative of the ability to experience and learn from these special moments that are far from my normal daily life.

My time in Tibet was a profound spiritual journey, with the opportunity to benefit from curiosity about matters that significantly impact the world but had been somewhat foreign to me. Rather than accept facile answers about Buddhism in a lecture hall, I journeyed halfway around the world to spend time with a practicing monk. For me, going deeper, pondering, and asking why again and again translates into a more spiritually nourishing life.

This adventure also further nourished my love of nature and trekking. I find that walking all day, in this case often behind massive yaks heavily burdened with supplies, can become meditative and contemplative.

Several years later I experienced the magic of Bhutan via a circumnavigation of sacred Mount Jomolhari. In the late afternoon of our first day of trekking, we reached the awe-inspiring and ancient Tiger's Nest Monastery, built on a precipice with dramatic scenery overlooking a beautiful valley. Also known as Paro Taktsang, Buddhism holds that Guru Padmasambhava brought Buddhism to Bhutan at this location. Our guides talked with us about Buddhism's seven types of happiness and enlightenment: mindfulness, investigation, energy, joy, tranquility, concentration, and equanimity. These principles were on our minds as our trekking continued for more than a week across high mountain passes, heavily forested lowlands, farming communities, and scenic villages. At a palace dinner, we heard the story of a declaration by the 4th king of Bhutan that "gross national happiness" is more important than "gross domestic product" as a measure of the country's success. This challenge to conventional wisdom has received great attention globally.

A companion on our Bhutan adventure later led me on a trek to the stunning monarch butterfly sanctuary in Mexico, where

Chapter Four - Cultivate Curiosity

he had played a lead role in protection as a United Nations World Heritage Site. The three to four-generation annual migration of these butterflies over thousands of miles is a marvel in the natural world. In Tibet, Bhutan, and elsewhere, I have found that trekking or hiking benefits clear and creative thinking, in the same way you can get lost in thought when you're driving for hours. Although my meditation practice is somewhat unconventional, it has deepened and grown over the decades. Today, I feel very fortunate that my experience in Tibet strengthened a contemplative practice that would help save my life, a story I will share later.

Cultivating and appreciating the benefit of curiosity led me to collaborate with my friend, John Hendricks, founder of The Discovery Channel, and film producer Steve Burns to explore and create retreats at his Gateway Canyons, Colorado resort, intended for deep dives into highly consequential issues of our times. Our vision was to gather top thinkers and scientists to discuss today's global concerns. We sought to inspire ardent learners with curious minds. As an advisory board member, I helped strategize about important themes, identify great speakers, and help with presentations. Our speakers ranged from authors Doris Kearns Goodwin and David McCullough to physicists Lisa Randall, Michio Kaku, and Brian Greene, internet gurus Vinton Cerf and John Seely Brown, journalist Carl Bernstein, psychologists and diplomats, and many others. The retreats were high-impact gatherings, and they became a launch platform for a streaming video-on-demand channel called Curiosity Stream. I'm proud to have played a role in this venture and to have some of my video content on this channel.

Takeaway: When you're on your phone, talking to a friend, listening to a scientific presentation, in a meeting, or watching a political debate, realize the immense value of challenging conventional wisdom and gaining personal conviction through critical thinking. Learn to champion that voice in your head whispering something similar to the quote popularly attributed to Mark Twain: "Whenever you find yourself on the side of the majority, it is time to pause and reflect."

Allow yourself to wander intellectually and perhaps even physically through travel to be sure you are thinking about your future in a rich and thoughtful way. Put more optionality on your radar screen. Don't be narrow. Explore. Dream. Ask: why?
Then, discover *how*.

interview at Curiosity Retreat

with Doris Kearns Goodwin

John Hendricks and Steve Burns

Wave Making
Timeline

1980
- Telluride, 1970
- State of Maine, 1975
- Down East article, 1977
- Agribusiness Associates, 1979
- IDEXX founded, 1983
- Jackson Laboratory board, 1989
- Maine Medical Center, 1989

1990
- Boston Marathon, 1990
- Kilimanjaro, 1991
- Carstensz Pyramid, Irian Jaya, 1994
- US-Israel Commission, 1994

2000
- Patagonia & Tibet, 2002
- Grand Canyon, 2002
- Harvard Kennedy School, 2003
- US Department of Defense, 2003
- Ironwood, 2003
- Venrock, 2005
- Bhutan, 2006
- Ikaria, 2007
- Life Science Hall of Fame, 2008

2010
- National Park Foundation, 2010
- Galapagos, 2010
- AAAS, 2010
- Ovation, 2010
- Covetrus & VFC, 2010
- Honduras & Viral Encephalitis, 2011
- Modern Meadow, 2011
- EM Shaw & Filmmaking, 2012
- Panama, 2012
- Seakeeper of the Year Award, 2013

2015
- Sargasso Sea Declaration, 2014
- Curiosity Retreat, 2014
- Cuba Science Diplomacy, 2014
- Machu Picchu, 2015
- Blue Ocean Award, 2016
- Sages & Scientists, 2016
- David E Shaw & Family Sculpture Park, 2017
- Hulaween & Bette Midler, 2017
- Palmyra Atoll, 2017
- Aspen High Seas, 2017
- White Shark Cafe, 2018
- Rwanda, Palau, 2018
- Sages & Scientists, Bentonville, 2019
- Antarctica Bicentennial, 2020

current
- Arctaris
- Black Point Group
- CEO.org
- Council on Foreign Relations
- Explorers Club
- GeoSure
- Itaconix
- IUCN
- Just Capital
- Leerink
- Maxwell
- MindUp
- Nautilus media
- Ocean Elders
- Polaris Partners
- Saildrone
- Second Century Stewardship
- Teddy Roosevelt Society
- UNE Shaw Fellows
- UNH Shaw Innovation Explorers
- USM Shaw Innovation Explorers
- US Olympic & Paralympic Museum
- Waterbear Network

Launch Wave Making Films

To YouTube

To Website

David Shaw with: gorillas in Rwanda, with shark in Honduras,
winter traverse of the Haute Route,
introducing Alan Alda at AAAS annual meeting,
diving with manta rays in Palmyra Atoll,
with US Interior Secretary Bruce Babbitt in the Grand Canyon.

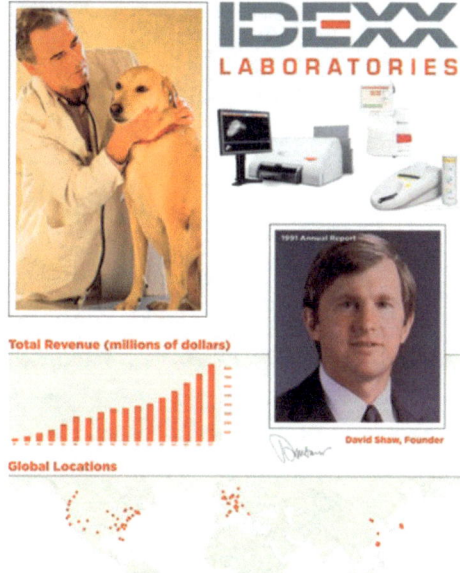

Early IDEXX team (then named AgriTech),
IDEXX 1991 annual report image, David Shaw
with Peter Crisp of Venrock, IDEXXers playing shoe golf,
David Shaw employee #1 badge

David Shaw with Deepak Chopra, Bette Midler, Mensun Bound,
Richard Rockefeller,
Superintendent Kevin Schneider, and Ocean Elders

Carstensz Pyramid, in Western Papua, with Dani tribe member, scuba diving with Palau President Tommy Remengesau and Sylvia Earle, with Thunderchief motorcycle group in Palau, with Jimmy Chin in Greenland ... and IDEXX golden claw award

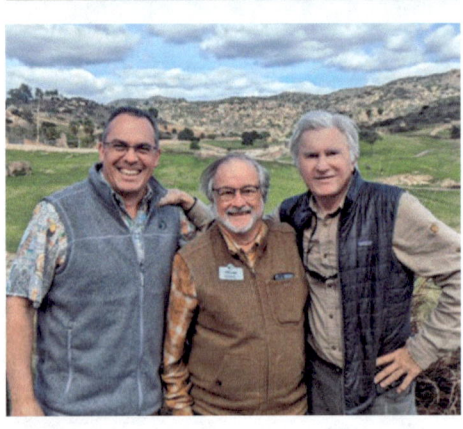

David Shaw ice climbing with Conrad Anker, with Supreme Allied Commander Europe General Jim Jones, David Shaw Amara sculptures, at San Diego Zoo Safari Park with Paul Baribault, CEO, San Diego Zoo and Wildlife Alliance, and Oliver Ryder, PhD, Director of Conservation Genetics, SDZWA, business logos, non-profit logos

Part Two
LIVE WITH INTENTION

Created by David Shaw in DALL-E

Chapter Five
Build a High-Performance Tribe

"What counts in life is not the mere fact that we have lived. It is the difference we have made to the lives of others that will determine the significance of the life we lead."
– Nelson Mandela

During my freshman year of college, I played for the UNH football team. I was a walk-on, playing offensive end, and the smallest player on a team consisting mostly of big, strong, outstanding athletes, including a Golden Gloves boxer.

The intense experience of being on a football team can cultivate friendships quickly versus just nodding to people in your classes or dorm. Great teams can coalesce as tribes in a matter of hours or days via the crucible of intense shared experiences. Some of my teammates were from South Boston, a long-established historically Irish enclave in Boston. They had grown up in a culture dramatically unlike Durham, New Hampshire—and their distinctive "paahk the caah" accent revealed that I was small but interesting to them. They felt almost like older brothers, and nicknamed me "Shawzy."

The season was going well for me until we played against the Dartmouth freshman team in Hanover, New Hampshire. The Dartmouth player opposite me weighed two hundred and thirty pounds and could outrun our halfback in the open field. He was also talkative at the scrimmage line, with some intimidating smack. I dished back and got some good plays on our side, including a pass I caught for yardage we badly needed as they dominated the game. This just escalated his threats. While his size was intimidating, I had found opportunities to counter that by being wily. That all ended after another good play on our side when he looked me in the eye and promised "your head is coming off." As the ball was snapped, I felt my helmet get stripped off my head with his right arm and then his left arm smashed into my face. I felt like a cartoon character, dazed, and confused with stars in my eyes, lying flat on my back. Jack, Bobby, and other teammates were standing over me looking down with worried faces. "Oh man, Shawzy," Bobby said, "Your nose is plastered all over your face!"

"Where's my helmet," I asked, trying to get up. "Time for revenge."

"You are not doing anything," Jack said, kneeling next to me. "You are going to lie down. ...We'll take care of this."

My pals restrained me while the medics sprinted onto the field with a stretcher to carry me off to the locker room. The Dartmouth player had indeed broken my nose, which would leave me with a deviated septum and a nasal voice for the rest of my life. But what I remember most from this experience was how great it felt to have protectors and teammates who were looking out for me. That game was our final freshman match and the end of my inglorious college football career. However, team members remained good friends for years, and experiences like that led to many new friendships. I also learned to better assess opponents before provoking a fight.

My friendship with Jack and Bobby led to a memorable night celebrating St. Patrick's Day with them in South Boston: "Southie." This was an offer I couldn't refuse: a trip to the famous "Southie" amidst the high-energy celebration of St Patty's Day, with two Irish friends who grew up there.

Despite being well aware of the famed "fighting Irish" culture of Southie, I wasn't prepared for the chaos that unfolded after we entered a local bar. Quicker than you could say "luck of the Irish" a bar brawl broke out, maybe sparked by some old animosity. Tables flipped, fists flew, and beer bottles became projectiles. Feeling the need to be a good friend, I joined the fray, only to be swiftly plucked away by Jack, and stashed in a corner. Just when I thought things

CHAPTER FIVE - BUILD A HIGH-PERFORMANCE TRIBE

couldn't get worse, police barged in and my head started spinning with the consequences of being arrested, going to jail, having a criminal record, and missing school. But instead of putting us all in handcuffs, one of the cops issued a threat that got Jack's full attention: "Jack, you get out of here now or we're gonna call Mom." "Mom?" I thought, then realized that the two cops must be Jack's brothers. Talk about buzzkill and instilling the fear of God! Jack pleaded with him, and we high-tailed it out of there, armed with tribal bonds of trust and loyalty cemented via a shared St Paddy's Day experience.

***

Strong community relationships and tribal organizations have played an important role in my life, so I seek to build and support them. From my days as a camper at YMCA Camp Belknap on Lake Winnipesaukee in New Hampshire, I've seen people unleash inner, sometimes hidden, superpowers when they feel they are part of a tribe. They build bonds via mutual values and beliefs, speaking the same language, and sharing experiences. Think of the warring Yankees versus Red Sox tribes.

When I started my own company, I was determined to create a culture where team members shared this same sense of community and tribal bonds. Where the traditional sense of employment and work was transformed into a sense of avocation, play, and belonging. We would empower community through culture.

In the process of deciding WHAT the company's business would be, I gave equal thought to WHO we would be, including the foundational values upon which the organization would be built. I had even envisioned what "a day in the life" of our company would look like. My process of creating a vision started with. identifying an ecosystem of values, virtues and principles that would support exceptional success. Then defining my leadership role and the company's cultural foundation. And then, envisioning what all of this would look like on a daily basis. In my mind's eye, I saw my role as the mayor of the community, the orchestra leader. Consistent with our intention to create and commercialize transformational products, we also had the inspiring opportunity, and need, to build a transformative entrepreneurial organization. We could reimagine work and not be bound by traditions that might encumber competitors. The accomplishment of great things would only be possible if we were a great organization, with great people, and great business practices aimed at accomplishing something bigger than all of us.

Apple Computer once celebrated the culture of disruptive entrepreneurial organization with this advertising campaign: "Here's to the crazy ones. The misfits. The rebels. The troublemakers. The round pegs in the square holes. The ones who see things differently. They're not fond of rules. And they have no respect for the status quo. You can quote them, disagree with them, glorify or vilify them. About the only thing you can't do is ignore them. Because they change things. They push the human race forward. And while some may see them as the crazy ones, we see genius. Because the people who are crazy enough to think they can change the world, are the ones who do."

The founding team at IDEXX agreed on things that we didn't want in our workplace. We didn't want time clocks for employees to punch in and out. We were wary of the negative impact of pyramid hierarchies —the big boss, the middle boss, the little boss, the workers— with me perched on top—or fancy offices for executives in suits. We wanted a caring meritocracy where everyone is encouraged to express their opinions and where the best ideas win. We wanted everyone to operate with an ownership mindset, making decisions in the context of what's best for our collective interests. I wanted to steer clear of the us-versus-them atmosphere I remember from when I worked in factory jobs growing up in Nashua. I can still recall the noxious ammonia stench of the chemicals used to remove hair from the hides soaking in huge subterranean tanks in the tannery where I worked.

Chapter Five - Build a High-Performance Tribe

Equally vivid in my memory was the way my fellow shoe factory workers and I were hunched over our leather-cutting tasks when management walked by in suits. At the tannery, there was never a sense that this was a collaborative enterprise with all of us united to produce the best leather possible that would result in high-quality shoes, wallets, or other goods. Our visibility only went as far as the raw material, the hides. We had little awareness of the end user, and I promised myself that if I were ever in charge of a company, everyone would always understand the purpose of their labor. On the floor of the tannery, there was a sense of class alienation. To me, this style of business seemed to be staid, traditional, uninteresting, and ill-suited to great success.

The golden age of entrepreneurship in our times offers an opportunity to devise something very different. I envisioned that IDEXX would be a group of people who were incredibly fulfilled by great collaborative achievements, making products for which they received intensely positive feedback. We embraced the idea that entrepreneurial companies can be highly fulfilling enterprises that don't fit a conventional image of traditional businesses. They can be a fantastic creative exercise, an efficient and effective way to express values, operating as a soulful, like-minded, self-empowered community. This is the reason we granted stock options to every employee at IDEXX. From day one, I wanted us to feel connected to each other—including financially. If the company did well, everyone profited, from the R&D staff to the receptionist to the line workers. This was going to be an organization of ownership-minded people.

While widely participative stock ownership has become more common recently, especially in entrepreneurial companies, it was less common in early IDEXX days. So it was important to regularly reinforce its meaning throughout the organization including at the time that grants were made. There were many memorable instances when we were able to demonstrate this value. I remember a conversation with a third shift "IDEXXer" in manufacturing who told me that his water heater had failed during a cold weather spell. I explained that exercising his stock options would easily pay for a new water heater and much more. It was an emotional and meaningful moment for him, demonstrating the value of having an ownership stake.

Our leadership group nurtured a high-performance team culture and community atmosphere through shared team building and social bonding activities such as white-water rafting, paintball battles, completing Outward Bound wilderness programs, and celebrating successes via awards like "The Golden Claw." This was a lobster claw that had been spray-painted gold and attached to a wooden base. Originally given to me as a joke, it became a highly coveted prize that was awarded periodically to the most outstanding team or team member in terms of performance exhibiting our shared values. This IDEXX equivalent of an "Oscar" traveled from proud recipient to proud recipient all around the world. Another award was called the 2X Award for a person or team that demonstrated "above and beyond" effort and performance, as the double X's in IDEXX exhorted us to do.

Working in an entrepreneurial high-growth company can be an intense "all in", "crucible" experience as the team seeks to collectively achieve audacious goals. Under the best circumstances, this intensity is welcomed by the team as part of a contagiously exhilarating and deeply fulfilling life experience. This can sometimes lead to people not taking vacation time. So it can be important to not only encourage vacation time but to establish a mechanism for more meaningful re-energizing breaks. To address

CHAPTER FIVE - BUILD A HIGH-PERFORMANCE TRIBE

this, we created an official sabbatical program where, based on tenure on the job, IDEXXers could have a month or more off to re-energize themselves. We called it PGL–Professional Growth Leave. This wasn't a vacation. It was an opportunity for people with more than 5 years of tenure to pursue intellectual growth and then bring this reinvigorated mindset back to IDEXX. The program benefitted employees and our company because returning PGLers often arrived back on campus brimming with ideas and enthusiasm for our mission.

To foster community, we created an in-house cafeteria where there were many opportunities for the kind of informal interactions that can enhance innovation and collaboration. The executive team sometimes served lunch as a gesture of service to the organization. We also encouraged people to mix up their lunch groups to foster new relationships, and I did this regularly. We also had several in-house bands that played at our high-energy parties.

From the beginning, investors and others had concerns about locating our company in Maine. The concentration of entrepreneurial companies in places like Cambridge and Silicon Valley reflects the importance of density as a success factor in many industries. This same phenomenon is true for music in Nashville, art in Miami, and media in Hollywood. One benefit of density is the ability to change employment to another company without relocating. Another benefit is the depth of a skilled workforce for growth and expansion, and a work culture that is consistent with the needs of entrepreneurial tech companies. In the state of Maine license plates have been promising VACATIONLAND since 1936. I discovered that new hires sometimes had misguided expectations that working for a company in Maine translated into a more easy-going, laid-back atmosphere than what they might encounter at a Boston or Silicon Valley biotech startup. We had to make it clear that, "at IDEXX, we are all in, all the time, and we expect the same charge-the-hill spirit from every team member."

It's important for leadership teams to visibly demonstrate

support for company initiatives including community service. One year, I announced a special prize for the IDEXXer who contributed most generously to a nonprofit that supports economic mobility, education, and health resources in the Portland area during their annual fundraising campaign. I would give the winner a ride to the cafeteria on my motorcycle. At noon on a designated day, the throaty sound of my Harley Davidson filled the corridor. Amid the cheers of onlookers, I rode up to the winner's desk, handed them a helmet, and gave them a ride to the cafeteria, where I treated them to lunch, before returning to work. I made this gesture to encourage a sense that we were all in this effort to care for others, both as a company and within the larger community. Many years later, stories like this have become part of the company's folklore.

As a group, our team strived to stay aware of relevant happenings to IDEXXers outside of work, demonstrating our appreciation of this community of people. This included weddings, graduations, births, and illnesses. When an employee in Italy was diagnosed with cancer, everyone in our Milan office shaved their heads in a show of empathy.

Our team made it a point to show appreciation in unexpected ways, such as arriving with pizzas to have midnight "lunch" with night crews. It can be important for tribes to have a clubhouse. With this in mind, I bought an old house about twenty minutes from our offices in Portland. The tribe wasn't just the top executives or scientists, it was many IDEXXers. One way of reinforcing our tribal spirit was a policy of promoting from within whenever possible, and also cross-training people to have experience in many different functions. This helped ensure that leaders reinforced our culture, captured in company folklore, which was passed from employee to employee. We spoke the same language, understood the acronyms, and shared inside jokes. We resisted platitudes and signs that trumpet, "We believe in customer service.", preferring to capture our beliefs in colorful stories such as superhuman efforts to get a customer what they need.

CHAPTER FIVE - BUILD A HIGH-PERFORMANCE TRIBE

It was important for our culture that everyone in the organization understand how their work contributes to key success factors including customer satisfaction. For someone in manufacturing, we wanted them to understand that somewhere in the world, someone was using a test kit they made. Maybe a vet was treating a family's beloved pet, or it was a water utility employee using one of our diagnostic tests that checked the *E. coli* levels in a city's drinking water. To help create the culture of customer focus we often invited customers to speak to people in the organization who don't normally have customer interaction. I wanted them to go home and think about the customers who benefited from the quality of their work. We also insisted that managers regularly visit customers in the field, and we applied the same customer focus to internal customers – ensuring for example that R&D should consider manufacturing to be its internal customer and that finance treat other departments as highly valued internal customers. Our leadership team adopted a practice of reaching out to IDEXXers around the world to show appreciation for their customer service efforts, and we often placed customer satisfaction as the first item in management meetings and business reviews.

We also sought to make the threat of competition very clear to people in all functions. Our view was that when even one customer somewhere in the world bought a product from one of our competitors, that was a real threat to all of us. It wasn't just economic. It threatened our competitiveness, the quality of our work, and the pride we took in our products. In a highly competitive world, the consequences of being even the second-place market share company can be very unattractive so it's important for everyone to understand the consequences of not being the best in the world in our business.

Little things can have great symbolism in a company. To everyone in the company, I was "David" and never "Mr. Shaw." And this applied to our leadership team members. We dressed in jeans and casual clothes versus the jackets and ties of bigger and more traditional businesses. I preferred not to always be at the head of the table or to be valued based on title or position. Wavemakers are set apart by what they do, not who they are or what their job title is. I prefer to intentionally create what I consider a radical meritocracy rather than establishing an authoritative or bureaucratic hierarchy. This includes generous acknowledgment of people who contribute the most in meetings, and who set examples for others.

Remembering our all-for-one spirit of the early years still makes me emotional. If the staffers were overwhelmed by the volume of customer phone calls, an SOS would come over the intercom. Top biologists, salespeople, accountants, me—everybody in the building—scrambled to the phones to deal with a customer service issue or take an order. The same camaraderie operated in the distribution center where sometimes you'd find many staff members packing and labeling until midnight with me leaving last to turn off the lights and lock the door. All the departments felt that we were in a firefight to survive and be great. For the R&D team, this resulted in a relentless embrace of innovation where every test and device was continually tweaked and improved upon. The sales team wasn't satisfied until every customer converted to IDEXX products and services.

And we took this passion for excellence and community on the road. Literally. One of our customer-focused rules at IDEXX was that when *anyone* in the company—not just salespeople—saw a veterinary clinic while driving, they were expected to pull over, go in, and demonstrate how they would benefit from our products. No exceptions. Including me.

I remember one year driving to my parent's home in New Hampshire. It was the Wednesday before Thanksgiving, and it seemed every family in New England was traveling for the holiday. My family and I had been on the road for two hours when I saw the sign of a veterinary clinic.

I pulled into the parking lot, grabbed my briefcase with

Chapter Five - Build a High-Performance Tribe

the IDEXX diagnostic devices, and walked in. After getting past a frowning receptionist, I asked the vet, "How do you perform your diagnostic tests?"

"We send them to the lab and get the results back in a couple of days."

"What if a pet owner brought their sick animal in, you took a blood sample, and five minutes later, you had the results?"

The vet looked at me with a cocked eyebrow, "That's impossible?" he asked.

"Let me show you. Do you have a blood sample from a cat you think might have feline leukemia?" I asked. A common cause of death among cats, after trauma, is an agonizing disease whose progress can be slowed by early detection and treatment, adding years to a cat's life.

"It's the day before Thanksgiving. I have sent all my samples out to the lab."

I opened my briefcase and gave the vet the diagnostic device and two vials of blood. After he poured each out, the one on the left turned bright blue, a positive result for feline leukemia. The vet turned to me, in surprise and said: "Amazing: where can I buy these?"

The following Monday when I returned to the office, I shared the story of that successful visit. Coworkers, in turn, gave their accounts of stopping at vet offices all over New England and beyond, recounting the reception they had received. Inevitably the results were positive when we were able to demonstrate our products because they had game-changing value that could be shown in just minutes. But getting the opportunity for those demonstrations, as an unknown company, in busy vet clinics, could often be very challenging. And this led to many amusing stories as well as shared suggestions about overcoming those obstacles. Years later, these early stories seem almost surreal after we built an extraordinarily powerful sales, marketing, and service organization around the world.

***

Not long ago, a colleague was driving me to Schiphol Airport outside Amsterdam, in the Netherlands after a week of investor meetings for Waterbear network, a novel impact media company that I'm supporting as an investor and advisor. As we approached the airport, we saw a large sign for IDEXX and realized that we were passing the company's European headquarters that I had established many years earlier. With time before my flight to ocean stewardship meetings in Monaco, I asked my colleague to detour into the IDEXX parking lot. We proceeded to walk into the lobby and, without disclosing my identity, I asked for several people who had been on my staff before I completed a CEO succession plan 20 years earlier, in 2002. Just by chance, a senior leader was passing through the lobby, heard the names I asked for, and informed me that these people had retired. She then asked who I was and the nature of my interest in IDEXX. Prepared for this, I showed a photo on my phone of my old IDEXX employee #1 security badge. Startled, she introduced herself and graciously explained that she was well aware of my role as founder and offered to provide a tour. As she escorted me into the office area I asked to see the warehouse. As we walked into the shipping room a forklift driver abruptly stopped his vehicle and shouted my name. "David Shaw!" he said, "I'm sure you don't remember me, but I've been waiting for this day for 20 years." By now several senior staff members had joined us and they looked bewildered by this scene. The forklift driver walked to me, took off his shoe, and said "Let's go." I proceeded to take my right shoe off, balance it on my right toes, and fling it through the air onto the seat of his forklift ~20 feet away. This produced gasps and laughter among the growing crowd of people who had joined us. To my surprise, the

CHAPTER FIVE - BUILD A HIGH-PERFORMANCE TRIBE

forklift driver matched my shot and squealed in delight. We were playing "Shoegolf" and had tied with hole-in-ones on the first hole. We agreed to play a second hole before I departed for my flight and his victory on that hole in front of so many colleagues produced a state of near ecstasy. By now we were running out of time for my flight and began to say goodbyes, with thanks for a very short, surprise visit. But my Shoegolf opponent insisted that I stop at his office area on the way out. Our growing entourage followed him to his desk where he displayed an enormous trophy with his name engraved on it. "Twenty years ago" he announced, "you gave me this trophy when I came in second in a Shoegolf match here. I think of that every day." And then he turned to the gathering crowd and said "this is the guy I've been telling you about. He founded our company, and it was always fun when he visited here." After several photos, I said goodbyes and dashed for my flight.

Shaw Shoegolf trophy

Wave Making : Inspired By Impact

As we sought ways to build a culture of purposeful playfulness, collaboration, competitiveness, and community at early IDEXX, we adopted Shoegolf as a tribal sport. Shoegolf is a game my brother and I invented as young teenagers to break up the tedium of walking to school in Nashua. We would pick targets such as trees, road signs, or trash cans and fling our shoes with our feet to hit those targets. Now trademarked and listed on the Urban Dictionary website, Shoegolf is played by flinging off your shoe at different predesignated "holes"—a fencepost, a mailbox, whatever. I had no idea at the age of twelve that it would turn out to be a lifelong sport. I have played the game with people from IDEXX in Maine, the Netherlands, and Japan as well as with Nobel Prize winners, media celebrities such as George Lucas and Steven Spielberg, government officials such as Commerce Secretary Penny Pritzker, and many others including my college-student mentees, and my grandchildren.

In my leadership capacity in various companies and organizations, the collective and distinctive ritual of Shoegolf was an easy and unorthodox way to break down barriers. It requires no previous training, no limit to the number of players, and no special field or equipment. However, a spare shoe might be needed if you happen to get your shoe stuck in a tree or kick your shoe into a swimming pool. This happened to actor and director Robert Redford the time we went toe-to-toe in a Shoegolf match at my home in Maine.

It was not surprising when I walked into our IDEXX office in Taipei, Taiwan many years ago that people were lined up, not to kiss the boss's ring but because it was "game on! Let's play Shoegolf." Everybody had their shoes ready. At that moment, I was not the company's CEO. I was not even at an elevated level. Instead, we were all part of the same tribe, and we were having fun, talking about how one person almost broke a window, how another lost their shoe up in a tree, how somebody else fell into a puddle or hit the forklift. Experiences like this help to humanize work relationships and create meaningful bonds with team members.

CHAPTER FIVE - BUILD A HIGH-PERFORMANCE TRIBE

It might be helpful to provide more examples of these experiences because of the important role that they can play in wave-making. A common practice for our family in Maine is to play beach bocce at low tide at the Prouts Neck beach. Important relationships are built quickly as teams compete to win a large gaudy championship trophy. Winners have ranged from friends and team members to National Geographic Society CEO Gary Knell, actress Bette Midler, and renowned violinist Charles Yang. At our annual Halloween parties, we ask attendees to be part of the entertainment, and this can include joining in on a chaotic dance performance of Michael Jackson's hit: Thriller. For his 70th birthday at Skywalker Ranch, I showed my appreciation for being part of the assembled tribe by showing a video of me as Darth Vader performing a hip-hop song entitled "Big Birthday, Seven Oh."

Here's another amusing example. When a gang of grey squirrels staged an invasion of my guest house at Prouts Neck one winter by climbing down the chimney, local police officer Peter Nappi helped me through a remarkably exasperating multi-day effort to remove them. But it quickly became obvious that when it came to pest control, we were about as clueless as two cats in a dog show. First, we tried the obvious things like closing the fireplace flue, since we weren't able to install chimney-top barriers during a snowstorm. After we released the first intruders, they came right back down the chimney, with reinforcements, and it was unbearable to hear their high-pitched squealing, stuck in the chimney above the closed flu. But we are not the kind of people to back down from a challenge. With professional help days away, and armed only with improvised capture systems like blankets and nets, we went full MacGyver on these critters. These totally failed on our first attempt and with the result that squirrels, covered in black chimney soot, raced around the house for what seemed like an eternity. Finally, we somehow succeeded in wrangling and evicting these grimy intruders but our fondness for grey squirrels was devastated. Turning this challenge into an opportunity, I recognized that this experience benefitted my friendship with Officer

Nappi. The next day, when my sense of humor returned, I bought a large, plush gray squirrel stuffed animal and left it on the front seat of Officer Nappi's empty cruiser, along with a framed certificate of commendation from the "North American Squirrel Association." This is just one amusing example of how small "thoughtful" gestures can build meaningful bonds with people in a world where so much interaction is conducted digitally.

Takeaway: It's human nature to have tribal instincts, to seek community, to want to belong to a group. This aspect of human nature can be a powerful force in building a cohesive company with a shared vision to create great value in the world. In this sense, WHO a company is can be even more important than WHAT it does. Conversely, success in WHAT a company does can be highly dependent on becoming WHO it needs to be in terms of organizational development, culture, values, and business practices. In my experience, when asked why people admire organizations, the answer is often about the character of an organization rather than the business it's in. So, an important success factor in wave-making is getting the character of the organization right to support the nature of the challenge, realizing that different challenges will benefit from different character traits. For the types of challenges I like to take on, I value a culture that blurs the distinction between work and play in pursuit of a highly fulfilling mission and disruptive goals.

> "Far and away the best prize that life offers
> is the chance to work hard at work worth doing ."
> - Theodore (Teddy) Roosevelt

Chapter Six
Capitalize on Critical Thinking and Constructive Debate

"The question is not what you look at, but what you see."
– Henry David Thoreau

An important role of art, in all its forms, is creative expression that helps us see the world differently through fresh and distinctive eyes, revealing new insights and perspectives. In 1981, for example, Maya Lin, then an unknown twenty-one-year-old college student at Yale University, submitted her design for the Vietnam Veterans Memorial in Washington, DC. She was not constrained by the classically inspired white marble and limestone buildings and monuments that dominate the National Mall—the wedding cake-like US Capitol, the Greek Parthenon-esque Lincoln Memorial, and soaring above them all, the Washington Monument, built in the style of an Egyptian obelisk. "I imagined taking a knife and cutting into the earth, opening it up, and the initial violence and pain that in time would heal," Maya once said of her concept, which consists of two polished black granite walls joined in a V and etched with the names of the more than fifty-eight thousand soldiers who died in the war.

The simplicity and power of Lin's submission resonated with the judges, who chose it unanimously over 1,421 others in the largest design competition at that time in US history. Upon its unveiling on Veterans Day 1982, however, the finished product was anything but universally well-received. Critics described it as "a black gash of shame" and demanded something more akin to the heroic bronze figures of traditional war memorials. Just such a representational statue, Frederick Hart's "Three Servicemen," was added to the site two years later. But as time has passed, it seems to me—and to the tens of millions of people who have visited The Wall—that Lin has succeeded in her mission. Over coffee after the 2021 opening of her Ghost Forest exhibition in New York's Madison Square Park, Maya told me that an important aim of her work is: to create a private conversation with each viewer.

Her point of view resonates with me due to my internal conversations every day with the art that inhabits my house in Maine. The works of sculpture that speak most deeply to me often involve the repurposing of everyday materials into objects of beauty. The remarkable transformation of those materials encourages me to think differently—to reimagine what is possible.

This important role of art in exploring creative perspectives has significant implications for high-impact wave-making in public and private ventures. Beneficial change in the world very often requires reimagining current circumstances, looking through new prisms, and abandoning old beliefs and ways of thinking.

One of my favorite artists, John Bisbee, from Brunswick, Maine, creates sculptures exclusively with metal nails. While for most of us a nail registers as an extraordinarily common item—if it even registers at all—John looks at nails and sees them for what he calls their "infinite potential." His Renaissance-era bust with a lavish "lace" collar sits on a table in my living room, and we installed his trumpet made of specially fabricated bronze nails as part of the David E. Shaw and Family Sculpture Park at the Portland Museum of Art. John describes his approach this way: "Taking the most ordinary, mundane of objects ... and spending my entire life trying to unleash it into its full capability and never fully getting there ... For me, it's about transformation and discovery and risk and failure—and occasionally reward."

My collection also includes the work of Chakaia Booker, who repurposes car tires, or "automotive rubber", to design large-scale abstract or semi-figurative sculptures. When Chakaia visited me in Maine for the opening of the David E. Shaw and Family Sculpture Park at the Portland Museum of Art, she inspired me to create my

CHAPTER SIX - CAPITALIZE ON CRITICAL THINKING AND CONSTRUCTIVE DEBATE

own art.

Another recent art project was my commissioning of a bust of the great Mark Twain by Taiwanese artist Long-Bin Chen, who crafted the piece from two boxes of books I provided that were written by or about Twain. It's meaningful to me, and of course to Long-Bin, that the medium for all of his sculptures are remaindered books usually related to the subject of the sculpture such as an Einstein sculpture made of Einstein books. He also uses outdated city phone books and other printed materials.

Great art calls forth new questions and provokes us to think in novel ways. It was a glorious day a few years ago when artist Peter Lundberg's larger-than-life bronze sculpture, "Return to the Sea," arrived in my driveway on the back of a flatbed trailer. The piece had traveled from China and roughly resembles a figure-eight set on its side—but with three loops instead of two. Peter describes sculpture as "an abstract language that we use to describe and to revel in the world, offering a view that you wouldn't normally see, and a way to appreciate things that come from the imagination ... It inspires, and it gives you something to play with in your mind ..."

Sculpture has had a profound effect on me due to its physical presence and also because it changes the way I experience a space. More than an object, it's the object's impact on the surrounding area that creates the deepest resonance, sometimes with spiritual significance. I have created my own sculptures with the hope of creating the kind of meaningful private conversations with viewers that Maya Lin speaks of.

To illustrate the importance I place on sculpture and its ability to move people, I also created a prominent outdoor sculpture park in the state of Maine. The David E. Shaw and Family Sculpture Park is outside the paywall of the Portland Art Museum so everyone in the city can enjoy this artwork in a natural setting. I believe this is a lasting gift to help future generations benefit from the gift of artistic inspiration.

Of course it is not just visual art that brings about new insights. Talented poets, writers, singers, and musicians can convey a thought or generate a mood in a few words or notes that reorder people's perceptions.

This discussion about the role of art in society is highly relevant to the art of becoming a successful entrepreneur or innovator. It is the ability to look outward or inward and see something differently, to gain new insight. Francis Bacon captured this belief when he reportedly wrote that "the job of the artist is to deepen the mystery." Sometimes success comes from observing or envisioning what other people cannot or do not. At other times, you see what everyone else sees but internalize it differently.

When I became a founding board member of the United States Olympic and Paralympic Museum in Colorado Springs, Colorado, I was inspired to get better acquainted with another group that often sees the world very differently from the rest of us, and from

CHAPTER SIX - CAPITALIZE ON CRITICAL THINKING AND CONSTRUCTIVE DEBATE

the way that we see them. I was in awe of the physical gifts and accomplishments of extraordinary Olympic and Paralympic athletes. But it was the private perspective through which they viewed their own accomplishments that most impressed and fascinated me.

Melissa Stockwell   Jackie Joyner-Kersee

It's common for media sources including TV sportscasters to focus on the "medal count" during Olympic Games, calculating that one country has won three more gold medals than another and perhaps creating drama about how disappointing it was for an athlete to have won a silver medal instead of gold. Of course, Olympians and Paralympians care about medals, but I've heard from many athletes that seeing everything through the prism of gold, silver, or bronze is a narrow view. A common view expressed to me is that the achievement these athletes are often most proud of is the mental mindset that it takes to reach this level of performance and competition… the ability to achieve the "mind of a champion." To reach the Olympics they have navigated their way through extraordinary challenges, and overcome many obstacles, in the face of potential failure. This accomplishment is a source of deepest satisfaction. These are the stories they love to talk about and share with others, be they young aspirants or fans of their sport in the Olympic Games. To triumph, these athletes require resilience, courage, and the ability to see the world through a prism utterly different from the perspective of winning versus losing. The battle, not the victory, is often of utmost importance to them.

Motivated by my interactions with Olympians and Paralympians, I've supported the creation of an educational program aimed at inspiring elementary, middle, and high school students. In a recently launched program called Becoming Your Personal Best (BYPB), Olympic and Paralympic athletes help teach life lessons, appropriate for each age group, about the six BYPB Resiliency Skills: Self-Identity, Mindset, Problem Solving, Perseverance, Relationships, and Confidence.

Via this program, we highlight how at some point early on in their lives, most not even out of elementary or middle school, these athletes—had decided to go for it! Only a few brave souls make that kind of big commitment at such an early age. The journey to becoming an Olympic athlete requires a great deal of struggle and sacrifice along the way. It's a daunting pyramid to climb. And before

Chapter Six - Capitalize on Critical Thinking and Constructive Debate

you even confront the athletic challenges, you need to master the myriad of mental challenges.

***

Being a disruptor starts with an idea—a "*what if*". You imagine something new that will create value in the world. Sometimes these ideas are highly audacious. They may be bolder than you think you're capable of executing—something that hardly seems possible. But it can be captivating to think, *If it were realizable, it would be transformative!* Then, you start to put together plans to convert an idea into reality, to understand the detailed operational issues required to fulfill your dream. Think of the printing press, which Johannes Gutenberg introduced in the middle of the fifteenth century. And, more than half a millennium later, an awe-inspiring slate of audacious modern technology companies such as Google, Facebook, Amazon, Tesla, and Genentech. The feeling of awe associated with observing the game-changing nature of these creative ventures can be inspirational and empowering to aspiring entrepreneurs.

Often, the best insights about ways to create value emerge from going out into the world and exploring unmet needs. Here is an example: In 1989, I became chairman of the board of the nonprofit The Jackson Laboratory, widely known as JAX, in Bar Harbor, Maine. JAX is a renowned research nonprofit institution with three inter-related missions. It has conducted cutting-edge research in mammalian genetics since its inception in 1929. It has a well-known educational program that was the starting point for three future Nobel Laureates. And it, uniquely, operates a robust and large-scale infrastructure that supplies customers around the world with many strains of mice with different genotypes (specific genetic configurations) that mimic human diseases. Among its many distinguishing achievements, research from the JAX has been connected to 26 Nobel Prizes, and scientists at the Lab have made numerous discoveries aimed at providing cures for cancer, heart disease, neurodegenerative illnesses, and others. JAX professor George Snell, Ph.D., won the 1980 Nobel Prize in Medicine for providing an in-depth understanding of the immune system's major histocompatibility complex, making organ transplants possible.

As the human genome sequencing project progressed through the 1990s revealing more secrets of DNA, and as it became feasible to engineer mouse genomes, —we found that customers were eager for JAX to offer a wider variety of mice strains and research services. Mouse models were playing an increasingly important role in biomedical research to understand the relationship of genetic composition to human health and to evaluation treatment opportunities. My friends at JAX were outstanding academics but working in an somewhat isolated research environment in Downeast Maine. The opportunity presented itself for me to bring business sensibilities from someone who had innovated at scale in biomedical entrepreneurship to build a global organization. This worked out beautifully. We recruited talented senior business managers such as Charles Hewett Ph.D. and encouraged a more customer-centric orientation without jeopardizing our academic edge. As a result, we expanded the service offerings to meet growing customer needs around the world, and revenues increased exponentially.

After implementing a succession plan for my role as chair of JAX's board of directors, I remained closely linked with JAX as a friend and advisor to subsequent leaders such as Edison Liu, M.D. To foster continued out-of-the-box and exploratory thinking, I recently endowed a chair at Jackson Lab for business and institutional innovation to fund, in perpetuity, a senior leader focused not on the mechanics of production, but organizational and business innovation in the nonprofit space. It has been inspirational to me to have a role in enhancing the ability of individuals on teams to see and think creatively, and to learn to look with fresh eyes.

Truly disruptive ideas, however, do not always come from interacting with customers about their unmet needs. Often, someone

Chapter Six - Capitalize on Critical Thinking and Constructive Debate

can describe what they think they're missing or what is making them unhappy with a product but not how to fill the gap or fix the problem. As the industrialist Henry Ford, whose Model T automobile revolutionized transportation in the early twentieth century, supposedly said, "If I had asked people what they wanted, they would have said faster horses." Similarly, we didn't recognize that we were dissatisfied with heavy luggage, flip phones, and motels before roller bags, smartphones, and Airbnb became available to us.

An entrepreneur can be anybody who spots an opportunity for disruption. History is full of stories of people who came up with a concept but who, for whatever reason, could not quite gain wide public acceptance for it. Henry Ford, for instance, was not the first automaker, but he perfected the assembly line and produced a vehicle that was widely accessible and affordable to mass markets.

Entrepreneurs and change makers often talk about pioneers as people with arrows in their backs who are killed because they went first, ahead of the next generation of innovators. Steve Jobs and Steve Wozniak did not invent the personal computer, but they transformed it into something beautiful and easy-to-use for a broad audience. Early-stage pioneers face the daunting task of proving a new concept and creating demand with customers who may be resistant to change. For example, the internet as an e-commerce platform was validated by others before Amazon built upon that pioneering experience and created a business of massive scale. Risks associated with development are usually far lower than risks associated with research.

Learning from pioneers, by reverse engineering their experiences, can dramatically de-risk a new venture.

When I got involved in the Portland-based carbon-capture company Running Tide in 2020, it was not the first-ever effort to attempt carbon capture at scale or combat ocean acidification. The company did an extensive landscape analysis of competitors, observed them closely, and gained valuable insights into difficulties associated with entering an entirely new market. Pablo Picasso captured an element of this approach when he reputedly said: "Good artists borrow; great artists steal." However, capital markets can be very challenging for new ventures of this kind and Running Tide has not been able to raise the capital necessary to accomplish its mission.

A subset of borrowing, or "stealing," is pattern recognition—seeing what works in one field or situation and adapting it to another, a skill I have developed and used throughout my career. It was pattern recognition that we put to use when we repurposed human diagnostic technology for animals to tremendous success at IDEXX. In formulating the business plan for IDEXX I realized that human diagnostic technology was highly applicable to the animal health market and that animal health was not a likely target for the large human-focused companies that were potential competitors. So we created a series of licensing and development agreements that provided us with outstanding technology platforms that needed to be customized for veterinary needs. One of our first partners was, Hybritech, a San Diego-based biotech firm that was commercializing a small handheld device as a home pregnancy test using urine. After a series of meetings, they saw the advantage of incremental revenue from a partner in a market that was a low priority for them. We signed a licensing agreement and began a very successful partnership.

About six months after our partnership got underway, our R&D team developed a way to improve the device to test whole blood instead of just urine. The way vets checked for feline leukemia in those days was a laborious process, often consisting of sending a sample to a lab and waiting a couple of days for the results. Our innovation meant timesaving convenience: a pet owner could bring their cat to the vet, and get a test result from our IDEXX diagnostic kit in just minutes during the patient visit. The vet could then treat the animal as needed before it went home. This was revolutionary: better medicine, better customer satisfaction, and more cost-effective. It is

Chapter Six - Capitalize on Critical Thinking and Constructive Debate

deeply gratifying when you can change the basis of competition, write new rules, and transcend the status quo. We would eventually use the same device to test for heartworm and parvo virus in dogs, and feline immunodeficiency virus among others.

Years later, I founded another animal health company called Vets First Choice (later evolved into Covetrus) with my son Ben and former IDEXX colleagues, to pursue a very large opportunity enabled by new technology. Survivors of the "dot-com bubble" had proven the immense practical value of the internet. Online shopping was taking off, and we realized that the internet could be utilized to disrupt the traditional distribution of veterinary drugs and related animal health products such as specialty pet food. This is a market that I had explored at IDEXX. We were well acquainted with the fact that veterinary clinics, unlike most human medical practices, inventory and dispense a wide range of drugs, nutritional, and other products to pet owners. While veterinarians are accustomed to operating these dispensing businesses, most prefer to focus on their medical practice. We determined that we could benefit the practice and pet owners by becoming an outsourced dispensing partner via sophisticated mail-order operations that we established around the world. Because we had access to patients records and practice management software systems, we went a step further as a prescription management partner, alerting vets when a prescription was due for a refill, automatically refilling it, and sending the medicine directly to the pet owner rather than requiring them to come back into the clinic. Eventually, we added other services including an extensive system of custom compounding pharmacies that supply veterinary clinics with a very wide range of drugs for specialized needs. Covetrus went public in 2019 with annual revenues exceeding $2B. It has since been taken private at an enterprise value of roughly $4B.

Seeing things differently does not have to apply only to a physical product. Another part of being an entrepreneur is shaping the way other people view things, or even shaping the way you view it. When starting IDEXX, I noticed that virtually every company in the field called itself a diagnostic business, and this framework felt too narrow. It described the function we performed—that is, what was happening in the test tube—versus the customer benefit we offered—the information about the animal's health obtained from the test. Was the animal healthy or sick? Based on that key insight, we redefined our business, calling it a healthcare information and decision support system, and this redefined the basis for competition.

Developing this new point of view led us to conceive of additional products and reimagine the kind of relationship we could have with customers—one that would be very different from that of competitors. In addition to selling diagnostic products to vets, IDEXX would create and sell the computer software management information systems that helped vets run their practices and integrated test results into the computer system, adding to overall efficiency. Soon we added clinical laboratories to our offering as well as remote cardiology and radiology services. Our relationship transformed from a vendor of diagnostic products to an indispensable partner of mission-critical products and services. We saw an analogy to the way that Apple Computer's business evolved with its ecosystem of game-changing products and services.

***

It's ironic to me that Mark Twain was a failure as an entrepreneur. He incurred daunting financial losses trying to launch an automatic typesetting machine and had to embark on an extensive speaking tour in Europe to recoup his financial losses, which topped over two hundred thousand dollars, or about six and half million dollars in purchasing power today. Where he excelled, though, was as a world-class noticer, whose keen and original observations—which he often delivered through humor—helped other people see society differently. It was Twain who said, "Travel is fatal to prejudice, bigotry, and narrow-mindedness."

Chapter Six - Capitalize on Critical Thinking and Constructive Debate

Just as art, music, and poetry can change our perceptions, traveling takes us out of our daily routine and our traditional ways of thinking and seeing. It means that your brain is not operating in the same old framework, a framework that might not serve a wavemaker well. Inspired by artists like Twain, I have developed certain habits of observation intended to enrich my experiences and to make them more memorable—especially while traveling. Strolling through the crowded medinas—or old parts—of Fes, Casablanca, and Marrakech during a recent trip to Morocco, for example, I forced myself to observe more intently by describing the scenes to myself using vivid language, and asking myself what would get my attention if I were a security guard, an artist, an investor, a city official, etc. Wandering through the colorful and inspirational Yves Saint Laurent Museum in Marrakech dedicated to the French clothing designer's work, I also attempted to view the experience through a variety of filters including even YSL himself. It's important for me to get the most out of an experience, and counter the human tendency of self-preoccupation, by spotting patterns or stories to absorb as much fresh knowledge and human connection as possible. This openness to experience and novel ways of seeing things can cultivate the beneficial emotion of awe.

Takeaway: When I was a teenager cutting scrap leather in a Nashua shoe factory after school, my co-workers and I sat in two lines facing each other at a table. Each of us had a piece of leather on a wooden cutting block, and our job was to hammer out as many decorative pieces as we could, making the most of each scrap. No one was giving me or us a holistic view of how our decorative pieces fit into the world. Our framework for understanding the value of our work was extraordinarily narrow – we didn't feel connected to the success of the greater organization and lacked the sense of purpose or fulfillment that might have been possible under other circumstances. This heads-down approach changed when I got to college and became friends with students who had work experiences that helped them understand the greater purpose of the organization.

I resolved to seek a higher level of awareness and even special insights relevant to my interests. Learn to see what other people might miss. To engage in the creative process is to pay attention to both the subtle details and the wider landscape, which affords us new perspectives. Insightful vision is an essential element to cultivate as an innovator, entrepreneur, investor, and wave-maker. Or as an artist.

Perhaps author James Joyce was addressing this issue when he wrote: "shut your eyes and see."

Created by David Shaw in DALL-E

Chapter Seven
Nurture Resilience and Courage

"Every time you are tempted to react in the same old way, ask if you want to be a prisoner of the past or a pioneer of the future."
– Attributed to Deepak Chopra

Sometimes, happenstance takes over in ways we cannot anticipate—forever changing how we experience the world. This happened to me in 2011. Oceanographer Sylvia Earle and I were on a scuba diving mission in Honduras to explore the health of the Mesoamerican Reef, the world's second-largest reef system stretching over 600 hundred miles from Honduras to Mexico. On our final dive, a group of large Caribbean reef sharks suddenly swarmed us. I instinctively started to push them away with my camera equipment as Sylvia took shelter under a coral ledge. But the sharks only grew more agitated, their thrashing attracting yet more sharks. Running low on oxygen in our dive tanks, we eventually escaped them and ascended to the safety of the dive boat.

my photo: one of the sharks swarming us

Back home in Maine soon afterward, I woke up in the middle of the night with horrific pain on the right side of my head. My hands were numb, and my vision blurred. After attempting to drive myself to the hospital, I turned around and called 911. I am a lifetime sufferer of migraine headaches, but this was an entirely different magnitude of agony.

Arriving long after midnight at Maine Medical Center by ambulance, I knew enough about diagnostics to insist the ER doctors check my spinal fluid for infection using a technology we had employed at IDEXX called polymerase chain reaction or PCR. This novel technology amplifies DNA in samples to improve sensitivity. The test came back positive, indicating that a virus was replicating in my brain. This emergency required specialists—and fast. In a race against time, I was administered an anti-viral drug named Acyclovir, loaded into an ambulance, and rushed—sirens screaming—to the world-renowned Massachusetts General Hospital (MGH) in Boston. Before departing Maine Medical Center I had sent an indication of my condition to friends in Boston, including Nobel Prize laureate Phillip Sharp who headed the McGovern Institute for Brain Research at MIT. I'm deeply grateful for the role that he and other friends played in my care.

AAAS chair emeritus Phillip Sharpe, and Susan Hockfield, president emeritus of AAS and MIT

Chapter Seven - Nurture Resilience and Courage

I was in a coma on arrival at MGH. The doctors there confirmed a diagnosis of viral encephalitis, a rare inflammation of the brain, with a mortality rate of more than 70 percent. Those who do survive are often permanently brain-damaged. My medical team theorized that my encephalitis was triggered by stress from the shark attack, which activated a dormant virus we all have in our nervous system. In my case, the virus traveled up my trigeminal nerve, which provides sensation to the face, through my right eye, and into my right brain. An MRI showed damage to my right frontal lobe, lateral lobe, and adjacent tissue.

When I finally emerged from my coma weeks later, it was hard for me to process what had happened. As I lay in the neurotrauma ward day after horrible day, I could not recognize visitors or comprehend what they were saying. My brain injury didn't cause me to lose existing memories, but I was unable to form new ones, which explains why most of the time I spent in the hospital remains patchy and vague. One of the few things I held onto was that my younger daughter, Eliza, was having her first baby in a few months. I wanted to stay alive to cradle this child in my arms, and provide helpful Shoegolf lessons in our highly competitive family. I also recall, without many details, how meaningful it was to have so many visits, calls, and cards from family and friends. One call came from television journalist Bob Woodruff who called at the suggestion of Tom Brokaw with a message of hope after recovering from

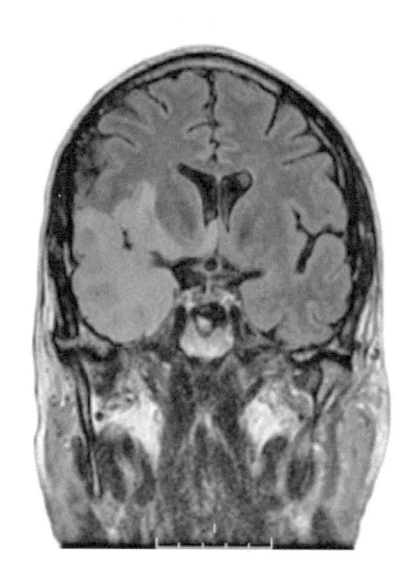

early MRI of my brain injury

a traumatic brain injury sustained in Iraq during the Gulf War. Bob also sent me the book he wrote with his wife: *In an Instant: A Family's Journey of Love and Healing.*

After two months at MGH, I was ready to be released, but almost everyone in my immediate circle, including family members and my medical team, felt that the best place for me to recuperate was at a nearby rehabilitation center. In that environment, I would receive twenty-four-hour care, the best therapists, and easy access to the world-famous Boston hospital. But I somehow knew that my recovery would benefit significantly by returning to my home life in surroundings I loved on the coast of Maine. I was grateful for the care I was receiving but also increasingly miserable with what I experienced as unpleasant and demoralizing cognitive therapy exercises, such as flashcards, in an institutional environment.

Upending the status quo, I prevailed, going home to face the most arduous six months of my life. Among many other skills, the right brain is responsible for spatial abilities and visual awareness, which is why it was difficult to find my way around my house. Nor was it possible to drive a car. Severe vertigo and headaches were a constant source of misery, and it was a struggle to focus. The smell and taste of food made me nauseous due to disrupted neural networks in my brain, and for weeks I subsisted solely on bottles of vanilla Ensure.

Recovering from viral encephalitis was an epic battle that would forever transform my world. During this time of despair and exasperation, my doctors, family, and friends were of tremendous help. But I grasped that I had to own my recovery—a scary but empowering realization. The only person who could make it happen was me, despite my deeply impaired cognitive capabilities. The infection forced me to draw upon reserves of resilience that I simply did not know I possessed. This expression attributed to British poet William Blake captures the challenge: "enlightenment means taking

Chapter Seven - Nurture Resilience and Courage

full responsibility for your life." He also reportedly wrote this about the human potential to rise to great challenges: "great things are done when men and mountains meet."

This is when I discovered that our brains are capable of healing themselves. Doctors now recognize the enormous potential of neuroplasticity–the ability of neural networks to remodel themselves. Dr. Rudolph (Rudy) Tanzi, one of my doctors at MGH puts it this way: neuroplasticity "says that every experience changes the connections between neurons in the brain. Even a thought or feeling can change things." All of us can employ self-directed practices or assisted therapy to build rich, new pathways throughout our lives. If you try to learn another language or play a new musical instrument, at first you can't. But when our minds create an intention and seek to act upon that, our brains have the capability to create enabling neural pathways. The world struggles to explain the distinction between the mind and the brain ... I began to think of the brain as the car and the mind as the driver.

A positive development that came out of my struggle was the necessity to immerse myself in a better understanding of the fascinating realms of human consciousness, behavioral health, and contemplative sciences. These new frontiers of scientific exploration are among the most important and fascinating issues of our times.

Cognitive therapy helped me develop a system for using my brain more purposefully and positively, and I became much more aware of the power of intent in shaping consciousness. Talking to yourself, and being self-aware, triggers brain activity in ways we still don't completely understand. For example, when I put down my cell phone, I made a conscious effort to remember where, often talking to myself out loud with the hope that this would create a memory: *I'm putting my phone on the kitchen table in front of me.* Sometimes it worked; sometimes it didn't, and I had to try again and again. It was one day at a time as I willed myself to recover.

with Rudy Tanzi and Deepak Chopra

In my recovery from encephalitis, I devoted hours to sitting quietly to take in nature's magnificence, often on the rocky ocean cliffs near my home. Like many others, my life has benefitted from the sense of wonderment and awe often associated with being in nature. I sought this calming benefit now, including the triggering of higher levels of oxytocin, to counter negative emotions brought on by my brain injury. I deepened my meditation practice in the spirit that Deepak Chopra reportedly expressed this way: "The purpose of meditation is to stop thinking for a time, wait for the fog of thought to thin, and glimpse the spirit within."

As part of my therapy, I embarked on several new activities, including learning how to play musical instruments, starting with drums. This was inspirational for two reasons. One was that acquiring a new skill helps to establish and strengthen new neural pathways. The second was because several of my doctors at MGH, including Ron Hirschberg, were musicians. They believed that music including drumming can help boost brain health in several ways, including enhancing sleep. I witnessed situations where patients with neurodegenerative disease were better able to walk to the beat of music, and able to sing despite difficulties talking.

Chapter Seven - Nurture Resilience and Courage

Not surprisingly, I discovered that drumming is about as easy as teaching algebra to a goldfish. When you watch people doing it with apparent ease it can be easy to imagine that you're capable of it as well. But when you first try to play the instrument, you realize it's remarkably difficult. One foot is doing one beat, and the other foot goes off on its own adventure. Then you have one hand doing a rock'n'roll beat, and the other thrashing a wild tango. Like many other worthwhile things in life, you try and try and try, and, eventually, you learn. Now, I can play basic beats reliably, as well as guitar and harmonica. I am grateful to my friend, and great harmonica player Mickey Raphael of the Willie Nelson band, for sharing his love of music and encouraging the life-enriching practice of playing harmonica.

Years later, while attending the Bohemian Grove's summer encampment in Sonoma County, California, I had a memorable meeting with Mickey Hart, world-famous drummer for the Grateful Dead. I was smoking a cigar, an occasional habit inspired by cigar aficionado Mark Twain, when Mickey and I met and talked long after midnight at the Owl's Nest Camp. Sitting with Dr. Bob Tjian, president emeritus of the Howard Hughes Medical Institute, I shared how drumming was helping me as a form of therapy to aid my recovery from viral encephalitis. Mickey was enthusiastic, well-informed, and supportive about the many health benefits of drumming, telling me "neurons that wire together, fire together" and "we've got to make music medicine." There's meaningful science to support this idea. I personally experienced the benefit of what's known as "brainwave entrainment," which is the concept that external stimulation at a certain frequency leads the brain's electrocortical activity to oscillate at the same frequency. Low brainwave frequencies, known as theta waves at 4 to 8 Hertz, are associated with sleep, and can be induced by external sounds at that frequency. Recent neuroscience studies show that brainwave manipulation to other frequencies can be beneficial for learning, reduction of anxiety, and other applications. I realized how right Albert Einstein was when he supposedly said, "in the middle of every difficulty lies opportunity."

After an arduous six months, I started to resume some of my previous activities with the belief that this would benefit my condition. It was important for me to test the belief that I could again be functional, productive, and impactful.

Perhaps the greatest test of this at that time was confirming my intention to join a 2012 ocean stewardship expedition to Panama that had been planned long before my battle with encephalitis. Less than a year after returning home from MGH my doctors were astounded when they heard about these plans, including my hope to scuba dive as part of the expedition. Encephalitis had damaged neural networks in my brain that impacted "executive function." This refers to a set of skills that enable us to plan, focus attention, remember instructions, juggle multiple tasks successfully, and understand potential future consequences of current actions. I was well aware of this and sought to regain this capability in my daily activities. My sense was that executive function was improving along with other cognitive functions. Upon hearing my plans the medical team at MGH was highly skeptical and sought to dissuade me from this trip. I took comfort from the likes of Ayn Rand who expressed this attitude: "The question isn't who is going to let me; it's who is going to stop me."

I am deeply grateful to our expedition host, my brilliant friend Bill Joy, co-founder of Sun Microsystems, for anticipating my special needs and assuring me that the risks were manageable. To avoid any risks associated with scuba diving, this included the use of a submarine for underwater exploration at depths of more than 1,000 feet. Our expedition was a success in many ways including very meaningful initiatives with the government of Panama regarding ocean stewardship initiatives, contributing to the creation of large marine protected areas. From a personal perspective, the experience was successful as validation that I could step back into a life I loved, with inspirational friends. I returned home with a belief in a bright future of impactful wave making, and with a profound sense that I should make the most

CHAPTER SEVEN - NURTURE RESILIENCE AND COURAGE

of the "bonus time" I was blessed with after surviving encephalitis.

exploring Coiba region of Panama by submarine

In 2015 I joined a Chopra Institute retreat in Kerala, India to deepen my contemplative science practices. This provided still more confidence-building evidence that I could transcend the challenges of encephalitis and transform these struggles into opportunities. Upon returning home, my struggle gained another layer of meaning when my doctors told me that my survival and recovery had served as inspiration for novel brain health initiatives including the creation of a center for integrated brain health at Harvard University and Mass General. By then I had become friends with Deepak Chopra, and he invited me to be a keynote speaker at the Chopra Institute's 2016 Sages and Scientists Symposium. It was a very gratifying convergence of circumstances when my panel discussion at the symposium also became the occasion for the new Harvard/MGH center for integrated brain health to be announced by Dr. Jonathan Rosand and Dr. Rudy Tanzi who had played key roles on my medical team.

My personal experience has taught me that we all have the capacity to improve our mind and brain health through practices such as embracing change, breaking out of old habits, and refusing to fall victim to negative emotions generated by the lower brain. Virtually anyone can benefit from developing a greater consciousness about brain health, which dramatically influences one's sense of well-being.

Another unexpected creative avenue opened in the exhausting early days after I returned home from Mass General. My phone rang. "I have some things that belonged to your great-great-grandfather, and I'd like to come see you," the caller said. He was a Civil War historian from Virginia whose expertise was the Tenth Maine Regiment, where my ancestor Elijah Morrill Shaw had served as a Union officer. To demonstrate the depth of his expertise, the caller informed me that he had collected more than 20,000 items from the Tenth Maine. Weeks later he arrived at my home carrying a few old letters, documents, and corps badges from the 10th Maine. We sat down to talk, and I quickly witnessed his extensive knowledge along with a realization that my cognitive deficiencies might keep me from remembering many details about matters important to our family. So, I instinctively grabbed my iPhone and hit record. "Please say your name and why you're here," I said. "Tell me what you know about my great-great-grandfather, E.M. Shaw."

"I feel a certain friendship with your great great grandfather," he said, choking up as he touched the Civil War uniform and sword I brought out for his visit. Because he had immersed himself in my great-great grandfather's handwritten letters, he felt a bond with my ancestor that crossed centuries. He told me that among other battles, E. M. had fought at Antietam on September 17, 1862, surviving the bloodiest day in American history where almost 23,000 soldiers were killed or wounded. The historian's hour-long visit became the basis of my first short-form film.

CHAPTER SEVEN - NURTURE RESILIENCE AND COURAGE

It was soon clear that filmmaking was wonderful therapy for the cognitive injuries sustained from encephalitis, and I embraced this opportunity for therapy combined with motivational impact storytelling. Today, I have made more than three hundred short films, some of which have been shown at film festivals. Besides being a conduit for my storytelling, they capture my travel, scientific endeavors, advocacy, and entrepreneurship, as well as the deep joy and pleasure I take in my family—which has expanded to include twelve grandchildren.

One film that combines many of the interests cultivated during my recovery is a tribute I made to preeminent American artist Winslow Homer (1836 -1910). His seaside studio in Prouts Neck, Maine, is just steps away from my back door. Homer who captured the death and degradation of the Civil War and its aftermath started his career as an illustrator for *Harper's Weekly*. But he is best known for the dozens of dynamic marine landscape paintings he completed during the last three decades of his life. This latter period reflects his fascination with nature's immense power. Many Homer paintings depict tumultuous scenes in the Atlantic Ocean—as well as human struggles with the elements.

After the Portland Museum of Art (PMA) acquired Homer's studio in 2006, curators discovered that this largely self-taught artist had scrawled the words "Turn, turn, tumble, tumble, tumble, turn" on interior boards in black chalk. Homer was "obviously deeply involved in studying the character of waves," a former director of the PMA notes in my film.

I often hike along the rugged cliffs depicted in his paintings, and sometimes photograph storm surf in an attempt to capture images of the kind that inspired Homer's iconic paintings. Watching the waves through his intense gaze gave me a new prism through which to notice the water's distinct movements. The sea is something that has been a part of my life from the days of my earliest childhood, but until I made this film, I had never studied waves so closely. In 2023 I had a solo photography exhibition at a gallery in Portland, Maine, and this included my photographs of massive storm waves crashing on rugged rocky cliffs in front of the Homer studio.

Beyond photography and filmmaking, I also used my time at home in these days to begin making my own sculpture. Examples of this are five-foot-high cast bronze figurative outdoor sculptures I've created to convey a sense of happiness. These sculptures are called Amara and they have been installed in groupings at the University of New Hampshire, the University of New England, and The Jackson Laboratory. My sculpture-making has continued with a very large-scale bronze installation at my home in Maine, and I attribute some of this artmaking to circumstances unexpectedly faced in my struggle with encephalitis.

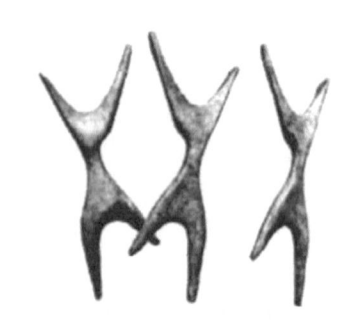

Amara cast bronze sculptures

Another health struggle played a role in the writing of this book. Emergency open heart surgery, including sextuple bypasses, in October 2023 saved my life (again) and caused me to take a "health sabbatical" at home, I benefitted by using some of that "off-the-grid" time to complete this book.

Visceral encounters with death of the kind I have experienced offer accompanying opportunities and challenges for "rebirth", self-discovery, growth, and belonging that have been the subject of immense curiosity throughout human history, including religious beliefs. The natural world provides powerful metaphors for human cycles of life and mortality such as annual seasons of Fall decline and Spring regrowth, and forests regenerating from the ashes of fires.

Chapter Seven - Nurture Resilience and Courage

Takeaway: None of us invite hardship or pain into our lives, but I know of no one who has sailed through life without adversity. My struggle with viral encephalitis plunged me into a terrifying vortex of despair and disability. But faced with this epic challenge, I uncovered deep and unexpected reserves of resilience that can strengthen ALL of us mentally and creatively. My friend Dr. Lisa Miller, author of *The Awakened Brain*, explains that "we are hard-wired so that our suffering brings us deeper, to discover larger meaning and purpose." While we are not always able to control circumstances, we have to ability to manage our reaction to them.

Suffering can cease to be suffering, and can become beneficial, when we choose to give it meaning. This is a lesson we must all learn, and sometimes re-learn. It was a happy surprise to find that working to overcome my illness helped me find artistic satisfaction as I pursued art, music, and filmmaking. Joseph Campbell captured this perspective of benefitting from struggles with this comment: "Any disaster that you can survive is an improvement in your character, your stature, and your life. What a privilege! This is when the spontaneity of your own nature will have a chance to flow."

Chapter Eight
De-Risk Through Superb Planning

"Security is mostly a superstition. It does not exist in nature, nor do the children of men as a whole experience it . . . Avoiding danger is no safer in the long run than outright exposure. . . Life is either a daring adventure or nothing."
– *Helen Keller*

"Why not go out on a limb? Isn't that where the fruit is?"
– *Attributed to Mark Twain*

I keep a glass trophy on my library bookshelf inscribed with the words "Mud, Sweat and Tears." It encases a palm-sized, pitted, gray rock that I brought back with me from the jagged, forbidding summit of Puncak Jaya in Western Papua, Indonesia. Almost unimaginably remote, Carstensz Pyramid as it used to be known, is the highest mountain between the Americas and the Himalayas. Standing at an estimated 16,023 feet, it is one of the " seven summits," the highest peaks on each of Earth's 7 continents. The challenges of this adventure included the location of Carstensz in the notoriously dense rain forests of Western Papua, and interaction with some of the world's most isolated native peoples who speak several hundred distinct languages and are unaccustomed to visitors. Even to reach base camp, our group of six, plus four guides and a dozen sherpas bushwhacked our way through dauntingly dense jungles, often in ankle-deep mud, for almost a week. We navigated treacherous mountain passes, sometimes following nothing more than the thin puffs of smoke far ahead of us that wafted from the campfire our guides built when they stopped to set up for the night.

Then, the summit. Setting out just after midnight, our ascent illuminated by headlamps, we took another fourteen hours to complete the cold, wet, physically demanding, technically difficult ascent to the top. At 2 pm that afternoon in May 1993 our group briefly sat on the jagged rock summit of Carstensz Pyramid, in bizarre weather that alternated between bright sunlight, snow flurries, and thunderstorms. For two of my fellow climbers, this culminated a long quest to reach the summits of the highest mountains on each of the planet's seven continents.

glimpse of Carstensz Pyramid summit

It's natural to view an adventurous expedition of this kind as risky. However, great preparation and planning can dramatically reduce risk. It can help us become comfortable with being uncomfortable. My experience suggests that anyone seeking high impact in the world, and the great rewards associated with that, must take full, proactive responsibility to wisely manage these risks through effective education and preparation. Of course, we sometimes confront the paradox that the more we learn the more we discover that we don't know.

Wave-making projects often start with creative musings and aspirational ideas. Sometimes these are the result of structured processes by an individual or teams, and other times they emerge at dawn, in showers, during walks in nature, or other times when the mind is relaxed and allowed to wander.

CHAPTER EIGHT - DE-RISK THROUGH SUPERB PLANNING

Asked once why he wanted to climb Everest, George Mallory, the most famous mountaineer among the first group of Westerners to attempt to summit Mount Everest, uttered the immortal words, "Because it's there." That spirit of exploration has always resonated with me, and it was during some early morning musings that I realized how much I wanted to join friends to climb Puncak Jaya. This was part of a bigger plan ... to roam the world, seeking out adventure ... observing and experiencing some of the earth's most fabled seascapes and landscapes. The idea of taking on a challenge just "because it's there" reflects a common human desire to explore and discover. My pantheon of heroes is full of adventurous explorers of all kinds and this desire has been a powerful force in my life. The concept of achieving what might appear impossible inspires me and many people I admire. I approached these kinds of adventures as a way to challenge myself, to grow, and to build a beneficial library of experience.

Adventurous entrepreneurship benefits from dreaming, but it is a common mistake for new entrepreneurs to overestimate the value of an idea and underestimate the work required to successfully execute that idea and bring it into reality. Capitalism provides a remarkably effective framework for testing the viability of ideas and companies. Capital markets judge the worthiness of ideas, plans, and organizations, including the ability to deliver results against stated goals. Competition relentlessly seeks to exploit weaknesses and opportunities. The discipline of business requires that hard questions be asked, answered, and stress tested regarding both big strategic issues such as business attractiveness and competitiveness, as well as critical operating issues such as the team's ability to formulate and execute plans. When I was in the thinking stages about starting IDEXX I was aware of the transformation taking place in human diagnostics as devices became more capable, convenient, and cost-effective. This knowledge provided confidence that we could do the same for veterinary medicine, with a very adventurous but low-risk plan. But opportunities of this kind can be seen and exploited by others so I knew I would have to work wisely, quickly, and quietly to win.

How do you live with the potential danger and uncertainty associated with an undertaking of this kind? The answer lies in the difference between *perceived* risk and *actual* risk. Something complex and challenging can in reality be low risk, and something easy and straightforward can be high risk. How does one spot the difference? Forethought, testing, and rigorous thinking. What makes something too risky is often ignorance, lack of analysis, or a failure to adequately plan.

Usually, the most perilous moment in any endeavor is the first time you try something. After that, with enough preparation and practice, you are able to mitigate the risk. There are many activities people undertake that seem unsafe or unsound, but if you seek to master them and develop appropriate skills, you can minimize the risk significantly.

The way I have learned to approach anything daunting is to deconstruct it into individual components and never look at it as if it were a single, impenetrable block of stone. This is an idea that Malcolm Gladwell helped popularize in his 2008 book *Outliers*: the theory that it takes ten thousand hours to achieve mastery of a skill. I am not sure the ten-thousand figure has to be taken literally, but I agree with the premise. It takes seeing or doing something repeatedly to get good at it—and to recognize the risks inherent in it. Gladwell's writing is supportive of the value of pattern recognition. This is the process of sifting and winnowing information and then putting that into the context of what you have learned in the past to make predictions for what might happen in the future. Sometimes this involves reverse engineering of analogous experiences of others.

That is exactly what I did before I journeyed to Papua. I didn't just walk out my door in Maine and start climbing one of the most forbidding peaks on the planet. I got there incrementally. I

Chapter Eight - De-Risk Through Superb Planning

deconstructed the expedition into its constituent parts and de-risked it chunk by chunk. Years before I embarked on the Puncak Jaya trip, I learned to rock climb on the famous peak Grand Teton in Jackson, Wyoming with renowned Exum Mountain Guide Nancy Feagin. I was coached by ski buddy Jimmy Chin, and I learned to ice-climb in Bozeman, Montana with my friends Conrad Anker and his wife Jenni. Conrad is considered one of the world's most experienced, and technically proficient high-altitude climbers. Among his many accomplishments, Conrad was on the 1999 research team that came upon the remains of George Mallory. The Englishman had been climbing Mount Everest–at 29,028 feet, the world's highest peak– before vanishing into the mist on June 8, 1924. The whereabouts of Mallory's body had remained a mystery for seventy-five years until Conrad and his group found it sprawled on an exposed ledge about two thousand feet from the top. It was decided that the British mountaineer had died after a bad fall, so they buried him on the mountain.

I had done a lot of climbing in New Hampshire's White Mountains as a teenager, and when I turned forty, I trekked to the top of Mount Kilimanjaro in Tanzania, the highest mountain in Africa and the highest free-standing mountain in the world. The snow-covered peak of this massive dormant volcano is a well-known image due in part to the famous Ernest Hemingway short story "The Snows of Kilimanjaro." The American writer considered the story, which depicts a novelist dying of gangrene on a safari in Africa, to be one of his great short narratives, incorporating the unconventional writing style that won him fame, including the Nobel Prize in literature. Even though Mount Kilimanjaro peaks at an elevation of nearly twenty thousand feet, it is not a technical climb, which makes it comparatively easy except for the high likelihood of altitude sickness from low oxygen availability. Scaling sheer, icy rock faces in the craggy Gallatin Range of the Rocky Mountains with Conrad was an entirely new level of difficulty.

"David, there's no reason for you to worry. I have everything under control," he promised. He lowered the danger quotient significantly by tethering me to him securely with a harness and rope—belaying, it's called. If I had lost my footing, I would have dropped no more than a foot or so before the rope arrested my fall. We persevered and I succeeded, with a reminder from Conrad that our sense of limitations can often be self-imposed.

Not only did I practice and prepare for Puncak Jaya, I also again put myself in the hands of the most competent guides available. The climb was led by Pete Athans, an extraordinarily skilled mountaineer, who earned the nickname "Mr. Everest" for successfully summiting that peak seven times.

Despite exhaustive planning, as we rappelled down from the summit of Carstensz in the dark and driving rain, we were within a couple of hours of reaching base camp when our luck turned. I heard a loud, cracking sound several hundred feet above me. With only seconds to react, I hugged the rock face as a shower of rocks pelted my helmet and upper body. After the initial burst of small stones, larger stones started hitting me—sledgehammers to my right shoulder and my helmet, at the base of my skull. The rest of that night is only a foggy memory. Our guides helped me safely off the mountain and into base camp around midnight, twenty-four hours after our climbing expedition began. The next morning, I woke up lying in a pool of blood and was unable to move my right arm. A puncture hole in my jacket marked the spot where a rock had broken my acromion, the bony tip on the outer edge of my shoulder. I had a nasty headache—probably a concussion. Another climber had injured one of his hands.

Our group decided that it was out of the question to retrace our strenuous, weeklong hike back to the small town where we had started. Instead, we hiked for help toward nearby Grasberg Mine, the world's largest gold and second-largest copper mine. We were aware that the Indonesian government strictly forbade visitors to

Chapter Eight - De-Risk Through Superb Planning

get anywhere near this enormously valuable natural resource area, but we had no other choice. Guards armed with automatic rifles confronted us as we approached, and we were not surprised when the next stop was the police station, where we were put behind bars. The police officers' attitude changed only when it became clear that I was seriously hurt, and they drove me to the nearby hospital. After that, we reconnected with our visas and passports that had been left in the small town we had embarked from. Finally, we flew from Jakarta to our different destinations, in my case, IDEXX offices in Australia. Years later I produced a short film of this adventure.

Although I eventually transitioned from mountain climbing to trekking, I still treasure these experiences, injuries and all. The rock that I picked up on the summit as a souvenir has a deep personal meaning for me because it is a powerful talisman, symbolizing the embracing of a challenge, preparation, perseverance, resilience, teamwork, and achievement.

I write here about mountain climbing because much the same combination of mindset, preparation, and expertise is necessary in business. I pride myself on aggressively pursuing business opportunities the same way I tackle adventures in the natural world. My motivation is accomplishment of course, and not thrill-seeking or risk-taking. I try to balance the need to be bold with the need for careful planning–something in business you want your team members and investors to fully appreciate. And it's not only for them, of course. Like with mountain climbing, it's the training and the hard work you put in that make these opportunities all the more rewarding for you. Albert Einstein allegedly captured his perspective on the importance of superb planning when he said: "If I were given one hour to save the planet, I would spend 59 minutes defining the problem and one minute resolving it."

Another critical success factor to manage risk in audacious ventures is to build a team with highly relevant and outstanding expertise and capabilities. Just as I was belayed by Conrad Anker in the Gallatin Mountains, Erwin Workman, a superb scientist, was essential to the founding and success of IDEXX. The journey to find him started with identifying the top companies in human diagnostics including Abbott Laboratories and Becton Dickinson – both considered "academies" for developing strong management teams. The next step consisted of finding a couple of people who had left senior positions in those companies and were willing to talk. I described my plans for IDEXX and asked if they would be willing to suggest former colleagues who would be suited to a more entrepreneurial venture outside of human diagnostics. It was informative to interview several highly qualified scientists, but when I met Erwin in a cocktail lounge inside the Chicago O'Hare International Airport, I knew he was ideal for this opportunity –brilliant and congenial, with stellar credentials, and great entrepreneurial capabilities. At the time, Abbott dominated the blood banking diagnostic business which involves screening donated blood for various diseases such as hepatitis and HIV before it can be given to a patient. Erwin was a leader in that important segment of the business. While joining a small startup may have seemed risky in contrast to his success in a large corporation like Abbott, he was able to dramatically impact those risks and achieve the fulfillment of building a highly successful enterprise of our own. As an additional resource, we assembled an informal scientific advisory board to challenge us intellectually about "what great looks like."

It is also essential to acknowledge what you *do not know* and to not be afraid to admit it ... to be willing to learn. In addition to recruiting Erwin, I brought in highly capable talent for sales and marketing and other functions. In a process similar to the one I employed to find Erwin, searches for key people often involve the identification of organizations that are outstanding "academies" for excellence in various functions. In the case of manufacturing, for example, I was well aware of the astounding innovations that Japanese companies were bringing to manufacturing and quality control processes in consumer electronics, automobiles, and other sectors. The power of

Chapter Eight - De-Risk Through Superb Planning

these innovations is reflected in the fact that the US market share for Japanese manufactured cars has more than doubled over 3 decades from ~20% in 1980, and this contributed to the ~$80B government "bailout" of US automakers including General Motors starting in 2008. Alarmed by this shift in power, I sought to gain the benefit of these capabilities and turn manufacturing into a powerful source of competitive advantage. This led to discussions and a meeting with the CEO of celebrated electronics company Motorola to hear and see how they were responding to this threat to their businesses in radios and mobile phones. Motorola had won the Malcolm Baldridge National Quality Award for performance excellence, and there was much to be learned from their experience. As a result, we recruited a manufacturing team from consumer electronics to bring that source of competitiveness to IDEXX.

Interacting with companies like Motorola at the leadership level benefitted from my membership in the Young Presidents' Organization (YPO), a global leadership community of CEOs with more than 35,000 members in over 140 countries. Learning from each other's experiences is a powerful benefit of YPO and this was the way that I connected with former CEO Chris Galvin at Motorola and many other CEOs who have become longtime friends. I continue to be an active member of YPO and am grateful that this has helped to shape my life in ventures of many kinds. I am also a member of the Chief Executives Organization (CEO) which offers similar benefits to be part of a community of people who have been leaders in YPO. In early 2024, for example, I was a keynote speaker at a CEO health and wellness gathering in Canyon Ranch Tucson, Arizona, and I serve on the organizing committee for our annual Global Technology Summit. Later in this book, I speak about the power of serendipity and synchronicity in life, and it's important to emphasize that membership in organizations like YPO and CEO enhances prospects for serendipity. I'm grateful for similar opportunities via the Explorers Club, the National Geographic Society, the MIT Media Lab, AAAS, Synergos, and others.

When I told my father I was starting IDEXX, he worried that I was taking on an inappropriate risk. I had started a family, and he was understandably concerned about our financial well-being. I fully appreciated that his perspective was influenced by living through the Great Depression, World War II, and other challenging times. But like most entrepreneurs, my desire for success and impact far outweighed my fear of failure. More importantly, through careful planning, I had reached a different conclusion than my father about the risks associated with investing my twenty-five-thousand-dollar life savings to get IDEXX off the ground.

I often think people have a misperception of risk in the world of entrepreneurship. If you have been diligent in building an entrepreneurial company, you may have more control over your own destiny than working in a large organization where decisions out of your control can lead to the elimination of your position or other unwanted consequences.

Just prior to IDEXX, I experienced something similar at Agribusiness Associates. Many countries have agricultural banks. In Europe, central cooperative agricultural banks such as Crédit Agricole, DG Bank, and Rabobank had formed an investment banking arm that hired our firm to help it break into the US market. Eventually, they concluded that there might be advantages to owning our firm and, before long, they bought out Ray Goldberg. At first, our team thought this was an attractive new relationship because we suddenly had an institutional parent company with huge reach into the international market for agriculture and food. Within a couple of weeks, though, our new owners introduced more central management of the kind they were accustomed to, and some of us perceived this as putting our success at risk via unnecessary micromanagement of our activities.

Under Ray's leadership, we had all worked extremely hard, but he had allowed us enormous latitude and independence. We interacted with our domestic and international clients in whatever

CHAPTER EIGHT - DE-RISK THROUGH SUPERB PLANNING

ways we thought were most effective. Fortunately, I had already concluded that I wanted to be on the other side of the desk, working not for clients but for myself, building my own business, creating my own products, and fulfilling my vision of what a company should look like. In this case, I perceived that the financial risk of leaving Agribusiness Associates was smaller than the emotional cost of being micromanaged, So I tendered my resignation and moved on.

***

At IDEXX and other companies I've helped create, we build backstops intended for risk mitigation. One of these is product line and customer diversity, the business equivalent of not putting all of our eggs into a single basket. Another is rigorous experimentation and training, analogous to staging a series of incrementally bolder mountain climbing experiences rather than attempting the most difficult climb first. This builds an inventory of strategies in the event of an emergency or surprise. The reason IDEXX wasn't at serious risk when the dairy antibiotic test did not go well is because my original business plan had optionality baked in. It contemplated that we would expand to address diseases in poultry, swine, and cattle as well as diseases and health monitoring in household pets and horses. We also designed a test to detect aflatoxins, a group of poisonous mycotoxins produced by certain molds that can grow in grains and nuts during production, harvest, storage, or processing. They are potent carcinogens and mutagens that can trigger liver disease, and cancer, as well as being linked to a devastating brain disease known as Reye's Syndrome.

Perhaps the most important risk management tool is open and honest but respectful communication. When you are scaling a mountain or scuba diving, safety signals need to be unambiguous and well-understood. The leadership team agreed that it was critical to encourage different points of view for the health of the business. For that to happen, you have to have trust and create a safe harbor for disagreements. No company can afford for team members to be reluctant to raise their hands or speak up simply because they disagree with the majority opinion. Just the opposite. You want people to see things differently and support critical thinking! I see it as my job to instill a culture of healthy debate, to amplify the outlier opinions. Even if counter viewpoints are not adopted, they can be incredibly valuable to consider in gaining conviction about important decisions.

The leadership team at IDEXX shared a belief about the importance of cognitive diversity … soliciting multiple perspectives and healthy debates on any important issues. Engaging the full interdisciplinary brainpower of a team creates competitive advantage. A strong team welcomes productive, solution-centric, critical debate of their work by colleagues, understanding that such feedback can sharpen their thinking and help them navigate around unseen, and potentially devastating, challenges. Some companies have a different approach and tend to encourage consensus decision-making. We found that people from those cultures didn't fit well with our needs.

In meetings, we encouraged constructive debate and candor of the kind I admire in science meetings where it is often fully expected that colleagues in the room will rigorously challenge your data, your analytical processes, and your conclusions in the interest of better science. For this peer review to work well, there needs to be a well understood psychologically safe environment.

While I believe in encouraging debate, personal attacks are not consistent with best practices in building high-performance teams. I admire leaders who employ other practices designed to support high performance. For example, I agree with the practice of dealing with difficult messages via statements of support before confrontation, and statements about accomplishments before disappointments. I appreciate leaders who focus on opportunities before challenges, and who present possible solutions when identifying problems. I think that organizations benefit immensely by learning from mistakes.

Chapter Eight - De-Risk Through Superb Planning

My experience also supports the practice of separating ideation meetings from meetings to judge ideas so that great idea generation isn't inhibited by immediate judgements. Great brainstorming and ideation can be a critical success factor and the process benefits from a supportive atmosphere. Once abundant ideas are presented, a second meeting, with different rules and purpose seeks to subject each idea to intense peer review so that only the best ideas survive. These "wargames" simulate the harsh realities of business where it is better to be your own toughest critic than to learn lessons via expensive failures.

Great organizations build thoughtful performance management systems and I enjoy playing a role in the design of these systems. A standard part of almost any performance management system is the evaluation of results against specific measurable goals. Beyond this, I have found it helpful to reinforce company cultural success factors by evaluating not just WHAT was achieved but HOW it was achieved. This can include evaluation by peers and subordinates of teamwork, innovation, ownership mindset, communication skills, and other factors. Providing feedback of this kind multiple times a year can reinforce behaviors and practices that drive success. I have played a role in the design of performance management systems for several different organizations, and I often consult with industrial psychologists as part of the process. A best practice is to frame disappointments as development opportunities for personal growth. Another is to discuss performance and the compensation implications of performance reviews in separate sessions.

Bottom line: it can be counterproductive to ideate and judge ideas in the same meeting. Think of it this way: one session is for generating fresh and creative ideas; the next is for challenging these ideas and prioritizing those that survive rigorous analysis. I have seen how this two-step process of open-ended imagination on the one hand and hard-nosed, results-oriented, critical stress-testing on the other gives you the best chance to arrive at the most successful outcomes.

Of course, risk management is an important fiduciary role of the board of directors of companies and non-profit organizations. So it's vitally important to create and manage a highly professional and competent board of directors to regularly review company performance. This requires proper board composition, appropriate governance structures including charters and self-assessments, clear rules of engagement, and well-understood business processes with leadership teams, and within the board itself. Serving on a board can be a high-impact opportunity, but also very challenging. I've been fortunate to serve on many boards, including in the role of chair. Great boards are carefully designed to support the success of the company via duties ranging from organizational development and financial reviews to technical and strategic evaluations, and enterprise risk management.

In my opinion, the single most important fiduciary responsibility of any board is to ensure that the CEO is capable of achieving the company's goals. I have served on boards that have overseen great challenges including strategic changes and CEO transitions. It's important to realize that if a board isn't highly socialized, well-organized, cogitative, supportive, and proactive, the quality of highly consequential discussions and the performance of complex duties can suffer. In any board, but especially in private equity-funded companies, it's not uncommon for directors to express views that reflect their ownership perspective rather than the required fiduciary perspective about what's best for the company and all stakeholders. In early stage, venture-backed companies, with newly formed boards, board governance can be particularly challenging, with risk implications for a company. Group thinking is a risk, and also behavior that amounts to performances for other directors versus more appropriate choice-oriented deliberations. Experienced leadership, just as in mountain climbing, can significantly de-risk these common hazards.

Several years after transitioning from my leadership role at

CHAPTER EIGHT - DE-RISK THROUGH SUPERB PLANNING

IDEXX, my position as a partner at Venrock Associates provided additional experience and new perspectives about risk management in the setting of venture capital investments versus an operating company.

Takeaway: The wave-making world-changing initiatives that I admire, and embrace, are inherently adventurous. And they can be very risky without proper preparation and planning. Even highly audacious plans can be preemptively de-risked by mastering a subject and rigorously stress-testing your assumptions and conclusions. Prepare as much as possible by breaking down risks, and then take the plunge, always recognizing that the biggest risk may be not taking risks. Take a chance on yourself.

"Risk comes from not knowing what you're doing."
- Warren Buffett

Created by David Shaw in DALL-E

CHAPTER NINE
DELIVER ON PROMISES

"It's the spouting whale that gets harpooned"
– Henry Hillman

Launching and leading adventurous, high-impact initiatives nearly always requires the communication of a bold vision, aspirational goals, hopes, and dreams. This is an important part of attracting resources needed for success. This phase of a venture soon gives way to the need to meet operating goals, ideally to under-promise and over-deliver. All entrepreneurs face various contours of this dilemma.

Leaders can take a cue about this from one of nature's most remarkable species–whales. Whales have unfortunately been hunted extensively by humans and they are at greatest danger when they spout. Henry Hillman, a Pittsburgh businessman, and philanthropist, whom the *Wall Street Journal* famously dubbed the "invisible" billionaire, reflected on this when he explained his reasons for keeping a low profile: *"It's the spouting whale that gets harpooned."*

I, too, often find it strategically useful to keep a low profile, to be underestimated by competitors. To under-promise and over-deliver to customers and shareholders. To operate in stealth mode when it's important to limit public knowledge of your plans. In the early days of IDEXX, we quietly pursued our goals because we knew this was an extraordinary, groundbreaking opportunity to dominate a sector that is critical to human existence. We didn't want to attract the attention of potential competitors with much greater resources, who could use brute force to defeat our insurgency. This approach extends to the way I present myself in the world.

At IDEXX, to combat the many looming threats facing an early-stage company, our leadership team continually evaluated vulnerabilities and challenges that could impact our success, preparing strategies to respond when and as needed. Sometimes we turned to a master of warfare for inspiration. Sun Tzu, the ancient Chinese general, military strategist, and author of *The Art of War*, penned, according to many historians, between 475 and 221 BCE. "All warfare is based on deception," he wrote. "Hence, when able to attack, we must seem unable; when using our forces, we must appear inactive; when we are near, we must make the enemy believe that we are far away; when far away, we must make him believe we are near."

What did this look like on the modern business battlefront? When I started IDEXX, the medical diagnostics business was dominated by large companies including Abbott Laboratories and Becton Dickinson. Armed with new generations of high-performance diagnostic technologies, these companies were battling over market share in the very large and growing human diagnostics business. Attracted by the size and growth of the market, many small biomedical startups sought to compete, often in specialized niches such as cancer diagnostics, diabetes testing, or home pregnancy tests. Our vision for IDEXX as an insurgent organization was to be a world leader in an important but underserved market, rather than launching frontal attacks on powerful, well-established incumbents. So, we quietly entered the diagnostics field by going into animal health rather than human health. In animal health, there were powerful global companies focused on pharmaceutical and nutrition products, with little if any capabilities in diagnostics. We sought to avoid competition with multi-billion-dollar incumbents both human diagnostic and animal health pharma. Sun Tzu's teachings are credited with supporting this strategy by endorsing the wisdom of "attacking unoccupied territory." And with this commentary: "Thus the highest form of generalship is to balk the enemy's plans; the next best is to prevent the junction of the enemy's forces; the next in order is to attack the enemy's army in the field; and the worst policy of all is to besiege walled cities." Importantly, he also addressed the issue of risk mitigation through planning by observing that "battles are won before they are fought."

Beyond keeping a low profile and downplaying the

Chapter Nine - Deliver on Promises

attractiveness of the veterinary diagnostic market, we developed a highly effective strategy of partnering with certain human diagnostic companies to commercialize their technology in our markets. This was often viewed by partners as a compelling proposition, offering them a way to generate incremental revenue without distracting our partner's focus from high-priority target markets in human health. Using this strategy we steadily built a portfolio of leading technology platforms, often paid for via royalties on product sales, versus the more expensive and higher-risk up-front research and development costs incurred by our partners. As our technology platforms expanded and our product lines became more extensive, we built exceptionally strong sales and marketing capabilities, and outstanding relationships with customers reflecting their appreciation of the transformative value that we were able to deliver. Eventually, as we emerged as the global leader in our markets, we were no longer a stealth player but many of our early vulnerabilities were far behind us.

Now our success attracted attention. When companies such as Abbott eventually decided to explore the newly burgeoning animal diagnostics market, we had already licensed the best technology from their rivals. I later learned that when Abbott business development staff came to a trade show and saw what we were doing, they reported back to their Chicago headquarters that an attack on IDEXX would now be fruitless. Yet our leadership position in these markets didn't change our view of the potential dangers associated with being unnecessarily promotional about our success or our plans. We were now a publicly traded company and still mindful that "it's the spouting whale that gets harpooned." Being a wave maker is not the same as being a noise maker.

***

In the wave-making world, possessing, and creating excitement about new ventures can be essential for success. An important trait for virtually every entrepreneur is passion and conviction about the prospects for their venture, notwithstanding daunting failure rates. This creates a situation where wisdom is needed to distinguish between success-driving excitement and superfluous hype. In business sectors such as biopharmaceuticals that require massive risk capital investments years in advance of product launches, companies remain "story stocks" for an extended time. An important consideration for me in building IDEXX, based partly on my aversion to hype, was the ability to be operational and generate revenues quickly with modest capital so that our results could speak for themselves. An amusing saying in the tech world is that ventures generate three types of products: software, hardware, and "vaporware". Every entrepreneur and wave-making organization must decide where to stand on "vaporware" or "hype" based on distinctive needs and cultures. I seek to stay out of the hype/vaporware business. Yet in the business world, hype is sometimes considered acceptable, even admirable, as an essential requirement for getting attention for capital and other needs. After all, virtually all entrepreneurial companies start as stories and plans, long before they are able to deliver the results they envision. Managing the transition from hopes, dreams, and plans to achievement and successful operations is a difficult chasm to cross.

After leaving Venrock, I continued to make many investments through my own firm, the Black Point Group, which I run today. Because of my operating and investment experience, as well as participating in thousands of presentations by entrepreneurs looking for capital, I have developed specific criteria to evaluate opportunities. Every evaluation includes an assessment of market attractiveness and organizational competitiveness – the ability to win. The most important criteria, and sometimes the hardest to assess objectively, is the quality and character of the team. Prior success means a lot, of course, as well as the way the team presents itself. These can range from matter-of-fact discussions by experienced domain experts to elaborate presentations and videos: hype. I've often found that hype is inversely proportional to substance, setting off alarms about getting into a long-term relationship. Having said that, I again recognize that

Chapter Nine - Deliver on Promises

enthusiasm, passion, conviction, salesmanship, and a whatever-it-takes mindset all play roles in the success of audacious, high-impact, wave-making ventures.

Capital markets can be a constant source of pressure to deliver good news, especially for public companies. Via earnings calls, or at investment conferences where hundreds of companies compete for investor attention, there's understandable pressure to stand out and create a positive impression about recent operating results and future prospects. Wall Street research analysts who publish reports on companies want the market to see that their insights are perceptive and accurate, and to have their recommendations validated. Yet predictability of results in a hyper-growth company like IDEXX can be very difficult, and this creates tensions about the prospect for disappointments. This is where the concept of under-promising and over-delivering becomes highly relevant, except that when analysts see a pattern of that they may just increase their projections to account for this management conservatism. Every public company has to find its way through this process and in too many cases the relentless pressure to deliver leads to improper behavior of the kind made famous with the WorldCom and Enron scandals of 2002.

No company is immune to the pressure to deliver against expectations and an incident of this kind led to a meaningful challenge for IDEXX amidst steep growth in 1997.

***

The top executives of IDEXX gathered in my house outside Portland for more than forty-eight hours to address an unexpected earnings shortfall in the context of our reputation for highly reliable performance. It was 1997, and we were missing the projections for our first-quarter revenues by a wide margin. Based on our stellar historical performance, expectations were very high, and early predictions of higher earnings created a crisis. Analysts had predicted earnings of twenty-one cents a share, and actual results were closer to just several cents per share. The cause was a recognition that distributors ordered excessive inventory of our products and that those sales distorted actual customer demand. It's a customary practice for distributors to seasonally build inventory of products ahead of high-demand periods to ensure product availability, and it can be difficult for a manufacturer like IDEXX to have access to data necessary to track actual customer demand. In this case, the IDEXX leadership team recognized that inventories were exceptionally high in relation to projected customer demand. This realization created an operational priority that also deserved to be shared with investors as a public company. I had stepped down as president but remained chairman of the board, and was touring colleges on the West Coast with my daughter Abigail when I got an urgent call to return to headquarters for team meetings organized to tackle this challenge.

The company had a history of high reliability, trust, and transparency with investors, and was faced with difficult decisions about how best to handle the inventory build as well as the communication of our plans for that. Many manufacturers face similar issues and it's not unusual to slowly bring inventories back to normal levels. Yet this results in future revenue shortfalls that must be explained to stakeholders. Another option is to share the high inventory realization publicly and take immediate steps to better understand and communicate true customer demand versus distributor purchases. The right strategy for this decision and others is highly influenced by the values and principles of a company and its leaders. Employing those here, the leadership team opted for high transparency, full disclosure of our findings, and immediate remedial actions to create systems and processes that would better serve our needs in the future. I was proud to be part of the team that once again derived decisions from our cultural beliefs about integrity, courage, and "what great looks like." Mark Twain captured this spirit when he allegedly wrote: "With courage, you will dare to take risks, have the strength to be compassionate, and the wisdom to be humble. Courage

Chapter Nine - Deliver on Promises

is the foundation of integrity."

The following Monday morning, I led our earnings call with investors as our leadership team provided an update on operations as well as details on our distributor inventory challenges. As a team, we took full responsibility for discovering and addressing this challenge, and we explained new processes and practices being put in place to benefit the company in the future.

Despite the company's continued growth and success, the inventory adjustment news caused our stock price to decline dramatically that day – plunging from thirty-two dollars a share to twelve dollars a share. Investors called to express their disappointment. Employees were shocked as they digested the news and saw the value of their shareholdings dwindle. Yet in company meetings over the next few days, there was a widely shared sense that we had done the right thing. We had once again demonstrated our commitment to mutually held values and principles that included transparency, trust, teamwork, courage, and continuous improvement. We had risen to yet another challenge of finding and fixing a business process issue that would now make us a stronger and better organization. As Nelson Mandela once said: "The greatest glory of living lies not in never failing but in rising every time you fall."

In the wake of these events, I returned as IDEXX's president to demonstrate support for the company and our outstanding future prospects. Over many years our leadership team had done an exceptionally good job of mastering the extraordinary challenge of building a successful high-growth organization with all the business processes and practices that are required for research and development, manufacturing, sales and marketing, information technology, financial and administrative systems, and all the rest. The distributor inventory issue required us to work as a team to institute better business information systems, processes, and controls. We communicated these to investors as the team addressed not only those issues but many others with implications for success as we continued our journey to global leadership in our industry. Like many other struggles the company had faced, the silver lining of this struggle is that it resulted in building a better and stronger company. Our candid and transparent handling of the inventory challenge rebuilt trust inside and outside the company as we returned to our historic pattern of under-promising and over-delivering even in a hyper-growth environment. Turning this crisis into an opportunity, we used our financial strength at the time to facilitate strategic entry into the veterinary clinical laboratory business that has subsequently become a great success.

Takeaway: An important part of building trust in business and elsewhere is based on reliably delivering on expectations and goals. There are many situations in life where it's tempting to create high expectations that may not be realistic. The world of hypergrowth tech companies is full of examples where bold, aspirational expectations are created as a critical part of envisioning game-changing success. Leadership teams have to make choices about how to build trust with their stakeholders. I've been fortunate to be a member of teams that seek to build trust by consistently delivering on expectations and being clear about aspirational goals versus more deliverable results. Recalling the well-known saying in the tech world about "vaporware", it's easy to find examples of tragic consequences. Beware of scaling beyond the speed of trust.

Chapter Ten
Keep the Mission and Vision Fresh

"It's better to be a pirate than join the Navy."
– Steve Jobs

As a tiny meditation every morning after a swim, I read the words painted on the wooden frame of a mirror in my pool house: "Live life to the fullest. Seek knowledge. Be creative. Do your best. Dream. Set goals. Be a friend. Know love. Eat good food. Cherish family. Go places."

These exhortations are a daily reminder to live life with intention, to continually search for meaningful new experiences, to seek change, and to stay adventurous. In other words, to keep everything in my life fresh and engaging.

Each New Year's Day, I revisit the set of personal goals I have consistently maintained over several decades, tweaking the goals as needed to reflect current circumstances: new ventures to explore, current ventures to support, new skills to master, new human connections to cultivate, special events with family and friends, and new adventures. Annually revising and updating this kind of personal statement can reaffirm the values embraced in life including setting clear intentions. It has been my intention to live a life of diverse experiences, with many chapters, and to be wary of the traditional societal convention of retirement as an end-stage in life. I seek new chapters and opportunities, resisting the concept of a finish line. I don't dispute that the concept of retirement can be the right thing for many people, yet I've seen too many instances where an abrupt shift from purposeful work to leisure has unfortunate consequences for mental wellness. Science increasingly reveals the importance of staying active socially, mentally, and physically.

Not long ago, an old friend described to me the stress of a new project he was working on and how he couldn't wait to finish it and have life go back to normal. While I sympathized with his sentiment, I suggested that it might be beneficial to reframe this challenge as an opportunity: to gratefully embrace the struggle of an adventure beyond his usual comfort zone. To understand that great achievements often require extraordinary effort, and that the sweetest victories often come from the hardest battles. The mindset of embracing struggles is a key success factor in high-impact ventures, and this philosophy has served me well including formative experiences working with agribusiness clients around the world with Ray Goldberg.

At IDEXX and other companies, an important priority for me as a leader was to ensure that team members were regularly offered personal growth opportunities. Sometimes this involved cross-functional experience such as transitioning someone from R&D to manufacturing, from sales to marketing, from US operations to international markets, and from management of one business unit to something completely different. For example, when IDEXX entered the water testing business, I asked a leader of one of our veterinary businesses to serve as general manager to commercialize our novel technology in drinking water utilities around the world. One example of these utilities was Thames Water—which serves sixteen million customers in the UK. Our test offers much more rapid detection of E. coli and coliform bacteria versus traditional tests. Beyond commercializing our E. coli test the newly appointed general manager was asked to expand our business with compatible products such as a test for a parasite found in water.

On a number of occasions, these new challenges involved overseas assignments designed to develop management experience, bring the DNA of our culture to remote locations, and create an appreciation for the global nature of our enterprise. Examples of this included Japan, Australia, and Germany where general managers were recruited from various functions in headquarters. These learning-by-doing experiences can result in a remarkable transformation in leadership and management capabilities due to the independent

Chapter Ten - Keep the Mission and Vision Fresh

nature of being a country manager as well as the appreciation that it creates for central services from headquarters.

Team members typically respond to these personal growth opportunities with a mixture of enthusiasm and apprehension because they understand both the benefits and risks associated with tackling a new challenge.

Experiential learning does something to your brain that observation just doesn't do. Nineteenth-century German philosopher Friedrich Nietzsche reportedly captured that concept with this phrase: "Only the doer learns." This benefit of broad experiential learning is also recognized through a doctrine known as the Lucretius Problem, named after the Latin poetic philosopher. Lucretius observed that our documented history can blind us, with uncertainty that we don't seem to grasp. For example, inexperienced people might be inclined to believe that the tallest mountain in the world will be equal to the tallest one they have personally observed.

At organizations I've helped to build, we've embraced innovative practices for team building and interdisciplinary teamwork. These have included mountain climbing adventures, white water rafting, paintball battles, and other activities including Outward Bound programs such as ropes courses. Beyond contemporary practices such as workplace design intended to enhance communications and collaboration, we have found that these more intensive extracurricular activities compress the learning curve to achieve our cultural objectives. It's very rewarding to have these practices result in new insights and collaborations.

We knew from feedback that our practices were working. Interdisciplinary interactions facilitated collaborative work, novel solutions, and out-of-the-box thinking. According to Walter Isaacson's biography of Steve Jobs, Apple's cofounder deliberately designed the Pixar building to facilitate employee interactions by putting an atrium in the middle. He believed "Creativity comes from spontaneous meetings, from random discussions."

Our leadership team at IDEXX operated with the belief that customer feedback and complaints were a source of great competitive advantage and innovation. So, rather than thinking of complaints as a hardship, we welcomed this gold mine of insights about how we could improve our products and services. Recognizing that this kind of input yields excellent benefits, I've embraced the practice of having all management team members regularly spend time with customers. Traveling and connecting with customers both in the United States and in countries around the world is a constant reminder of our top priority, resulting in a pervasive highly beneficial frontline mentality. I admire leaders and organizations that encourage a spirit of play as part of their company culture–and this has contributed significantly to the success of my organizations. Approaching business like a great game engages team members in a different way than a framework of drudgery. As groundbreaking American psychologist Abraham Maslow supposedly said: "Almost all creativity involves purposeful play."

performing at an IDEXX event

Chapter Ten - Keep the Mission and Vision Fresh

To incorporate the benefit of gamesmanship into a company culture, leaders have to lead by example, sometimes embracing practices outside their own comfort zones. Here is an example of what I mean: For quarterly company meetings at IDEXX, we would all gather in an auditorium to hear news and updates across the company. I knew that many team members tended to tune out during financial updates because finance was foreign to them, so we would sometimes give one day's notice to a group in manufacturing or R&D, that they would be presenting financials. They would then scramble overnight to actually understand the financials well enough to communicate to the whole company, often in very amusing ways. Audience comprehension tended to skyrocket. And the teaching and communication role also created important learning for the presenters. Senior leaders would also participate, often announcing awards for outstanding performance, and telling the associated stories with the aim of adding to the company's "folklore" about who we were and what we valued.

Sometimes my role was focused on our vision for the future and the exciting opportunities ahead of us. In one instance, I asked if anyone in the audience had a contradictory perspective about an opportunity I had described. An outspoken IT team member raised his hand and sought a debate. Amidst this, I interrupted and asked him to come up on stage so that we could settle the issues properly. Two sumo wrestling suits were brought on stage so that we could determine through a sumo wrestling match whose perspective would prevail. The audience howled with laughter as we stuffed ourselves into these suits and bounced around the stage until I finally triumphed. Eventually, I expressed my appreciation for his suggestions and bowed to the audience. It was funny, playful, and the perfect kickoff to the weekend. The IDEXX staff went home and told their friends and families about this crazy but wonderful place where they worked.

This kind of personal performance didn't come easily for me, and I know that it can be a challenge to others. Yet the impact on culture can be very significant. The organization can benefit from leaders pushing themselves into the spotlight and welcoming new experiences like being center stage—even if these occasions are challenging. Forcing ourselves to try things that don't come naturally can be consistent with our expectations for all team members in an enterprise whose goals included the creation of exceptionally fulfilling careers. So, leaders sometimes need to fulfill a variety of roles such as ringmaster, motivator, cheerleader, orchestra conductor, and wave maker, personifying traits and values supportive of our culture and our success. Often this involves DOING versus simply SAYING: walking the talk. For example, demonstrating frontline, customer-focused priorities by calling on customers, versus simply stating its importance.

Another example of this approach at IDEXX is when I was invited to join the 30th-anniversary celebration at headquarters in Westbrook, Maine. I hadn't seen many people in my IDEXX tribe since putting a CEO succession plan in place a decade earlier. It didn't seem right to just attend the celebration in a routine way versus a demonstration of my profound gratitude to IDEXXers in an impactful and memorable way. This led to a surprise musical performance, that included riding up to the stage on my Harley, with "Ride of the Valkyries" blasting from my motorcycle's speakers. Then I stepped up to a microphone with an in-house IDEXX band and my then-wife, actress Glenn Close. As the crowd cheered and joined in, we all belted out a song I had composed for the occasion: "IDEXX Rocks You" to the tune of "We Will Rock You" by Queen. It was an impactful, emotional, and memorable reunion that added to IDEXX folklore about "what great looks like." As educator and author Stephen Covey and I once agreed in a memorable meeting: "What you do is far more impactful than what you say."

Chapter Ten - Keep the Mission and Vision Fresh

performing with IDEXX band

This same approach has been effective for me in areas outside of work as well. Upon being asked to deliver the commencement address at the University of Southern Maine, I did a survey of my friends. This revealed that few could remember the names of those who spoke at their college graduation, and none could remember anything said in these commencement speeches they had sat through with their proud families on such a big day in their young lives.

So, in reflecting on typical commencement speeches and this feedback on their impact, it became clear to me that a non-conventional approach was needed to make it more impactful, ideally stating several points and then doing something to demonstrate those points. This line of thinking led me to focus on just two points in my commencement address: 1) the value of always challenging convention, and 2) the importance of operating with a framework of "what great looks like" in every endeavor. To demonstrate "challenging convention" my speech would include a musical performance. And to demonstrate "what great looks like" the musical performance would, hopefully, include vocals by the graduating student scheduled to sing the national anthem.

The day before graduation I composed new lyrics to Beethoven's "Ode to Joy," renaming it "Joyful, Joyful Graduation" for this occasion. Several minutes into my graduation speech I paused and asked the national anthem singer to identify herself in the audience, and she then joined me at the podium. As university trustees on stage watched nervously, I handed newly composed lyrics to the singer, took a harmonica out of my pocket, and played a few notes to be sure we would be in the same key. The two of us then launched an energetic rendition of Joyful Graduation and received a standing ovation. We succeeded in connecting with an audience of thousands, and many comments over the years from audience members are testimony to vivid memories created by this unconventional approach.

my musical commencement speech

As another example, a friend and I decided to give a toast at dinner for our friend Sylvia Earle's birthday. Rather than the usual spoken toast, we composed lyrics for "Sylvia Save the Sea," which used the tune of The Beatles' song "Let It Be." That performance years ago is still remembered and appreciated by Sylvia and others. Likewise, when we received FDA approval for our first drug

Chapter Ten - Keep the Mission and Vision Fresh

(Linaclotide, trade named Linzess) at Ironwood Pharmaceuticals, for gastrointestinal applications, we celebrated at a winery in Napa Valley. As people made heartfelt but conventional toasts at dinner, another board member joined me in scribbling the lyrics for a musical toast, and we then stood up and sang "God Bless Linaclotide." Our performance was video recorded, and this celebratory anthem was seen and appreciated by virtually everyone at Ironwood. To the tune of God Bless America, our lyrics started this way: "God bless Linaclotide, drug that I love. Take a capsule, and then you'll feel the movement coming down from above," etc.

A similar thing occurred upon my election as chairman of the board of The Jackson Laboratory (JAX) in Bar Harbor, Maine. These were exciting times in the world of genetics research and at JAX – a period when the workforce grew exponentially from less than two hundred employees to more than two thousand. I was eager to be more immersed in the culture of the lab than is sometimes the case with outside directors. This led me to visit JAX far beyond board meeting occasions, and it was gratifying to get to know many staff members involved in our genetics research, impacting a very wide variety of human conditions. These personal interactions are highly motivational for me, and our discussions covered many topics, ranging from their specific research interests, to funding issues and collaborative opportunities. As at IDEXX and other companies, there was a tendency for scientists to stay somewhat siloed in the labs, with little interaction with other disciplines. Yet when these interdisciplinary interactions occurred, they were sometimes magical in terms of solving problems and fostering innovation. It was my good fortune to be working with a newly appointed CEO named Kenneth Paigen who was eager to find innovative ways to advance research at JAX. One day we were discussing the interesting phenomenon that many staff members had musical skills but were not aware of the musical skills of others, even in nearby labs. And we agreed that music can be a great way to build relationships. Before long we had initiated something called the Right Brain Café, whereby staff members began to gather for weekly jam sessions and get to know each other in ways far different than normal daily work interactions. This concept had a very significant impact culturally because, suddenly, team members began to see each other in a fresh way; not as people you pass in the hallway and nod to while walking to your lab but as fellow musicians.

Another example: when a group of UNH students came to my home for dinner, we didn't simply call a caterer and order a meal. Instead, it seemed more meaningful to retain a professional chef to show all twenty of us how to make pasta from scratch. Then she supervised us as we worked together to prepare our shared meal. This mindset of exploring opportunities for novel and unique experiences has served me well in life.

Playwright George Bernard Shaw (no relation!) famously made this thought-provoking statement about shaping our lives versus passively searching for identity: "Life isn't about finding yourself. Life is about creating yourself." This offers a useful framework for living a life of impact via proactive strategies for personal growth and self-discovery. With this in mind, an important way of creating ourselves is through embracing change, adapting to new circumstances, and taking on fresh challenges and new behaviors.

Consider the example of Teddy Roosevelt. A sickly child plagued by asthma, the future Rough Rider, rancher, writer, twenty-sixth US president, noted conservationist, Nobel Peace Prize winner, and all-around "man in the arena" reinvented himself and embraced a life of extraordinary vigor. He remains one of our most inspiring and remarkable leaders. That's one reason that it meant so much to me to be inducted in 2016 into the Theodore Roosevelt Society at his rambling estate Sagamore Hill in Oyster Bay, New York, overlooking the Long Island Sound.

Chapter Ten - Keep the Mission and Vision Fresh

Teddy Roosevelt Society

***

To remain fresh and focused on important priorities in a rapidly changing and media-saturated world, it is necessary to be adept at discerning signals from noise. The signal is the critical information you require to understand, to advance, to grow, to gain insight. The noise is the non-essential information including the mental clutter that is so prevalent today thanks to the ceaseless flow of information from social media and news outlets, each one competing to attract more attention via powerful sales and marketing strategies. So I admire people who train themselves to effectively distinguish signal from noise in their professional and personal lives. In my struggle to survive viral encephalitis, I decided to enhance happiness by subtracting the disruptive noise of much retail news from my life. After several years of far more selective choices about news, I now sometimes find myself in conversations with people who are surprised to discover that I do not have an opinion on the latest fill-in-the-blank scandal. And I have a new awareness of how often news noise occupies a prominent position in social conversations, often intruding on and drowning out more substantive signals. I worry about young children, including my grandchildren, being inundated twenty-four/seven with frequently toxic and utterly trivial news. Noise which overwhelms signal.

In this context, we must all be very aware of forces in a world designed to steal our attention for their benefit. This creates a great need to protect our mental space and keep our minds clear of pointless detritus so that we can focus on what is important in life.

***

By nature, I usually find myself on the side of those who want to change things in the world–the rebels, the innovators, the insurgents. It inspires me to reflect on how George Washington and bands of citizen soldiers and militias won the Revolutionary War by defeating the British in the battle of Yorktown. This extraordinary accomplishment occurred after suffering major losses in New York and surprising the British in the pivotal battle of Trenton. When Washington was informed that water damage in a cold night crossing of the Delaware had rendered their gunpowder unusable, he reportedly responded: "Use the bayonet. I am resolved to take Trenton."

As IDEXX succeeded as an insurgent force and grew at a meteoric pace, we faced the risk that many successful organizations face: the prospect of complacency associated with an incumbent mindset. No longer the underdog, we had become the market leader in our field and an authority on veterinary diagnostics. The rebels amongst us began to sympathize with the statement attributed to Albert Einstein: "To punish me for my contempt for authority, Fate has made me an authority myself."

Not surprisingly, board of directors meetings regularly included conversations about improving near-term profitability by slowing down investment spending in R&D or other functions such as international expansion. These are important strategic choices and our leadership team nearly always urged continued investment spending to create value via expansion into future opportunities.

We resisted the temptation to become self-satisfied and were determined to encourage the innovative vigor and fresh thinking that

Chapter Ten - Keep the Mission and Vision Fresh

had created our successes. We envisioned a world full of expansive opportunities to leverage the extraordinary platform we had created. At the same time, we recognized that some stakeholders prefer increased near-term profitability. Balancing this competing perspective is a matter we took very seriously.

A critical priority of a leadership team in these circumstances is to maintain a hungry, insurgent, energetic, and high-performance culture rather than having success lead to comfort and contentment. One strategy to achieve this is to identify bold new goals and opportunities, and to view past successes largely as launch platforms for even greater future initiatives. Veterinary pharmaceuticals, for example, is a market exponentially larger than diagnostics.

Because my leadership beliefs included the importance of regularly reimagining what great looks like, I eventually found myself faced with a difficult decision that I had long anticipated. As a leadership team, we had worked hard to build an organization with a deep bench of talent and succession planning such that we weren't dependent on any individuals for our success.

From the beginning, I had believed that the ultimate proof of IDEXX's success would be seeing it flourish without me. I never thought it was best for the company for me to be its CEO for life. I thought the true test of whether I had succeeded at IDEXX was if I could leave and the company wouldn't need me—that it had perpetual life and was self-sustaining. I didn't want IDEXX to be dependent on any one person, including me. As our staff grew to thousands of people I became increasingly concerned when I experienced situations where my personal knowledge and capabilities seemed to create dependencies.

This is a critical question: can a founder-built company prosper without the founder?

Having studied other founder-led companies I realized that no one, including me, would be able to answer that question until I actually stepped away from the company and saw what happened. I grasped that I had to leave. This was an important family for me and an integral part of my life. The struggle to create a great company had been epic. It was astounding that so many things had gone right, despite the odds. We had not just survived, we had thrived. By our 40th anniversary celebration in 2023, IDEXX revenues exceeded $3B with an enterprise value at year-end of roughly $40B. I had stood on stage with my friend and Kleiner Perkins co-founder Brook Byers for induction into the Life Science Foundation Biotech Hall of Fame. The Maine state economist had announced in Maine's bicentennial video that the creation and success of IDEXX marked the transition of the state's economy from natural resources to modern technology, now estimated at nearly 20% of the state's gross product.

Chapter Ten - Keep the Mission and Vision Fresh

I recognized that if I stayed at IDEXX, my presence could become a liability. I also realized that leadership of an incumbent organization wasn't a great fit for me.

Because insurgency is part of my nature, it was time to move on, knowing that it wouldn't be easy. For one thing, our board, employees, customers, and investors sent gratifying signals about my leadership. But at a deep level, it seemed clear to me that a succession plan was best for the company and a new adventure was best for me.

Making the decision to leave IDEXX was both hard on one hand and simple on the other. However, executing that decision became incredibly complicated and time-consuming. Finding the right CEO to take over-involved multiple searches and several very difficult failures. Finally, in January 2002, we had a new CEO installed. That's when I jumped on my Harley-Davidson Road Glide and pulled out from the IDEXX parking lot for the last time. That same evening, I boarded a plane to Patagonia and then trekked with friends through this stunningly beautiful and remote region at the tip of South America.

***

On return from Patagonia, I joined the faculty of Harvard's Kennedy School of Government, in Cambridge, Massachusetts, as a Senior Fellow, and I continued my practice of guest lectures at MIT's Sloan School of Management. Beyond that, it was exciting to become engaged in several new entrepreneurial ventures in the famous Kendall Square innovation hub. These included two cancer diagnostic companies.

At the Kennedy School I worked with the Center for Business and Government on corporate social responsibility issues, and to address public policy and corporate governance issues associated with a wave of corporate "creative accounting" scandals of those days.

These included the high-profile collapses of WorldCom and Enron. In reaction to these scandals and the resulting confidence crisis about corporate governance, the US Congress enacted legislation for accounting reform and enhanced investor protection. The Sarbanes-Oxley Act of 2002 set new standards for all U.S. public company boards, management, and public accounting firms.

More enthusiastically, I developed a strong working relationship with the Center for Public Leadership , led by David Gergen, to further its mission of inspiring and developing principled, effective public leadership. David is a well-known political commentator, author, and presidential advisor who served Ronald Reagan, Gerald Ford, and Bill Clinton. He is an astute student of leadership, including this statement, relevant here: "Leadership is a journey. Each one of us has to take our own path, and get there our own way". Emphasizing impact, David went on to say that "Leadership is about calling people to do things beyond themselves."

As a faculty and advisory board member, I collaborated with David and students to identify admirable public leadership qualities and showcase people who embodied these qualities in a program we created called "America's Best Leaders". The experience opened me to a wider world, taking on fresh, new challenges, and getting ready to change in ways I could not predict.

One of these new experiences happened in conjunction with my Kennedy School affiliation. I was asked to spend time with the US Department of Defense as it

Press coverage of our leadership program at Harvard's Kennedy School of Government

Chapter Ten - Keep the Mission and Vision Fresh

grappled with the aftermath of the September 11, 2001 terrorist attacks. Here is an excerpt from my account of that experience published in the Spring 2004 issue of this Harvard journal: *Compass, A Journal of Leadership*. One of my goals was to highlight leadership practices that the military and private sector can learn from each other.

Published Spring 2004, Vol. 1, No. 2

COMPASS: A Journal of Leadership
Center for Public Leadership
John F. Kennedy School of Government
Harvard University

Harvard Kennedy School

Generals and Admirals as CEOs
The business world has long looked to the military for important lessons about leadership and strategy. Now military leaders are learning from the private sector, and generals and admirals sometimes sound like CEOs. An entrepreneur comments on some recent experience with the military's transformation.

By David E. Shaw

Just after sunrise on June 9, 2003, 40 tired American civilians were huddled near a remote airport terminal when the deafening scream of low-flying A-10 and F-15 fighter jets shattered the morning quiet. In two lightning-fast passes, the jets attacked and destroyed the airport's defense capabilities. Moments later a giant C-130 aircraft rumbled into sight. Soon the sky was filled with dozens of paratroopers, who quickly took possession of the airport. Less than 30 minutes after the first air strike, the American civilians were safely in the hands of U.S. troops and ready for evacuation.

I was one of those jet-lagged civilians, and this, fortunately, was only a mock anti-terrorist attack and extraction exercise at a NATO base in Europe. Standing with me as the exercise concluded, United States Marine Corps

Wave Making : Inspired By Impact

General James Jones, Supreme Allied Commander, Europe, spoke quietly but passionately about transformational challenges faced by the U.S. military in a post-9/11 world. "Our vision for the future has to recognize that threats to American safety and freedom are very different now," said Jones. "Business as usual is not an option."

We listened attentively as the general listed prominent new challenges including growing political instability and rogue nations, tensions with traditional allies, proliferation of terrorism and weapons of mass destruction, expanded military involvement in humanitarian actions, and management of all-volunteer US armed forces. His views about the urgent need for transformational leadership and strategies were similar to views expressed to us just days earlier in briefing at the Pentagon by others including General Richard Myers, chairman of Joint Chiefs of Staff, and Deputy Secretary of Defense Paul Wolfowitz. It was surprising how often these military leaders frequently referred to high-performance business practices as a source of inspiration for the transformation they envisioned. This included familiar business terms such as delivering stakeholder value creation, return on investment, customer satisfaction, competitive advantages, and leadership practices that are less autocratic and more motivational in keeping with a volunteer workforce. New leadership practices that are less autocratic and more motivational, team-oriented, and collaborative. Aboard the USS La Salle, flagship of the U.S. Sixth Fleet, Admiral Greg Johnson, Chief of Naval Forces Europe, helped me understand a changing perspective in the military, to better "meet shareholder expectations." He explained that military leaders are increasingly focused on return on investment without the benefit of being able to relate input to output in the same terms as the private sector. We heard that traditional military "output" in terms of readiness to win wars or avoid wars through deterrence often made cost a low-priority consideration. However, in the context of scarce resources, military leaders are adopting more business-like analyses that contemplate the cost and benefit of many different scenarios of readiness.

Chapter Ten - Keep the Mission and Vision Fresh

Throughout my business career, I have developed great admiration for many aspects of military leadership thinking, and I have hired hundreds of military alumni for a wide variety of responsibilities. Many share highly desirable leadership qualities such as a disciplined approach to achieving results, a passion for winning, and a strong focus on team building.

It was an honor to have this experience with US military forces and I have continued to interact with military leaders for many years including hosting former Secretary of Defense General Jim Mattis at our Leerink Partners Healthcare Summit in Napa Valley.

with Jim Mattis

***

I was proud of our work at the Kennedy School, but had completed my role there and was ready for a dynamic next step.

In 2005, my friends at Venrock Associates invited me to become a partner. Of course, I knew them well via IDEXX and had invested in their fund. Upon acceptance of their offer, my center of gravity shifted to Manhattan for several years of fascinating and intense immersion in the world of venture capital. Beyond the professional challenge, it was fulfilling to be immersed in the invigorating energy and sense of endless possibility in New York City. This included meeting people from all over the world and relishing the mix of high and low culture. Manhattan is the perfect place to witness what great looks like in terms of art, music, dance, and theater. And as the global finance capital, New York City is also the place to see and take part in what great looks like in terms of investing.

One important achievement in those times was my leadership role in the creation of Ikaria Holdings, an inspirational biopharmaceutical venture I will discuss later. This became a significant venture for Venrock. During my time in Cambridge, I joined the board and invested in an early-stage biopharmaceutical company called Ironwood Pharmaceuticals. This was another shared investment with Venrock.

As a partner at a prominent venture capital firm like Venrock, there is massive deal flow to manage, and you find yourself in a position where you must decline all but a few of the most attractive ventures out of hundreds or thousands that seek funding. And this is an industry where the success rate of ventures that get funded is daunting. Many ventures struggle or fail, so financial returns are usually dependent on rare "unicorns": game-changing, superstar companies like Apple, Intel, Amgen, or American Superconductor. IDEXX was and is one of these. It was a big mental shift for me to go from leading a company, with a significant ability to manage our prospects for success, to funding high-risk ventures without the same direct management control. This leads to an investment focus on backing great management teams and so unicorns are most often comprised of the rare combination of great management teams and great ideas.

I am grateful for my time at Venrock, but realized after several

Chapter Ten - Keep the Mission and Vision Fresh

years that my interests and abilities were better suited to building and managing ventures, versus finding and funding.

***

Since departing Venrock and the Kennedy School faculty, its been a blessing to have had many inspirational opportunities to engage in impactful ventures.

As an advisor to the San Diego Zoo Wildlife Alliance, I have collaborated with CEO Paul Baribault in the transformation of a traditional zoo to a powerful force in global wildlife conservation including the protection of endangered species.

As an advisor to Saildrone, I have supported the company's innovative vision of a healthy ocean and a safe, sustainable planet through our autonomous wind and solar-powered fleet of boats. These unmanned surface vehicles provide intelligence and insight for challenges from maritime defense and seafloor mapping to earth system processes such as weather forecasting, carbon cycling, and sustainable fisheries management.

As an investor and Advisory Board member of Nautilus, I'm inspired to share stories that take readers into the depths of science, and spotlight ways that its power profoundly impacts our lives and cultures. At a time of significant anti-science public sentiment, we aim to make science highly understandable, interesting, and relevant. Beyond our major focus areas of oceans and neuroscience, we venture into the fields of anthropology, geology, astronomy, genetics, and physics. My friend John Steele, Publisher of Nautilus, has described our mission this way: "we're embarked on a voyage into the wonders of the universe."

As a member of the Council on Foreign Relations (CFR), I seek to understand and impact the global character of many of the most pressing issues of our times, and the impact of US Foreign policy on issues that matter to all of us. One example of this was authoring a 2014 *Science & Diplomacy* article about high seas protection, and participating in a CFR symposium on global ocean stewardship.

Through the Global Philanthropists Circle at Synergos, with more than 400 members in over 30 countries, we engage in peer learning, collaborative communities, and special events to share ideas and inspiration on ways to impact society's most pressing needs. Founder Peggy Dulany summarizes our work this way: "Synergos is a global organization that has pioneered the use of bridging leadership, which builds trust and collaboration to solve complex problems."

As a member of the Advisory Council of the Nationhood Lab at Salve Regina University's Pell Center, I support work to counter polarization, disinformation, and authoritarian threats to American democracy by developing, testing, and disseminating a renewed civic national narrative for the United States. We are encouraged that our research shows that most Americans across nearly every demographic category favor a civic national story based on the inspirational ideals of our Declaration of Independence rather than on authoritarian ethnonational, religious, or heritage-based assertions. Young people demonstrated the greatest commitment to civic ideas.

In collaboration with The Goldie Hawn Foundation's MindUP program, I support the delivery of contemplative science services to address urgent emotional and behavioral health issues in schools. These issues are part of a larger global mental health crisis, and our experience demonstrates that this crisis can significantly be impacted by enhancing awareness and providing remedial practices.

On advisory boards at the MIT Media Lab, the National Geographic Society, and WaterBear I have the opportunity to think creatively about the future of media and its role in society, including best ways to harness the highly impactful power of storytelling. At the

Chapter Ten - Keep the Mission and Vision Fresh

MIT Media Lab, we have research groups focused on several dozen subjects ranging from transformative solutions for climate and energy, to digital technologies for mental and physical wellbeing, applications of artificial intelligence to the human experience, and other initiatives to invent a better and more just future.

Takeaway: Exploration and discovery are important characteristics of the human spirit. It can be very beneficial to nourish these forces to live a fulfilling and impactful life. I seek, and admire others who seek, to adopt a mindset of creativity and curiosity with frequent encounters of new ways of doing something, a new subject or theory to explore, or a new field of inquiry to delve into. Recently, for instance, I examined the intersection of spirituality and artificial intelligence (AI). The rapid progress of AI has ignited a flame of curiosity and awe, as I marvel at these technological wonders and seek to understand how two seemingly distinct realms intersect. We are coming face to face with sublime questions about the nature of consciousness, what it means to be human, the authenticity of human relationships, and our ability to decode synthesized reality and perceive powerful new modes of persuasion.

*with John Steele, Publisher of Nautilus,
and Ellen Windemuth, Founder of Waterbear Network*

PART THREE
DO GOOD AND PURSUE ADVENTURE

Winter surfing in Maine

"The harder the conflict, the greater the triumph."
– *George Washington*

Chapter Eleven
Be Bold

"What you can do, or dream you can, begin it. Boldness has genius, power, and magic in it."
– John Anster inspired by Johann Wolfgang von Goethe

Love, reverence, and gratitude for the ocean have been a constant in my life. I have had adventurous experiences in spectacular seascapes around the world and have had the opportunity to contribute to global ocean stewardship. When I am at home in Maine, I am seldom out of earshot of ocean waves crashing rhythmically onto rocky shores and sandy beaches. But over the years, I grew increasingly troubled by the catastrophic deterioration of ocean health around the world. This includes overfishing, pollution including agricultural runoff and vast plastic waste, dramatically increased acidity due to carbon absorption, higher temperatures, deoxygenation, seabed mining, and ominous changes in ocean currents. The United Nations is one of many organizations that has documented these threats including the addition of more than 17 million metric tons of plastic waste. UN Secretary-General António Guterres and his predecessors have repeatedly warned of an "ocean crisis."

This evolving crisis is why, in April 2010, I sailed among the Galápagos Islands on a four-day voyage aboard the *National Geographic Endeavour*, joining my dive buddy and fellow steward of the sea, oceanographer Sylvia Earle, and other marine activists. Hailed by the US Library of Congress as a "Living Legend" and named "Her Deepness" by *The New Yorker*, Sylvia had won a TED Prize a year earlier, granting her "one wish to change the world."

In her powerful acceptance speech, she told the TED audience, "I wish you would use all means at your disposal . . . to ignite public support for a global network of marine protected areas–hope spots large enough to save and restore the ocean, the blue heart of the planet." Speaking in her expressive alto voice, Sylvia concluded: "We

with dive buddy Sylvia Earle

need many things to keep and maintain the world as a better place. But nothing else will matter if we fail to protect the ocean. Our fate and the ocean are one."

For most of history, humanity often imagined the deep sea as a dark, largely empty void, or worse, a place of terror filled with sea monsters. Only quite recently have scientists revealed that the ocean teems with life, top to bottom, and it reaches depths of almost thirty-six thousand feet–deeper even than Mount Everest is tall. Yet National Geographic Society estimates that more than eighty percent of Earth's oceans remain unexplored. This remarkable ecosystem accounts for 70 percent of the earth's surface, and it is the environment where the majority of life exists on our planet. About half of the oxygen we breathe comes from the ocean–primarily from ocean-dwelling plankton. The ocean also efficiently stores heat and carbon dioxide, thereby helping to mitigate the effects of climate change. But as greenhouse gasses from the burning of fossil fuels, methane generation, and other sources heat the environment, nature's cooling system is breaking down, leading to higher temperatures, rising sea levels, and increased acidity. Still, at the time Sylvia made her speech,

CHAPTER ELEVEN - BE BOLD

less than 2 percent of world oceans were protected versus more than 15 percent of the world's land, usually referred to as the "terrestrial" world.

On the *Endeavour*, I found myself among marine scientists, prominent businesspeople, policymakers, and philanthropists like my close friend and neighbor Richard Rockefeller, a practicing physician, and an ardent conservationist. Also with us were musicians including Jackson Browne, and media personalities including Edward Norton, Daryl Hannah, and Leonardo DiCaprio. When Leo and I were dive buddies, it was interesting to learn more about his enthusiasm for our work. All one hundred people aboard the ship shared Sylvia's goal of saving the ocean and it was an honor to be among them. The creative and intellectual energy produced by such a diverse range of perspectives was electric, and I made a conscious decision to be open to potential opportunities that each encounter might offer in terms of imaginative thinking and perspective-shifting ideas.

Part of Ecuador and perched astride the equator, the Galápagos is an archipelago with more than 100 islands in the western Pacific Ocean. It was inscribed as a UNESCO World Heritage site in 1978 and is a naturalist's dream, famous for several species of marine and terrestrial wildlife found nowhere else on Earth. I was happy to see saltwater iguanas, blue-footed boobies, and Galápagos giant tortoises. And it was rewarding to see the place where, in 1835, English naturalist Charles Darwin made some of his ground-breaking observations about the role of natural selection in evolution.

Our days were split between dives in pristine aquamarine waters and provocative work sessions on the ship where people stepped up as "idea champions," advocating for their particular ocean conservation strategies. Creativity was percolating on the decks, in the lounge, and during dinners aboard the *Endeavour*, with people sharing ideas enthusiastically. Standing at the lectern in the *Endeavour*'s lounge one afternoon, speakers held forth animatedly about the urgency of preserving marine ecosystems such as Monterey Bay, with its vast kelp forests and enormous subterranean canyon rich with fish. Seventy-five miles south of San Francisco, it encompasses an area larger than Yellowstone National Park.

From past experience including my role as a presidentially appointed trustee of the US National Park Foundation, it was widely recognized that protection for specific marine ecosystems could contribute to better ocean health. But I was also well aware that the ability to protect discrete marine ecosystems was a much different proposition than for the terrestrial world because of the vast inter-connectedness of oceans. The way I saw it, plans for discrete ecosystems had to ultimately be linked to a plan for far broader ocean stewardship. In that context, it's important to understand that close to two-thirds of the world's oceans lie beyond the jurisdiction of any country. These High Seas, as they are called, represent Earth's largest ecosystem. And leaving those vast High Seas unprotected makes it extraordinarily difficult to safeguard adjacent ecosystems like Monterey Bay.

If the purpose of our gathering was to determine what great looks like for the health of world oceans, it worried me that our thinking and our plans might not yet be matching the vast scale of the challenges and opportunities that we faced. So, with others, I raised the issue of much more expansive thinking, suggesting that to achieve the goal of wise global ocean stewardship it isn't nearly enough to preserve Monterey Bay or any other specific bay, inlet, cove, or estuary since all of these are interconnected. Instead, perhaps now is the time to create an audacious plan for stewardship of all of the world's oceans, including the planet's vast high seas, which extensively intermingle via a global network of powerful ocean currents.

***

Conventional wisdom often urges us to take things one step at a time, to believe that slow and steady wins the race. It warns against

Chapter Eleven - Be Bold

getting too far out over our skis. Beyond that, insufficiently developed social trust and unclear rules of engagement in group discussions can inhibit the expression of dissenting or contrary opinions. This can create a tendency for people to "play it safe" in expressing their opinions. However, I have spent most of my career in cultures where critical thinking and contrarian views are viewed as essential for success. Big challenges benefit from bold and innovative thinking, and open discussions.

My experience in government, academia, and the private sector has also made me very aware of two fundamentally different mindsets that influence the nature of these discussions. In many "traditional" settings, perspectives about opportunities are strongly bounded by what resources are available to accomplish a goal. However, successful entrepreneurship often requires a different mindset. Rather than asking what resources are AVAILABLE, the entrepreneurial perspective focuses on what resources are NEEDED to achieve a goal. It is a mindset of abundance with the assumption that needed resources can be marshaled for a compelling plan.

This was one of those circumstances. Our group needed to give ourselves permission to think about solutions at the right scale ... perhaps as dramatic as a challenge to the viability of life on Earth.

Discussions of this kind are seldom easy. It's quite natural for thoughtful participants to develop views that differ from a group, but to be cautious and conservative in expressing these views. For important decisions, it's critically important to encourage diverse and contrary perspectives. And to ensure that a prevailing perspective doesn't inappropriately dominate group thinking, or drown out minority opinions.

Great challenges such as protecting our oceans, reversing climate change, and making the world economy more equitable will only be addressed successfully by encouraging bold and innovative thinking by diverse, highly engaged, and courageous visionaries among us. Renowned anthropologist Margaret Mead is credited with capturing this belief beautifully with this statement: "Never doubt that a small group of thoughtful, committed citizens can change the world: indeed, it's the only thing that ever has."

***

My most vivid early memories of the ocean are of walking down a beach at dawn with my mother's father, Walter Evans, and his dog Mandy, to a scenic tidal pool near his cottage in southern Maine. He and my grandmother had owned this cottage on Drakes Island, near Kennebunkport, for many years and it was a treat to visit them. Nearby, the Rachel Carson National Wildlife Refuge stretched across more than 5,000 acres of marshes and estuaries. As if it were yesterday, I can still smell the salt in the air as we set out in the early summer mornings, weaving through the dune grasses. A highlight was spotting seals as they lounged on the sand and rocks, or popping their heads out of the water while swimming. My grandfather brought binoculars so I could observe but not bother these remarkable marine mammals with their whiskered faces and dark button eyes.

It was on Drakes Island as a young boy that I hunted for crabs and starfish in seaweed-laced tidal pools. Later, I learned to body surf and snorkel. I was fourteen when I got my scuba diving certification, paying for it with money from my paper route. I wanted to explore the world, and I reasoned that you cannot fully explore the world without going underwater. After some freshwater dives in quarries around Nashua I ventured into the magical world of the Atlantic Ocean. It wasn't like the warm Caribbean, with its technicolor showcase of exotic fish, sponges, and coral. It was freezing cold, and wetsuits were needed. But it was stunning, and I was hooked.

This passion for the ocean was the reason I was on Sylvia's TED-at-sea expedition. At the beginning of the voyage, I was focused

Chapter Eleven - Be Bold

on the Arctic Ocean, the smallest of the world's oceans, surrounding the North Pole. Our group worried that as the sea ice melts and ship traffic increases, the Arctic Ocean, once protected by its isolation and brutally cold temperatures, would become more and more exposed to manmade dangers.

However, as I listened to different speakers, my focus shifted to a more expansive strategy. The perils to one ocean often relate to dangers faced by other distant globally interconnected ecosystems. Conceptually, it seemed that the best solution was the almost absurdly bold challenge of protecting all of Earth's High Seas. These are the deep and open international waters that lie beyond the two-hundred-nautical-mile economic zone of each country's coastline—where national jurisdiction ends. Comprising well over half the planet's biosphere, the high seas belong to no one and, therefore, are vulnerable to legal and illegal fishing as well as mining and pollution, such as the oil discharge and sewage from industrial tankers and container ships. In other words, this is a largely lawless expanse where anyone can do what they want, despite the consequences for life on Earth.

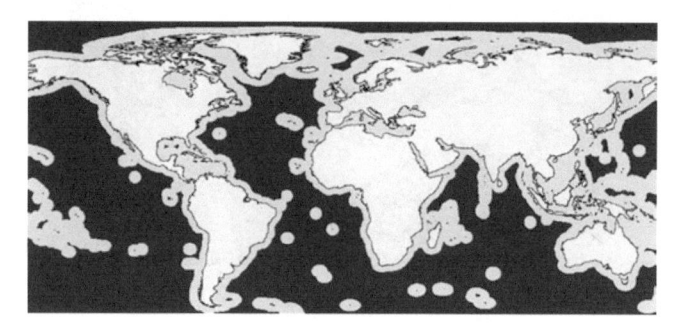

"High Seas"

Turning to my friend Richard Rockefeller I quietly expressed concern about the logic of our discussions "What about the High Seas?" I asked. "How can we ever protect world oceans without stewardship of these interconnected ocean ecosystems that represent the majority of world oceans? Won't all other efforts ultimately be futile if we don't protect the high seas?" Knowing that others in our discussions had extensive expertise in ocean stewardship, and that high seas protection wasn't a new idea, we posed this strategic question to the group, with mixed results. While some signaled appreciation for the framing of our challenge, others expressed concern that such an audacious idea would distract our attention from more practical initiatives. In the midst of our deliberations the then-premiere of Bermuda, Ewart Brown, made a video presentation featuring the Sargasso Sea which occupies some two million square miles of high seas in the North Atlantic Ocean. All other seas are contained by land boundaries. Think of the Mediterranean or the Black Sea. But the Sargasso Sea, named for its swirling and floating sargassum seaweed is bordered by neither continents nor countries. Uniquely, its ever-changing boundaries are shaped by five ocean currents, including the Gulf Stream, which create a massive clockwise gyre.

map showing Sargasso Sea

    Bermuda is the largest island near the Sargasso Sea and is the only government with jurisdiction over it. Bermuda's Exclusive Economic Zone extends into the Sargasso Sea, influencing a signification portion of this unique marine area. This led to a discussion about the prospect of working with Bermuda and other governments to create a high seas protection mechanism for the Sargasso Sea that

Chapter Eleven - Be Bold

might be a launching platform for the protection of all high seas. This might be the precedent-setting breakthrough that we were seeking.

By the time the voyage ended, a group of us had embraced the idea. I flew with Richard Rockefeller and Ted Waitt, co-founder of Gateway, Inc., to Bermuda for a meeting with its premier. Citing the country's great heritage in maritime affairs, we outlined our perspective on the nature of this opportunity. As part of making this case, we shared our view that playing a leadership role in protecting the Sargasso Sea would create an opportunity for Bermuda to gain global recognition for tackling one of the great challenges of our times. In the Pacific, President Tommy Remengesau Jr. of the island nation of Palau, was demonstrating similar inspirational leadership.

We offered to collaborate in realizing this historic opportunity, and we outlined a concept to establish a new conservation model that would combat the threats of overfishing, climate change, and sargassum harvesting, as well as the devastating accumulation of garbage, including plastic. The Bermudian government enthusiastically signed on and, as founding chair, I worked with Sylvia Earle, Richard Rockefeller, and others to establish an organization for our work: the Sargasso Sea Alliance. Along with officials from Bermuda, philanthropists, and key scientists, our newly constituted team included a leading international marine environmental lawyer from the International Union for Conservation of Nature (IUCN). Dedicated to protecting nature, it functions like the United Nations of the global environmental community, bringing together more than 1,400 groups.

I made a conscious decision to challenge conventional wisdom by looking beyond marine conservation experts to recruit an executive director. Instead, I searched the world of terrestrial conservation and ultimately recruited a conservation lawyer at the World Bank as our executive director. The terrestrial world has a long history of conservation and today more than 15% of the planet's terrestrial world is protected in some way. The marine world lags behind; at that time less than 2% of oceans were protected. My logic was that our pioneering initiative in marine conservation would benefit from advances already proven effective in a more advanced domain. By doing that, we brought innovation to our work, and we weren't stuck with status quo thinking about what marine protection should look like. American journalist H .L. Mencken recognized an aspect of the challenge we faced when he supposedly wrote: "For every complex problem, there is a solution that is neat, simple, and wrong."

Over time, humanity has developed a variety of methods to protect land. Zoning laws are one way. Other approaches include the designation of national parks, national monuments, wilderness expanses, and acreage overseen by the Bureau of Land Management. But in terms of protecting the High Seas, the Sargasso Sea Alliance was blazing a new path. We wanted to provide protections similar to those enjoyed by such biodiverse land preserves as the Serengeti National Park in Tanzania.

Like the Serengeti, the Sargasso Sea is an oasis of biological diversity. Thus, one of our most pressing priorities was to produce and broadly share scientific studies highlighting this critical role. Known as the golden floating rainforest of the ocean, this body of water is the only free-floating seaweed habitat in the world. As *National Geographic* describes it, the sargassum is both "a mobile shelter and a movable feast"–a mustard-hued, nutrient-rich canopy for more than a hundred species, including endangered turtles and eels, as well as migrating sharks and humpback and sperm whales.

A treaty is the highest level of commitment countries can make. A declaration, which sometimes precedes a treaty, is generally less binding. A treaty is enforceable, whereas a declaration is a statement of intent or principles and is usually not enforceable. In the spirit of "starting by starting," I knew that our needs would be best served by taking a realistic first step in formalizing our collaboration by

Chapter Eleven - Be Bold

designing an appropriate declaration for our multi-nation consortium of supportive nations. So, we assembled a group of legal experts, and they set to work. Simultaneously we built a strong science case in support of our work, and I personally made a film to help the world understand this spectacular but remote ecosystem that few would ever see in person. This was my first attempt at filmmaking for advocacy and I was gratified that it got great recognition including an award at the Blue Ocean Film Festival and Conservation Summit.

A VIDEO TRIBUTE TO PROTECTION OF THE SARGASSO SEA
by **David Evans Shaw**

SARGASSO SEA ALLIANCE

    Leading a bold venture of this kind doesn't necessarily require exceptional subject matter expertise. It requires the capability to assemble an outstanding team and oversee a successful process. Soon we were sharing the science case, the film, and the draft declaration with leaders in countries adjacent to the Sargasso Sea and the North Atlantic Ocean to gain their support as signatories to this precedent-setting initiative. We were fortunate to have the support of leading conservation organizations such as the National Geographic Society and IUCN, and we were gratified by responses to our proposals as a powerful consensus developed in support of the declaration.

    Four years after our Galápagos expedition, on a balmy day in March 2014, I stood on a perfectly manicured, emerald green lawn of Bermuda's Castle Harbor for a celebratory group photo with our board members, and representatives of prominent conservation groups and diplomats from different countries. Earlier that day we had the great satisfaction of watching representatives from Bermuda, the United States, the United Kingdom, Monaco, and the Azores sign the Hamilton Declaration on Collaboration for the Conservation of the Sargasso Sea. This historic agreement established the Sargasso Sea Commission to exercise a stewardship role to benefit future generations.

Before signing the Hamilton Declaration, Craig Cannonier, Bermuda's Premier, said, "As lead government of the Sargasso Sea Alliance, Bermuda is proud to be a part of this great initiative.... I really want to say a heartfelt thank you for what this means to future generations ... that the world looking on, seeing us come together in a collaborative way to ensure that there is a future in our waters for all of us."

It was an enormous accomplishment when, in subsequent years, other countries signed on, including the Cayman Islands, Canada, the Dominican Republic, the Bahamas, and the British Virgin Islands. It was an honor for me to present our accomplishments and our plans for global high seas stewardship to a gathering in New York City at the Council on Foreign Relations, where I am a member.

Reflecting on the success of the Hamilton Declaration, I realized that the pivotal moment occurred when we intuitively sensed the need to lift our perspective from individual bodies of water—the Arctic Ocean, Monterey Bay—to the vast and utterly unprotected High Seas. Training yourself to think as broadly as possible, and to mentally scale to the right level for every opportunity, is a critical tool to develop for wave making at the magnitude needed to address many of today's most pressing challenges.

***

The Hamilton Declaration had just the ripple effect we had hoped for .... and a "ripple effect" is the right way to think about progress because it often occurs in ways you can't fully anticipate.

Chapter Eleven - Be Bold

Among many other factors, an article I wrote for the AAAS journal Science Diplomacy contributed to this ripple effect.

> **SCIENCE & DIPLOMACY** **AAAS**
> A quarterly publication from the AAAS Center for Science Diplomacy
> ADVANCING SCIENCE, SERVING SOCIETY
>
> David E. Shaw, "Protecting the Sargasso Sea," *Science & Diplomacy*, Vol. 3, No. 2 (June 2014*). http://www.sciencediplomacy.org/letter-field/2014/protecting-sargasso-sea.
>
> Protecting the Sargasso Sea
> *David E. Shaw*

In 2006, President George W. Bush established Papahānaumokuākea Marine National Monument surrounding the northern Hawaiian Islands as a Pacific Ocean sanctuary that was larger than all other US parks combined. After being appointed by President Bush to the board of trustees of the National Park Foundation in 2010, I became part of a group advocating to expand Papahānaumokuākea, and I also served as a leader in the US National Park Service Centennial in 2016. I was thrilled when President Obama, who was born in Honolulu, subsequently used executive power under the Antiquities Act to quadruple the Papahānaumokuākea marine monument's size to 582,578 square miles, an area nearly the same size as the Gulf of Mexico. It is now one of the largest marine protected expanses in the world.

Another reason to celebrate occurred that September in Washington, when Obama, speaking at the Our Ocean Conference hosted by the US Department of State, announced the designation of the first-ever marine monument in the Atlantic Ocean, 130 miles off the coast of Cape Cod. Here, in the final months of his second and final term, the president delivered words that perfectly encapsulated my own hopes for the years to come: "So if we're going to leave our children with oceans like the ones that were left to us, then we're going to have to act," he said, seeming to be speaking not just as a head of state but as the father of two daughters. He continued, "And we're going to have to act boldly. . .The ocean's health is our health ... Probably the most important thing that you can do on this planet Earth is to make sure that you're making it just a little bit better for future generations."

Several ocean activists who were in town for the conference discussed what we should tackle next. These included me, Sylvia, and Dr. Barbara Block, an oceanographer at Stanford University famous for her research tracking white sharks and other marine animals. With Barbara's help, I succeeded in putting tracking tags on great white sharks and an 800-pound bluefin tuna to discover their migration patterns. We all agreed that the Hamilton Declaration had signaled that vast ocean protection was possible, and that it was time to leverage that experience on a global scale.

As our planning began for the next chapter of high seas stewardship my phone rang one day. The International SeaKeepers Society, which encourages research, stewardship, and learning about the ocean in the yachting community, was calling with the news that they proposed to honor me as the 2013 International SeaKeeper of the Year, an award recognizing those who have made exceptional contributions to the protection of the world's oceans. Among the previous honorees were, Sylvia Earle; Prince Albert II of Monaco; filmmaker James Cameron, and oceanographic explorer Jean-Michel Cousteau. The son of the legendary oceanographer, Jacques Cousteau, Jean-Michel is an accomplished filmmaker, oceanographer, and environmentalist in his own right.

Because I have always believed that it's far better to give recognition than to receive it, I told SeaKeepers that I could only accept the award if other members of the Sargasso Sea Alliance

Chapter Eleven - Be Bold

leadership team were recognized along with me. They expressed their policy of honoring individuals and thanked me for considering their overture as they proceeded to consider other worthy candidates. The call ended cordially, and I felt good about the conclusion.

Refusing personal recognition for a team effort has always felt right to me. Focusing on *we* instead of *me* was a reminder to myself of the importance of standing up for what I value—in this case, the crucial importance of teamwork. For example, once when the governor of Maine called to tell me that IDEXX had been named the Maine Business of the Year and invited me to come to the state capitol to accept the award. I requested instead that he come to our cafeteria at IDEXX, stand up on a lunch table with me, and present the award to the entire company. Our success was a team accomplishment, and it was vital that the governor and I convey that message to everyone. That is exactly what happened.

Even so, I was a little surprised, and pleased, when a week later, the SeaKeepers phoned again. "You catalyzed a dynamic and provocative discussion among the members of our board," the caller said. "It caused everybody to think, *Well, of course, great things get done by teams.*" This sequence of events reveals that a gesture does not have to be big and bold to have a lasting impact.

Sargasso Sea Alliance team at 2013 Seakeepers Bal de la Mer

The atmosphere for the awards ceremony at the St. Francis Yacht Club was charged with excitement, partly because San Francisco was hosting the thirty-fourth America's Cup sailing race. On stage with my colleagues one night in September, I told the audience, "We believe that a protection declaration for the Sargasso Sea can become an island of hope, inspiration, and exemplary stewardship in a vast sea of perilous complacency and ominous threats." In advance of this award ceremony, I had given considerable thought about ways to make it special, beyond the fact that the amazing America's Cup races were happening all around us. Drawn that evening partly due to the race, attendees at our event included prominent Californians, national park trustees, and ocean stewards from around the world.

I have long been a fan of The Beach Boys and mused about the significance of The Beach Boys supporting ocean stewardship. So, I reached out to renowned Beach Boy Al Jardine to see if he might like to figuratively step off the beach into the ocean -with us at the SeaKeepers event. Introducing myself to Al, I described the opportunity. Al enthusiastically accepted my offer and added to the festivities that night by performing an original song: "Don't Fight the Sea." We were all grateful for his contribution to the evening and I feel fortunate that we have been friends ever since.

with Al Jardine at 2013 Seakeepers event

Chapter Eleven - Be Bold

Later that year our work was honored again when my film about the Sargasso Sea won an award at the 2016 Blue Ocean Film Festival and Conservation Summit in St. Petersburg, Florida. This included recognition for the soundtrack which was composed and recorded in my home music studio in Maine. Each year ocean conservation leaders are recognized at this Summit. My friend Nainoa Thompson, president of the Polynesian Voyaging Society, was honored with the 2016 Legacy Award, and it was a wonderful surprise that I was recognized with the 2016 Making Waves Award. In my acceptance remarks, I commented that it was humbling to be singled out as a wave maker in a room with so many impressive ocean stewards. In response to this, my collaborator and dive buddy Sylvia Earle grabbed the microphone and announced that I am "the tsunami among wavemakers."

Making Waves Award, presented to David Evans Shaw
award for exceptional leadership
in environmental stewardship and public engagement
2016 Blue Ocean Conservation Summit

***

Soon the original Sargasso Sea team regrouped to take our high seas stewardship initiative to global scope, leveraging lessons learned in the North Atlantic. Less than a year later, in the summer of 2017, Sylvia, Barbara, and I were sitting on the stage at the Aspen Ideas Festival in Aspen, Colorado, along with a young climate leader, Esau Sinnok, who belongs to a native tribe in Alaska. Enhanced by glorious blue skies and clear mountain air, the annual festival is a gathering of national and international A-listers, thinkers, and doers drawn from a vast array of fields that include economics, science, culture, the arts, philosophy, politics, and religion. We were invited to publicly unveil our imaginative and ambitious new High Seas project, unprecedented in its scale and scope.

One very important element of our plan was to persuade the United Nations to create a new leadership position for ocean stewardship: a special ambassador, or envoy, for oceans. In our planning sessions, we learned that since its founding in 1945, the UN had at various times created special envoys for urgent issues such as AIDS/HIV in Africa, global education, and negotiating the end of apartheid in South Africa. Given the vast importance of our work and the critical role that the UN could play, we resolved to make this a top priority of our work. The fact that UN Sustainable Development Goal #14 is about "Life below water" was consistent with our intentions. The official wording is to "Conserve and sustainably use the oceans, seas, and marine resources" for sustainable development.

Soon I was spending time at the United Nations to understand the process of creating the "special ambassador" position, and searching for great prospects to take on this responsibility. Our search quickly focused on Peter Thomson, the UN ambassador from Fiji, due to his reputation as a highly respected ambassador and powerful advocate for ocean health. A consummate diplomat, he helped organize the first UN Ocean Conference in June 2017 to support Sustainable

CHAPTER ELEVEN - BE BOLD

Development Goal 14. Fiji, which Peter represented at the UN, is a magnificent archipelago of more than 330 islands in the South Pacific that is particularly vulnerable to flooding because of rising sea levels, coastal erosion, and extreme weather including more frequent and more violent tropical cyclones—"big blows," as Peter calls them. When we approached Peter about this opportunity, he was positive and gracious, saying in his clipped accent, "No kidding! I'm game!" Peter's daily mantra is, "You cannot have a healthy planet without a healthy ocean. But ocean health is in decline." After the UN told me there was no money to fund a Special Envoy for the Ocean, I collaborated with Prince Albert II of Monaco, a noted environmentalist, to donate initial funds, and other sources eventually followed suit.

with Sylvia Earle and Peter Thomson, UN Special Envoy for Oceans

Another objective for us was to prod UN member countries to formalize an international treaty to enforce the protection and sustainable use of marine biodiversity in the High Seas. To reduce overfishing of high seas we joined other organizations to pressure the World Trade Organization to dramatically reduce counterproductive commercial fishing subsidies.

After our launch at the Aspen Ideas Festival, the enthusiasm for our High Seas initiative was palpable. Sylvia had announced on stage in Aspen that this could be the biggest idea of all time. Ocean stewardship was deservedly getting greater public attention and the connection between climate change challenges and human health was increasingly apparent. Now, we agreed, was the moment to galvanize the public globally to restore oceans to health in support of life on Earth. We expanded our capabilities in several ways including advisory relationships with former Secretary of State Madeleine Albright, and Paul Baribault, Vice President of Disneynature. After our initial collaboration with the Aspen Institute, we resumed more independent activities consistent with the entrepreneurial nature of our mission.

On a personal level, I continued to find collaborative opportunities, including expeditions, that encouraged ocean stewardship. I flew with The Nature Conservancy to Palmyra Atoll National Wildlife Refuge, situated halfway between Hawaii and American Samoa. Composed of approximately fifty islands roughly in the shape of a horseshoe, Palmyra's most beautiful feature is its thousands of acres of unspoiled coral reefs in waters that range from vivid turquoise to deepest blue. I thought Sylvia got it just right when she said, "You'd have to dive more than fifty years ago to see marine life like this."

The land, which sits mere feet above sea level, now hosts a rotating group of scientists and visitors like me who participate in research efforts. There are no permanent inhabitants. This is a dramatic change from the disruption it suffered during World War II, when the US military built an airstrip and installed as many as six thousand personnel. With their naval ships, came rats which ran wild, multiplying and eating bird eggs. To restore the avian populations, these invasive rodents had to be exterminated. Today, Palmyra is a thriving, pristine wildlife ecosystem—an inspiring model of sustainability and an exemplar of what great looks like for the rest

Chapter Eleven - Be Bold

of the world. It is a beacon of hope to illuminate what happens when a group of committed environmentalists strikes out boldly.

The film I made of our experience at Palmyra Atoll has been watched tens of thousands of times due to its compelling depiction of an inspirational stewardship success story.

Another source of inspiration at this time was leadership shown by my friend, and collaborator Tommy Remengesau Jr., former President of the Pacific island nation of Palau. I enjoyed our work together and, at his invitation, traveled to Palau to discuss new opportunities, and scuba dive in the pristine waters now protected via his leadership. It was an unforgettable experience to have this courageous and charismatic leader as a dive buddy, and I made a short film to commemorate our time together. Unexpectedly the president also organized a motorcycle ride with a group of his friends known as the Palau Thunder Chiefs, and I had the great honor of being inducted, as a foreigner, into this distinguished tribe of fellow motorcyclists!

As part of Palau's immigration process, visitors are asked to take the following "eco-pledge" which is stamped into all passports: "Children of Palau, I take this pledge as your guest; to preserve and protect your beautiful and unique island home. I vow to tread lightly, act kindly, and explore mindfully. I shall not take what is not given. I shall not harm what doesn't harm me. The only footprints I shall leave are those that will wash away."

I continued ocean stewardship adventures in Belize, Raja Ampat Indonesia, Australia's Great Barrier Reef, Hawaii, and other special places. In the winter of 2020, I visited Antarctica at the bicentennial of its discovery for a first-hand experience in a place that is extraordinary in many ways. This includes the vital role it plays in the planet's ecosystem including ocean currents. It is a place of awe-inspiring natural beauty including spectacular wildlife. Governed by 56 nations, it is the coldest, windiest, and driest continent on Earth. It has been the scene of extraordinary exploration and discovery including the famous Shackleton expedition. Today it is a place of terrifying change in a warming global climate. Temperatures on our arrival day were the warmest recorded in Antarctic history. Scientists traveling with us conducted studies on whale migrations, krill abundance, and other subjects, and I made a film to share impressions from our visit.

My advocacy for ocean health persisted in my roles as a Trustee of the US National Park Foundation, as Treasurer of the American Association for the Advancement of Science, and as a National Fellow of The Explorers Club. Additionally, I have served as a member of Ocean Elders, and a Patron of Nature at the International Union for Conservation of Nature. These organizations include other dedicated stewards of the natural world including Queen Noor of Jordan, Ted Turner, Richard Branson, Jane Goodall, Sylvia Earle, Prince Albert of Monaco, Greg Carr, Bertrand Piccard, Nainoa Thompson, Sven Lindblad, Bob Weir, Jackson Browne, Gerry Lopez, Jean-Michel Cousteau, Prince Carl Philip of Sweden, and others.

(Left to Right:)
with Queen Noor of Jordan and Palau President Tommy Remengesau
with Jane Goodall
with Prince Albert II of Monaco

Chapter Eleven - Be Bold

To expand the role of science in the stewardship of nature and the management of national parks, I launched the Second Century Stewardship program in collaboration with Acadia National Park, the Schoodic Institute, the Carnegie Institute, and the National Park Foundation. In working with such dedicated people, I sometimes recalled Lucille Clifford's remark that "nature is not asking us what we are doing ... nature is asking us who we are being." I had an opportunity to discuss the deep spiritual connection between humans and the rest of the natural world on stage with Deepak Chopra at the 2019 Sages and Scientists symposium. The meeting was hosted by our friend Alice Walton at her remarkable Crystal Bridges Museum in Bentonville, Arkansas.

In November, I traveled to Cape Breton, Nova Scotia's northernmost island, to participate in a project to place tracking tags on Atlantic bluefin tuna as the fish swim from Canada and Ireland to spawning grounds in the Gulf of Mexico and the Mediterranean. Since ancient times, human beings have been fascinated by these remarkable warm-blooded beings as they roamed global oceans with their incomparable strength, beauty, and speed, which can reach over forty miles per hour. Today, this species of tuna ranks as the most valuable fish in the world because it is so prized by sushi and sashimi chefs. A single bluefin in 2013 fetched more than $1.75 million. Because of its value, blue tuna has been dramatically overfished in the past but recent regulations and sustainable fishing practices have reversed the decline.

This trip was part of a program called Tag-A-Giant, developed by Barbara Block's lab at Stanford to research threatened fish populations. It was a blustery day, and we scanned the choppy slate-gray water for tuna, when suddenly I felt one grab the line and then pull hard as it tried to swim away. Ninety exhausting minutes later, I reeled in the bluefin that the team onboard estimated to be about twenty years old and to weigh close to eight hundred pounds. Throwing a wet cloth over its eyes to keep it calm, we quickly tagged this athletic creature with its glimmering iridescent skin and got it back in the water. I named the tuna "Blue Magoo" and was able to track its migration via our satellite and acoustic tags. The experience of being actively engaged in a hands-on, high-impact, technology-enabled conservation effort for these remarkable and threatened creatures provided a great sense of fulfillment. Throughout my career, it's been important for me to combine strategic and policy-level impact contributions with hands-on field experiences…. keeping it real.

I also felt elation and a sense of accomplishment in spring 2023 when I flew to Monaco for a lunch hosted by Prince Albert II at his magnificent palace, which the Grimaldi family has occupied for more than seven hundred years. We gathered as global leaders in the conservation of nature to celebrate the formal adoption of language for the UN Biodiversity of Areas Beyond National Jurisdiction treaty–known as the High Seas Treaty. This historic breakthrough to protect biological diversity in the High Seas occurred after all-night negotiations several months earlier at the United Nations headquarters in New York City. A milestone in itself, it is also a critical component in reaching the UN 30 x 30 pledge, which promises to protect one-third of the world's ocean and one-third of the world's land by the year 2030.

The sense of fulfillment of "doing well and doing good" is an important element of human nature. The world is full of inspirational stories of people who contribute to our common good. I feel very fortunate that my life has been enriched via the opportunity to contribute to global ocean stewardship, knowing that life on Earth depends on healthy oceans. We live in a time where amazing modern technology provides us with knowledge of the great challenges we face, and with the ability to meet those challenges. I hope that sharing my experiences in ocean stewardship and other endeavors provides a sense of hope and motivation for a life of impact just as others have been inspirational to me.

Chapter Eleven - Be Bold

Takeaway: Life is a great adventure, and I admire those who use their time to live to the fullest in the service of creating a better world whether in healthcare, living standards, public service, arts and literature, conservation, or otherwise. George Bernard Shaw famously had this to say about that:

"This is the true joy in life, the being used for a purpose recognized by yourself as a mighty one . . . being a force of nature instead of a feverish, selfish little clod of ailments and grievances, complaining that the world will not devote itself to making you happy. . . I am of the opinion that my life belongs to the whole community and as long as I live, it is my privilege to do for it what I can. I want to be thoroughly used up when I die, for the harder I work, the more I live. I rejoice in life for its own sake. Life is no brief candle to me. It is a sort of splendid torch which I have got hold of for the moment and I want to make it burn as brightly as possible before handing it on to future generations."
- Attributed to George Bernard Shaw

Chapter Twelve
Harness the Power of Partnerships

"Sticks in a bundle are unbreakable."
– Kenyan Proverb

"The strength of the team is each individual member.
The strength of each member is the team."
– Attributed to Phil Jackson

    In the predawn dark on June 18, 2021, I walked across a dew-dampened meadow to join a group of public officials and scientists gathered in Maine's Acadia National Park. A magnificent forest of soaring evergreen trees surrounded the grassy field where chairs were set up, waiting to be filled. Secretary of the Interior Deb Haaland, a member of the Pueblo of Laguna and the first Native American to serve as a US cabinet secretary, was making her inaugural visit to a national park since her appointment by the Biden Administration.

*with Interior Secretary Haaland
and SCS science fellows*

Wave Making : Inspired By Impact

I was seated with Secretary Haaland, Maine Governor Janet Mills, and the state's congressional delegation when we heard the distant sound of percussion music. Soon, members of the Wabanaki Confederacy, the area's first inhabitants, emerged from the woods where their ancestors had lived and gathered sweetgrass for centuries. Dressed in brightly colored ceremonial garb and accompanied by wooden flutes and leather drums, these "people of the Dawnland" singers performed a traditional chanting ceremony to welcome the rising sun, their resonant voices ringing out in the cool morning air just days before the summer solstice.

Suddenly, a different and more familiar sound reached us. World-famous classical cellist Yo-Yo Ma joined the Wabanaki musicians, his bow gliding swiftly across the strings. A rich duet rippled across the meadow-turned-concert-hall, as the sun, now fully up, warmed our group.

The unique melody they produced represented the extraordinary melding of two distinct traditions playing together. The artistic collaboration produced an unforgettable melody, and there was a multiplier effect from the partnership compared to a solo venture. Ma was there as part of a project he conceived and created called Our Common Nature, a collaboration with Indigenous and other musicians from Maine to Hawaii. The goal of this creative project is to pay homage to distinctive voices and cultures, and to honor the central role of nature in human life.

I was attending this daybreak ceremony as founder of the Second Century Stewardship (SCS) initiative , launched in 2016 to mark the centennial of both the US National Park Service and the establishment of Acadia Park. A cherished part of our country's shared fabric, the National Park System is made up of more than 400 parks, monuments, and historic sites–safeguarded areas of special significance in every state and as well as in four US territories. These parks receive more than three hundred million separate visits each year, a higher

Chapter Twelve - Harness the Power of Partnerships

level of visitorship than all US major league sports combined. Teddy Roosevelt is known as "The Conservation President" for his outsized impact on protecting some of America's most treasured natural monuments and federal properties. Yet he wasn't the first president to delineate land for a national park. That honor goes to Ulysses S. Grant who signed the Yellowstone National Park Protection Act into law on March 1, 1872. – Roosevelt established approximately 230 million acres of public lands between 1901 and 1909. These included five national parks, eighteen national monuments, 150 national forests, and 55 federal bird reservation and game preserves. He once said of our national parks: "We have fallen heirs to the most glorious heritage a people ever received." Roosevelt recognized how fortunate and unique it was to have land designated as belonging to all the nation's citizenry instead of being solely reserved for the pleasure of royalty, nobility, and the wealthy. Pulitzer-Prize-winning novelist Wallace Stegner echoed this sentiment decades later in a speech when he described our national park system as "the best idea we ever had. Absolutely American, absolutely democratic, they reflect us at our best rather than our worst."

As mentioned earlier, President Bush had appointed me to the board of trustees of the National Park Foundation for a six-year term that culminated with the 2016 National Park Centennial. I was already a lifelong devotee of national parks in America and around the world. One of many memorable park experiences was a whitewater trip I took with my son, Ben, on the Colorado River through the Grand Canyon. In California, I bicycled hundreds of miles across Death Valley and hiked in Joshua Tree, Redwood, and Yosemite parks. Other US national park experiences include Everglades in Florida, Haleakal in Hawaii, Katmai in Alaska, Yellowstone and Glacier in Idaho, Wyoming, and Montana, Rocky Mountain and Black Canyon in Colorado, Acadia in Maine, Great Smokey Mountains in North Carolina and Tennessee, Big Bend and Guadalupe Mountains in Texas, Zion and Arches in Utah, Mountain Rainier and Olympic in Washington State, Grand Teton in Wyoming, and many others.

Internationally I have been inspired by my visits to marine and terrestrial parks across Asia, Europe, South America, Australia, and Africa. These include special places like Mt Kilimanjaro in Tanzania, Machu Picchu in Peru, Torres del Paine park in Patagonia, the Haute Route from Chamonix to Zermatt, Australia's Great Barrier Reef, and parks in Bhutan, Tibet, Morocco, Scotland, France, Italy, Egypt, Gabon, South Africa, Canada, Greenland, Iceland, Panama, Costa Rica, Mexico, India, China and other countries. One memorable visit to Cairngorms National Park in the highlands of Scotland included a pilgrimage to castle ruins on an island in Loch an Eilein, Rothiemurchus. The ruins are said to be the ancestral home of Shaw family forebears who immigrated to America in the 1630s.

In creating the Second Century Stewardship initiative, I wanted to honor the rich legacy of America's national parks and improve future prospects for protecting these special places by using the lens of science to create a deeper and different relationship between people and parks. I intended to help build a bridge from a traditional emphasis on magnificent landscapes and special places of geography or culture, to an expanded emphasis on the most important and transformative force of our times: science.

I envisioned an opportunity for US parks to expand their role as classrooms and laboratories.... places for visitors of all ages to learn more about our natural world through the lens of science. We were enthusiastic about creating opportunities to experience the beneficial emotion of awe, and for park staff to add an additional layer of science to their research, storytelling, and policymaking. With their vast visitorship and high accessibility, national parks are an ideal venue for enhancing public appreciation of science. The scenic beauty of parks is well known and beneficial to visitors, but we envisioned the opportunity to enhance visits by using the lens of science to better understand that beauty and look beyond pretty scenery to unleash curiosity about the natural world. Zion, for example, was shaped by an arc of erupting volcanoes and the thrusting of geological uplift over

Chapter Twelve - Harness the Power of Partnerships

millions of years.

In my announcement of the Second Century Stewardship initiative, I emphasized the important role of science: "Modern science provides us with unprecedented ability to be wise stewards of these special places and cultural treasures, for the benefit of future generations." We live in an era with notable anti-science attitudes and beliefs that deny climate change, dismiss the importance of vaccines, or otherwise create the risk of undermining the evidence-based foundation of science. There are far-reaching implications for society when discourse and actions are based on personal beliefs versus the benefit of evidence-based critical thinking, peer review, and other foundations of science. After a lifetime of business entrepreneurship, and conservation advocacy interwoven with science, I have witnessed benefits to society from the disciplined, evidence-based, rational approach of scientific inquiry —the step-by-step process by which scientists observe, evaluate, disprove, and improve. Science has been responsible for so many previously unimaginable advances in human civilization and has yielded enormous prosperity and well-being. We live longer, healthier lives thanks to medical breakthroughs like antibiotics and vaccines. We are able to fly around the world, experiencing extraordinary places, thanks to engineering. We hold smartphones that put more information in our hands than is contained in the world's greatest libraries, and we are able to talk, email, text, and video chat with people across the globe as easily as though they were next door, thanks to technology. Embedded in every aspect of our lives, science has transformed our world for the better.

These are great accomplishments of our times, in contrast to perhaps our generation's biggest failure: the devastation of our natural world. Of course, the impact of humans on the natural world extends tens of thousands of years. In the current geological period where humans have had a dominant influence on Earth, known as the Anthropocene, our impact on the planet's ecosystems has been profound.

Effective impact activism for parks or other matters benefits immensely from powerful storytelling to educate and influence audiences. For this reason, an essential element of impact campaigns like Second Century Stewardship is communications training. For my own advocacy work, I continue to support the development of powerful impact communication skills and media knowledge as a member of advisory councils at the National Geographic Society, Waterbear, the MIT Media Lab, the Synergos Global Philanthropists Circle, Sustainable Harvest International, and other organizations.

To fulfill its important mission, and support the scale of the opportunity, Second Century Stewardship (SCS) was conceived and launched as a partnership between several organizations with complementary capabilities. Practices and learnings from SCS now inform local programs in numerous parks.

As a Fellow and Treasurer emeritus of the American Association for the Advancement of Science (AAAS), the world's largest general science society, I felt strongly that AAAS would be a great partner for Second Century. With more than 120,000 members around the globe, AAAS would give us rigor, scale, and instant credibility. AAAS in turn would benefit from the collaboration with us because we would provide new forms of engagement at a time when the organization was searching for fresh ways to involve younger scientists. The National Park Foundation partnered with us, contributing funds and its unsurpassed, in-depth knowledge of the parks. Research Learning Centers in eighteen parks across the country provided another partnership opportunity. The largest of these, Schoodic Institute, is based in Acadia National Park and was able to share its science education and outreach capabilities. Other collaborators included the Alan Alda Center for Communicating Science. Founded by the acclaimed actor most famous for his role in the long-running TV series M*A*S*H, the organization reflects Alda's lifelong passion for science and his deep desire to help scientists share their unique insights with the public. I had the honor of introducing

Chapter Twelve - Harness the Power of Partnerships

Alan as a keynote speaker at our AAAS annual meeting in 2014. His group helped us design workshops for SCS scientists and park staff to learn how to tell their park's science story to visitors in novel and creative ways, including public communications. We also partnered with the Carnegie Institution for Science. With a gift of ten million dollars in 1902, industrialist Andrew Carnegie set up an organization that has been at the forefront of research ever since with a special focus on providing scientists the freedom and resources to pursue their individual interests.

Second Century Stewardship started with one park–Acadia, known for the towering beauty of its rocky headlands, which rise above the Atlantic coast. Just a three-hour drive from my home near Portland, Acadia, midway up the Maine coast–an area known as "Down East"–covers roughly half of Mount Desert Island as well as other nearby scenic points and islands. Acadia gets its name from the area including Nova Scotia, Prince Edward Island, and New Brunswick where approximately ten thousand French Canadians, Acadians, settled and whom the British expelled in the 1750s during what Canadians called "The Great Upheaval." Some resettled in what later became Maine, and others traveled further south to Louisiana and became known as "Cajuns."

Our plan was to set up a pilot project to demonstrate what great looks like before scaling the program nationally either under the Second Century brand or via similar local programs. Observing how our pilot project was thriving was one of the reasons Secretary Haaland and the other dignitaries came to visit.

***

Partnerships have played an important role in my career. As IDEXX grew, I sought out partners to provide strategic capabilities needed to support our success.

Here is an example: I was having difficulty breaking into the Japanese animal health market because of regulatory hurdles. So, we entered into an agreement deal with one of the biggest Japanese animal health companies for them to distribute IDEXX products in their country. An important provision of the agreement was that it granted exclusive rights to our partner *except* that IDEXX could sell its *own* Japanese products in Japan. In other words, the Japanese company was our distributor unless we distributed the products ourselves. Like many small companies, we had been thrilled to sign with a pharmaceutical giant in a foreign country, but this enthusiasm can be short-lived when a small entrepreneurial company finds that its products don't get the attention hoped for by the larger partner. Of course, we worked hard to improve our partner's performance through sales training and other strategies. Yet results remained disappointing.

At a trade show in Tokyo, I briefly encountered a Japanese woman executive named Eiko Ohnishi, who operated a twenty-person clinical laboratory for veterinary medicine in Tokyo. Although we merely bowed and exchanged business cards, I immediately knew that here was an entirely different kind of partner. I was impressed that Ohnishi was succeeding as a woman entrepreneur and CEO in a male-dominated economy like Japan's. Back in Portland, I decided to call Ohnishi to discuss a "partnership", with the hope that this might eventually take the form of an acquisition. With the assistance of a Japanese translator, we reached Ohnishi in Tokyo. I had explained to my translator that I would speak in direct American style with the expectation that my message would be translated in keeping with the Japanese culture, including an emphasis on courtesy, knowing that a get-to-the-point style might be considered rude and inappropriate.

"Hello Eiko, it's David Shaw, I hope that you remember me," I began. The translation of this took considerable time as the translator added cultural niceties. Eiko then made a long response that translated "in American" to "hello David, nice to hear from you."

Chapter Twelve - Harness the Power of Partnerships

Next, I said to the translator, "I wonder if we could talk about the possibility of collaborating." It took a couple of minutes to translate this. The translator was asking questions—or so I assumed—and Eiko was replying in Japanese. Because I thought she couldn't understand English, I verbalized my concerns and intentions to the translator. "Now we're going to talk about getting her to host me for a visit. So please say to Ohnishi-San, 'I wonder if you'd be willing to meet with David in Japan sometime soon? It could be in the next couple of weeks.' This resulted in a long response. Our conversation continued in this way until, in the midst of a long translation, Eiko said in clear English: "David, I can understand everything you're saying."

"What?" I replied in astonishment.

"I want you to know that I'm not speaking English because I'm feeling very rusty."

We both laughed as her pronunciation of "R" in "rusty" sounded like "L".

"I'm going to fly to Tokyo for a visit in a few days," I told her.

"Yes please," she said. "I look forward to seeing you."

This was the beginning of a beautiful partnership. I admired what she had achieved, and I loved her sense of humor. I flew to Japan, and with the help of an extraordinary executive assistant named Shizue Baba, I negotiated to buy her company, called AMIS, and put Eiko in charge. Baba-san and I then visited our distributor in Osaka and informed them that IDEXX was launching its own Japanese product line via our wholly-owned subsidiary, AMIS. Sales immediately began to grow rapidly with this small but great, and mostly female, team in Tokyo. Eiko and her dynamic colleagues were happy to be unleashed by new American colleagues who admired what they did. The success of our product launch was critical to the success of the combined company. She and I went out on calls together as partners, and we closed every customer we visited, partly because it was easy for customers to see our deep conviction that they would benefit immediately from having the capability to perform diagnostic tests in their clinic. It was a happy and successful experience and a great example of the power of a partnership.

IDEXX had previously created a partnership in Japan to commercialize our avian diagnostic products, and we continued that relationship with Gensuke Tokoro, based in the small town of Gifu. In Europe IDEXX originally contracted with large well-established animal health companies for distribution but, as in Japan, we found that replacing those partnerships with our own staff dramatically improved sales and customer relationships. These experiences made me wary of setting high expectations of partners based primarily on their size and market power. Instead, we find that a crucial predictor of performance is the relative importance of our relationship with a partner.

These examples of building in-house sales and marketing capabilities highlight an important strategic issue for me. I've witnessed three major business models for analyzing business expansion opportunities: leveraging R&D/technical capabilities, leveraging customer insights and distribution capabilities, and leveraging management systems. In my businesses, I regularly seek to find attractive growth prospects that especially focus on the first two models: selling more to the same customers and finding new customers and markets that leverage product and technology strengths. The expansion of IDEXX in Japan was initially driven by the power of our technology and products. As that power drove success, we built distribution strength and deep customer knowledge. This market power then provided the opportunity to add new products and technologies for the same customer base and distribution channel. Becoming masters of these two business models can be a source of exceptional success and most companies I admire adhere to these

Chapter Twelve - Harness the Power of Partnerships

strategies. 3M is an example of a company that leverages coatings technology capabilities in multiple markets. Johnson and Johnson is an example of a company that leverages customer and distribution strengths to sell a wide range of products.

***

Whether it is a not-for-profit organization like Second Century Stewardship or for businesses including the many I have founded or advised, a common strategic choice is whether to make or buy the capabilities needed for success.

A good example of this was a series of decisions that famed investor Warren Buffett made in the early 2000s. Following in the footsteps of Microsoft co-founder Bill Gates and his then-wife Melinda, Warren Buffett pledged to give away more than 99 percent of his wealth during his lifetime or at his death. Because of his vast wealth, this was headline news in itself. But to me, what made Warren's decision especially unusual was his announcement that instead of starting his own charitable foundation and taking on the responsibilities of distributing and administering his fortune to philanthropic causes, he would donate tens of billions of dollars in Berkshire Hathaway stock to existing philanthropic organizations such as the Bill & Melinda Gates Foundation. A longtime friend of Bill Gates, Buffett said, in effect, that he supported the Gates Foundation's mission of combating global disease, inequity, and poverty and saw no benefit in duplicating their efforts himself. Years later I had an opportunity to talk with Warren about this and to get the perspective of our mutual friend Carol Loomis at *Fortune Magazine*. He reiterated his belief that this partnership was the right "make or buy" decision. When Buffett resigned as a Gates Foundation trustee at the age of ninety, he again confirmed this stance, telling reporters that his goals were "100 percent in sync" with the Gates Foundation's CEO. Whatever his metrics were for success, he had clearly found a partner that aligned with them.

Like Buffett, I look for attractive collaborative outsourcing opportunities, and resist unnecessary duplication of effort. Rarely do entrepreneurs have all the capabilities they need in-house to be successful, so it is wise to broadly explore meeting needs via partnerships. We did this at Ironwood Pharmaceuticals in Cambridge, Massachusetts when we partnered with Forest Laboratories to access their extensive sales and marketing capabilities for our pioneering drug Linzess, for gastrointestinal applications.

At Waterbear, we are harnessing the power of impact media to create a global community of activists in support of the United Nations' sustainable development goals. This includes partnerships with leading brands and more than 100 NGOs worldwide to expand our impact storytelling reach. A recent partnership with the Ellen MacArthur Foundation is aimed at accelerating a global transition to a circular economy. Our film, Going Circular, documents the vital importance of a circular economy to support life on Earth. Consistent with our mission, Waterbear is a Certified B Corporation that adheres to high standards of social and environmental performance, public transparency, and legal accountability to balance profit with purpose. We created the Resilient Foundation as a non-profit film studio to partner with Waterbear and our ecosystem of partner organizations to produce impact films intended to inspire and support activism for a better world as envisioned by the United Nations Sustainable Development Goals.

At Ovation, a genomics company, we partner with clinical laboratories and biobanks to advance human health in support of the emerging historic opportunity for life-changing individualized, or "precision", medicine. Using our distinctive human genomic data linked to rich, longitudinal phenotypic data at scale, life science companies are uncovering insights that accelerate drug discovery and development. Just as the causes of human happiness are more personalized than standardized, modern science helps us understand and create healthcare practices, including drugs, that benefit from

Chapter Twelve - Harness the Power of Partnerships

personalization to individual circumstances.

At Itaconix we have partnered with the University of New Hampshire to create a new generation of high-performance, safe, and sustainable biobased polymers for applications ranging from personal care and home care to industrial uses. Our expansion has been an example of leveraging core technical strengths with itaconic acid to produce products for diverse market segments. We are proud of our role in the important global movement to decarbonize everyday products.

Another case in point is Modern Meadow, a biotech company where I am a founding investor, director, and advisor. In 2011, the co-founder, Andras Forgacs, launched the company with the idea of creating a laboratory-grown sustainable material that looks, feels, and in some cases even smells like leather. After a number of years of innovative research by a remarkable team, the moment eventually came when the company crossed the threshold from vision to reality, from research to development. We had created a platform of sustainable "biofabricated" materials and now needed to make products to put into the hands of consumers —as well as in their pockets, on their wrists and feet, and over their shoulders, in the form of wallets, watchbands, shoes, handbags and more. For Modern Meadow, as in many start-up enterprises, this next leg of the journey– often known as the last mile– would be a critical stage for reaching success.

The quandary facing us: should the company build its own factory and hire the designers and technicians to take the products to market? Or should it instead find a partner to play a lead role in productizing our innovative materials —a company with proven expertise to turn our raw materials into finished luxury goods? Should we make or buy this capability in the context of all of our other priorities? At Modern Meadow, we went about answering this question in much the same way that I have found partners in other businesses such as IDEXX—we consulted people with lifetimes of experience in the fashion industry. We sought to determine who has the greatest expertise. Who are the most respected vendors and why? Who might be interested in the concept of sustainability and willing to take on the challenge of an unconventional product? Who is an innovator, not just doing what is asked of them but suggesting ways in which something might be done even better?

Armed with Excel spreadsheets full of partnership prospects and selection criteria we conducted this critically important decision process knowing that great partnerships can be elusive for many reasons including human chemistry. For us, the holy grail was a relationship with a productizer that also fit well with design and marketing partners.

I still remember the day Modern Meadow found our perfect match: a generations-old, family-owned company named Limonta. Located outside Milan, in northern Italy, they were highly skilled at turning animal hides into beautifully crafted consumer goods and had an unparalleled reputation in the marketplace among luxury goods companies. Importantly: they were as excited about working with us as we were with them.

The famous blues musician and singer Robert Johnson supposedly said, "All business is personal. Make your friends before you need them." We took that approach with Limonta, signaling to them that we were looking for a relationship that was professional, but we also wanted one that included the added benefits of social and personal dimensions.

Our partnership with Limonta led us to another rewarding alliance—this one with Tory Burch, the luxury lifestyle brand that draws from Burch's own rich sense of color coupled with design elements from her wide-ranging travels and her remarkable eye. The fashion company has begun offering several of its bags, including one

Chapter Twelve - Harness the Power of Partnerships

of the company's most popular totes, made from Modern Meadow's sustainable material, the plant-based, leather-alternative Bio-Alloy™.

I am pleased to say that our collaboration worked out smoothly, with the result that Modern Meadow and Limonta created a profit-sharing partnership named BioFabrica. Modern Meadow creates the formula, while Limonta produces the bolts of material and then cuts the sustainable "leather" to Tory Burch's specifications, including the colors and textures. I have great admiration for the Modern Meadow team that created this partnership with two top-of-the-line partners–Limonta and Tory Burch–each with their own superlative skills that complemented ours.

Recently, I had to smile when I took my daughter Eliza and her family out for dinner and she showed up proudly wearing the Tory Burch crossbody handbag I gifted her, crafted from Modern Meadow's plant-based substitute for leather. She and the bag both looked beautiful.

Modern Meadow is an example of a company that has leveraged strong technical expertise to address opportunities in several markets including sustainable fashion and healthcare.

***

Forming a partnership is of course just the first step in long-term success. Partnerships can be hard work and there are best practices for sustaining and improving partnerships. At Acadia National Park, for example, not every original Second Century Stewardship partner went the distance. Yet the initiative yielded outstanding results.

Clear roles and responsibilities are critical along with outstanding communications including conflict resolution processes. Anticipating partnership challenges is the reason why, at various companies and organizations I've been part of, we seek to turn partnership management into a science informed by best practices.

We establish management frameworks and teach people the necessary skills. A partnership team leader receives training about what great looks like in this realm and is assigned responsibility for achieving partnership goals.

Supported by the Second Century partnership, there have been 5 years of expanded scientific ventures in the park. There might be a fourth-grade class collecting dragonfly nymphs, part of a nationwide project to track airborne mercury pollution which is primarily generated by burning coal and mercury-contaminated waste as well as by manufacturing chlorine. The toxin ends up in the freshwater habitats where dragonflies lay their eggs—our streams, lakes, and rivers—and the contaminated water can eventually flow into the oceans, spreading the toxin further. This program grew to involve a hundred national parks. Another effort taking place might be citizen scientists from a local community college measuring the height of an ancient midden formed from clam, oyster, and mussel shells—a prehistoric version of a garbage dump—to track erosion of the shoreline. Scientists have also studied how the growing number of tourists and hikers is affecting the topography of Cadillac Mountain, which at just over 1,500 feet, is the tallest peak on the United States' Atlantic seaboard. During the winter months, it is also the first place in the country to observe sunrise.

Second Century Stewardship fellows, selected annually, have studied tick-borne diseases, as well as the connection between park visitation rates and fall foliage patterns, which are changing because of the climate crisis, among other scientific and social science questions. One Second Century fellow, Bonnie Newsom, an Indigenous archaeologist on the faculty of the University of Maine and a member of the Penobscot Nation, used her grant to discover how the original inhabitants engaged with the land that now forms Acadia National Park prior to European contact by studying the park's archeological sites, an increasing number of which are underwater due to rising sea levels.

CHAPTER TWELVE - HARNESS THE POWER OF PARTNERSHIPS

Since its launch, our fellows have been trained to convey their knowledge to visitors in person and to extend their reach by using traditional media—writing, giving print and TV interviews, and engaging with ever-changing and growing social media platforms. The result has been many deeply gratifying and inspirational stories, shared with more than a million people. With tears in their eyes, park rangers and volunteers have told me about middle and high school students from Maine's impoverished interior who, despite growing up in VACATIONLAND, have never set eyes on the Atlantic Ocean or breathed in salt air. The students' excitement is palpable, the rangers tell me, as these teenagers glimpse for the very first time a teeming tidal pool or spot a spouting whale. "It can be life-changing," an older woman volunteer told me, "when they suddenly realize that there is a big world beyond the confines of their small hometowns."

Second Century Stewardship has expanded beyond Acadia National Park, operating in more than sixty parks, and in many cases morphing into analogous local programs including the Shaw Fellows program at the College of the Atlantic in Maine. Of particular note, the program has supported researchers conducting work on public lands. Most importantly, this partnership has helped to develop creative and original guidelines for communicating with the public about science, and engaging visitors in ways that stimulate their interest in the natural world in parks across the country. It is my own hope that this initiative will encourage young people to grasp how incredibly interesting and dynamic science is. Perhaps the Second Century Stewardship or similar initiatives will inspire some of them to consider careers in STEM—science, technology, engineering, and mathematics. For our nation's future health and prosperity, we must have more students engaged in these critically vital fields.

The impact of Second Century Stewardship was summed up well by professor John Anderson at the nearby College of the Atlantic. He uses Acadia National Park to train his students to monitor a species of petrels —seabirds—that make their nesting site there. "It's so, so important both in terms of education and also just a general understanding of nature to actually get out and experience it firsthand, and so this is what Acadia gives us, this wonderful gift of being able to do," he said. "We're in a living laboratory where everything's happening. It's not in textbooks; it's not in video. When they ask me, 'what are we going to see today?' I can honestly say, 'I don't know.' And that's why it's science."

Acadia Superintendent Kevin Schneider and Schoodic Institute director Nicholas Fisichelli added this important perspective in a recent meeting: "there is no better place than parks to advance science for nature and public engagement."

Takeaway: Mastering the skills of partnering is a critical success factor for tackling great challenges and opportunities. I've heard it said that individually we are drops of water, but together we can be an ocean. All great achievement is the result of collaborations and partnerships. That concept is captured in this well-known African proverb: "If you want to go fast, go alone. If you want to go far, go together." The keys to an effective partnership often start with answering the question: make or buy? If a partnership will give you a multiplier effect you cannot achieve on your own, the road to creating a successful relationship includes having a shared vision for success, determining complementary capabilities, building mutual respect and empathy, clearly defining roles and responsibilities, establishing effective practices for transparent communication and conflict resolution, and avoiding asymmetrical commitment. Here's an old joke about asymmetrical commitment : in a ham and egg omelette, the chicken is involved and the pig is committed.

Chapter Thirteen
Seize and Savor Serendipity

*"... in the shaping of a life,
chance and the ability to respond to chance are everything."*
– Attributed to Eric Hoffer

In a lifetime of sailing, kiteboarding, swimming, and scuba diving all over the world, one of the most magical moments I have ever experienced occurred right in front of my house in Prouts Neck. It was on a cool, clear day in May as I stood gazing out at the blue-gray waves of the Atlantic Ocean.

Amid the squawking seagulls and pungent salt air, something startled me—a hissing hydraulic sound. I wondered if there was a truck with brake problems going down the hill when I suddenly realized the noise was coming from the water. Running out on our dock I saw what appeared to be a small white submarine glide by. And then it circled as though, somehow, it sensed I was there. "Don't go away!" I called as I ran to my house across the street to get my mask, snorkel, and wetsuit.

Returning a few minutes later, several neighbors had gathered with the dock attendant

"we think it's a beluga whale" I shouted, "Does anyone have a camera? I'm going in!"

"Be careful out there," someone warned. "It might be a great white shark."

Now in the warmth of my neoprene wetsuit, I jumped in. The whale started interacting with me including swimming side-by-side and a memorable face-to-face encounter captured on camera. Known as the "canary of the sea" because of its ability to vocalize, this chirping beluga whale snuck up behind me and gently nudged me along the surface. Then it flipped upside down and swam under me. This serendipitous interlude lasted for about half an hour before the whale swam off, leaving me in a state of wonder.

with beluga whale at Prouts Neck

I had unexpectedly experienced a magical moment between myself and a sea creature whose life is usually spent far north in the Arctic Ocean. When I told the story to Sylvia Earle, she explained that belugas are known to be social with humans. "It's very special that a whale chose to call to you from the water!" Years later I took family members to remote Somerset Island in the Canadian high Arctic to witness a gathering of an estimated 1000 belugas along the Northwest Passage.

Celebrating and appreciating life's fleeting beauty is part of my personal philosophy, which emphasizes the importance of being in the moment at all times. While a resolute spirit and striving with great intention are very important in achieving life goals, I have also

Chapter Thirteen - Seize and Savor Serendipity

witnessed firsthand how important it is to be open to serendipity. I love the idea that you can be going through your routine day and activities and then, in an instant, something unexpected happens that creates new opportunity. Serendipity benefits from a purposeful mental matrix of alertness, curiosity, keen observation, and openness. A windfall can only come about if the person recognizes the opportunities contained within the situation. The following story is an example of this.

I had been elected a Trustee of The Jackson Laboratory (JAX) for several years when, in 1989, I was selected to become chairman and we started conducting a search for a new lab director. JAX is a world-renowned independent, nonprofit biomedical research organization that harnesses the transformational power of modern genetic science for the mission of improving human health. The laboratory was founded in Bar Harbor, Maine, in 1929, with a gift of fifty thousand dollars raised from benefactors including Detroit businessmen who vacationed there. These wealthy men wanted to support the pioneering work of scientist Clarence Cook Little who was researching genetics and its connection to cancer and had established a summer lab in Bar Harbor. The group included automakers Edsel Ford, who took over the Ford Motor Company from his father Henry, and Roscoe B. Jackson of the Hudson Motor Car Company. The institution was named for Jackson, who died suddenly in 1929.

Today JAX researches the genetic causes of various human diseases, including cancer, heart disease, Alzheimer's, and diabetes. Beyond its in-house research, JAX provides more than thirteen thousand strains of genetically specialized mice, which are used in research at over 2,400 institutions in sixty-eight countries. Because mice share 90 percent of the same genes associated with disease as humans, and their life cycles are measured in months rather than decades mice have long served as a leading model for studying human genetics.

In the spring of 1989, a star candidate for the lab's directorship,

Professor Kenneth Paigen, flew to Bar Harbor from the University of California, Berkeley, where he chaired the genetics department, for an interview and a tour of the facilities. Knowing that he and his wife were passionate sailors, we happily pointed out the tempting waters of Frenchman Bay that surround Mount Desert Island where the lab is located. The visit went exceptionally well. We were impressed with Ken's relevant domain knowledge, his communication skills, his leadership capabilities, and other qualifications for the exciting future ahead. So, we told Ken we would be in touch soon with an offer to lead JAX. We just didn't know how quickly "soon" would be.

Several hours after Ken's departure, as he arrived at Bangor Airport for his return flight to the West Coast, we received urgent news that a fire was suddenly engulfing a building at JAX, and emergency responses were underway. I quickly learned that, while the fire threatened important research assets, people had been rapidly moved to safety, and injuries to JAX team members and construction workers were very minor.

As the JAX leadership team continued in crisis management mode, we quickly came to agreement that Ken Paigen should be paged at the Bangor airport to be apprised of this unexpected crisis. It's a testimony to Ken's great character that he returned hours later to JAX to support us in this time of need. Soon after he joined JAX as our new CEO.

Those of us who have some experience with crisis management realized that while we faced the challenge of a significant crisis, it could also be a moment of opportunity. This perspective was well expressed by Albert Einstein when he supposedly observed, "In the midst of every crisis lies great opportunity," Ken Paigen took over within days as director of the Jackson Lab, a post he went on to hold with extraordinary success for thirteen years, until his retirement in 2003.

Chapter Thirteen - Seize and Savor Serendipity

my tribute to Ken Paigen

This was a moment of serendipity for The Jackson Laboratory, which could now reinvent itself in the midst of one the greatest scientific revolutions of all time. The historic first sequencing of the human genome was just years away and this would usher in an unprecedented era of individualized "precision" medicine. I was fortunate to play a leadership position on the board, with Ken Paigen as our new CEO. Turning the crisis into an opportunity, the board, the staff, public figures, and friends of JAX across the world scientific community collaborated to build new facilities, expand research programs, and rise to the challenge of great opportunities ahead. To fund this rebuilding and expansion, I joined with Maine's US Senator George Mitchell—then US Senate Majority Leader—and other benefactors to raise about seventy million dollars including insurance proceeds. JAX's revenues jumped exponentially from fifteen million dollars then on to more than five hundred million dollars today. I'm grateful for the unexpected circumstances that resulted in my leadership role in this amazing institution, starting with the introduction by my friend Bob Kinney. I never would have imagined during my work at General Mills that its CEO was born in Bar Harbor, Maine, and was a close friend of JAX founder Clarence Little.

Throughout my life, moments of serendipity have led to positive outcomes, whether in the water with a beluga whale or rebuilding a world-class research institution in Maine. Like the double strands of DNA, serendipity and science have been intertwined for centuries, sometimes also benefitting from synchronicity. A famous example of this occurred in early September 1928, when a moment of serendipity transformed modern medicine and launched a lifesaving revolution.

Alexander Fleming was a Scottish bacteriologist who lived from 1881 to 1955. On September 3, 1928, he returned from a family holiday to his lab at St. Mary's Hospital in London where he found that a Petri dish of the bacteria *Staphylococci*, he had left unattended in a corner was now contaminated by a blue-green fungus. This mold, which a less attentive scientist might simply have tossed out, had stopped the bacteria's growth. After musing, "That's funny," the scientist set to work to discover why. The mold produced a substance that turned out to be an antibiotic, which he eventually named penicillin. Later Fleming wrote, " ...I certainly didn't plan to revolutionize all medicine by discovering the world's first antibiotic, or bacteria killer. But I suppose that was exactly what I did."

Used to treat formerly incurable infections such as septicemia, gonorrhea, meningitis, pneumonia, rheumatic fever, and a host of other diseases, it is estimated that penicillin has saved the lives of more than two hundred million people. It is the single most important medical discovery of the twentieth century, and it all happened because someone was able to take their eyes off their own agenda and pay attention to what was going on around them. Mark Twain once observed: "the greatest of all inventors is accident."

Two other scientists played vital roles in taking penicillin from the lab into the hospital wards by 1943, where it was critical in treating wounded Allied soldiers: Australian pathologist Howard Florey and German-born British biochemist Ernst Boris Chain, who isolated

Chapter Thirteen - Seize and Savor Serendipity

and purified the antibiotic. Fleming, Florey, and Chain shared the Nobel Prize for Physiology or Medicine in 1945. In his Nobel Lecture, Fleming noted, "...penicillin started as a chance observation. My only merit is that I did not neglect the observation and that I pursued the subject as a Bacteriologist."

The seventh of eight children born to hill farmers in Scotland, Fleming's powers of observation were honed during his childhood. An *Encyclopedia Britannica* entry about him reads, "His country upbringing in southwestern Scotland sharpened his capacities for observation and appreciation of the natural world at an early age."

The lesson here is clear: serendipity can only make a difference if you are open to it. Had Fleming, upon returning from vacation simply thought, *Dammit! They wrecked my experiment. I'll never leave Petri dishes out unattended again when I go on holiday*, we may have had to wait decades for antibiotics to be discovered. Instead, Fleming pauses, thinks, ascertains, and is credited as one of the greatest scientists—and Scotsmen—in world history.

It's so easy to miss things, especially if you are busy juggling jobs or projects, rushing to make dinner for your family, or feeding your pets. I am a habitual noticer of sunsets, taking great joy in the oranges and pinks that streak across the sky over the water in front of my house. But as with anything, if you're not paying attention, it passes you by. Every once in a while, you have to stop and say, "Wait a second. Maybe I should double down."

You can only open the door and invite serendipity into your life; you cannot force it to enter. John Lennon offered a perspective on serendipity when he said: "Life is what happens to you while you're making other plans." And many people have remarked on the phenomenon of "luck" with comments along these lines of this quote often attributed to golf champion Gary Player: "the harder you practice, the luckier you get."

Takeaway: Hard work, intention, persistence, and planning are important drivers for success. But always be vigilant for serendipity: surprising moments of magic and wonder where chance and readiness intersect in unexpected ways. My experience is that a mindset of exploration and discovery improves prospects for serendipity, and the accompanying rewards. Why leave serendipity to chance?

Chapter Fourteen
Be a Purpose-Driven Force for Good

"What counts in life is not the mere fact that we have lived. It is the difference we have made to the lives of others that will determine the significance of the life we lead."

– Nelson Mandela

"Pencils down, everyone," I said. "We have some important visitors here today." I was addressing the staff of New Jersey-based INO Therapeutics for the first time as its new CEO and board chair. Days earlier, in my position as a partner at the venture capital firm Venrock Associates, I had led the acquisition of the company, from the large Germany-based industrial gas company Linde. INO Therapeutics produced inhaled nitric oxide, an FDA-approved gas-form drug used in hospitals to dilate pulmonary blood vessels. Upon acquisition, we immediately combined INO with an early-stage biotech company called Ikaria which I had co-founded with Venrock. Ikaria's technology was created by Seattle-based biochemist Mark Roth who had induced hibernation in mice by exposing them to minute amounts of hydrogen sulfide. With support from several sources including the Defense Advanced Research Projects Agency in the US Department of Defense, we were pursuing important medical applications for this novel technology and saw synergies with the gas-based medical technology at INO. The combined company was renamed Ikaria Holdings.

An immediate concern as the company's new leader was my conviction that the previous corporate owner and leadership team had inadequately engaged the hundred-plus employees sitting before me in the inspirational purpose of the company's life-saving mission. The German parent company had seemingly managed INO very actively, and I wanted to immediately introduce a different paradigm that reflected our new circumstances. It was important to me and to the

Ikaria's INOmax inhaled nitric oxide drug

company's success that team members care deeply about our mission and come to work every day spiritually connected to the importance and purpose of our products.

Standing on stage in the corporate auditorium, I asked a physician and a young couple to join me. The physician, dressed in casual business attire, explained in a warm and sincere tone of voice that he worked in a neonatal intensive care unit (NICU) and had brought the parents of a patient with him for this visit at my request. The woman was holding hands with a young child who was trying to pull away from her. "I can hardly believe I'm here," she began, with a voice full of emotion. "You're the company with the miracle drug. Our baby, Allen, had just been born, and he was having a hard time breathing. I wasn't able to see him and heard that he was in critical condition. I felt completely helpless." Her voice cracked, and she began to sob.

Her husband put his arm around her and continued telling their story. "I was looking through the window of the neonatal intensive care unit, and I could see Allen, who had turned a horrible blue color. I'd been a father for only a few minutes, and already we thought we were going to lose our baby. I was terrified. The NICU pediatrician told us that Allen had a condition called hypoxic respiratory failure,

Chapter Fourteen - Be a Purpose-Driven Force for Good

which means that he was unable to oxygenate his blood. One drug offered hope. The nurses put a mask over his nose and mouth and administered your drug. It was a miracle! I watched as Allen turned pink. Without nitric oxide, our baby boy would have died. Thank you, thank you, thank you," he said, choking up.

I watched the audience as the parents spoke and young Allen roamed around the room. Row upon row of employees had tears in their eyes. By the time Allen's father had emotionally expressed his gratitude, many employees were quietly sobbing. Allen came back to his parents for a hug. After a short break, we reconvened, and I urged everyone to remember this moment anytime they wondered about our purpose as a company.

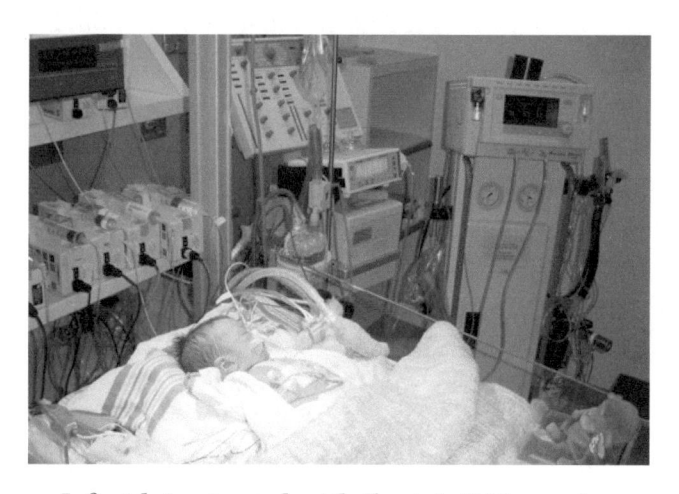

Infant being treated with Ikaria's INOmax drug

It was a culture-shifting moment. Team members better understood important implications of the company's new circumstances. As an independent company, there was no longer a distant parent company sending dictates from headquarters. We needed to navigate by a new north star, and we would thrive by being more emotionally connected to our mission to save babies' lives and provide benefits for cardiac surgery and other applications.

It was 2007, and I wanted very much to leverage my experience at IDEXX, to prove to myself that its exceptional success could be replicated in other domains. In these times of transformational advances in biotechnology, I was particularly interested in having the experience of building a pharmaceutical company. Ikaria Holdings represented this kind of opportunity, and a new entrepreneurial spirit swept through the company as we became masters of our own destiny armed with purpose, exceptional people, profits from INO sales, a pipeline of new products, and a belief that success in business can and should be measured in ways far beyond the prevailing single-minded metric of shareholder value. We supported a high-spirited tribal culture at Ikaria through Outward Bound team-building exercises, paintball battles, and, of course, frequent Shaw-style Shoegolf tournaments. For a company party, the senior management team joined me in creating customized lyrics for the song Age of Aquarius by The 5th Dimension, and we regaled an employee gathering by singing "Age of Ikaria."

In this chapter, I will share my beliefs about business and the important role of capitalism in society. Like many others, I am motivated by business ventures that create exceptional value for many stakeholders in society and always operate with the conviction that business can be a force for good.

***

At IDEXX, Ikaria Holdings, and other enterprises, I seek to create exceptional long-term value for customers and employees as a top priority. My experience has led me to believe that a company can only achieve superlative success via a community of exceptionally motivated mission-driven employees. An organization of outstanding people in a purpose-driven culture is needed to deliver exceptional customer value which drives success. Investors and other stakeholders benefit from customer success driven by great teams. Only after that did I prioritize investors and shareholders. Our approach was less a matter of chasing profits and shareholder value creation, and

Chapter Fourteen - Be a Purpose-Driven Force for Good

more a matter of passionately pursuing vision, and having economic rewards ensue from our business achievements. Larry Fink, CEO of the investment firm BlackRock, expressed an important perspective on profits and purpose with this comment: "Purpose is not the sole pursuit of profits but the animating force for achieving them. Profits are in no way inconsistent with purpose – in fact, profits and purpose are inextricably linked."

In the early days of IDEXX, our leadership wasn't primarily motivated by the dominant Wall Street philosophy of "shareholder primacy" which contends that shareholder profits are the sole measure of success in capitalism. We were deeply committed to creating exceptional shareholder value and we sought to have all IDEXXers be shareholders and operate with the mindset of owners. However, we didn't believe that profits and shareholder value creation should be the sole measure of business success. This concept gained traction in 1970 with the publication of free-market economist Milton Friedman's *New York Times* essay, "A Friedman Doctrine: The Social Responsibility of Business Is to Increase Its Profits." Quoting from his book *Capitalism and Freedom*, Friedman asserts that social responsibility is " a 'fundamentally subversive doctrine.' " He goes on: " '... there is one and only one social responsibility of business– to use its resources and engage in activities designed to increase its profits . . .' "

At the time of the essay's publication, the concept of shareholder primacy was considered to be so unorthodox, as David Gelles writes in *The Man Who Broke Capitalism: How Jack Welch Gutted the Heartland and Crushed the Soul of Corporate America–and How to Undo His Legacy*, that the theory had not yet made its way from academic circles into the public consciousness. For most of human history, the vast majority of businesses have been family-owned, whether they were farms, inns, shops, or everything in between. It wasn't until the Industrial Revolution in the eighteenth and nineteenth centuries that work really started to become corporatized and workers became cogs in a larger whole. Thomas Edison–whose innovative contributions included advancements such as the improved incandescent light bulb and early power plants, founded General Electric (GE) in the late nineteenth century. Edison was as inventive in the way he ran the company as he was in his R&D lab. One of the earliest companies to offer retirement plans, profit-sharing, and health insurance, GE was affectionately known among employees as "Generous Electric," Gelles writes. But it was not the only US corporation back then that looked out for employees and the broader community's well-being. This ethos was enshrined in American business for decades. During the Cold War, many corporate leaders believed that a strong middle class made up of well-compensated, long-term workers, including those who worked in manufacturing, was critical to social stability and served as a bulwark against the spread of political unrest and communism.

According to Gelles, all of that began to change at GE in 1981 when Jack Welch took control as its new CEO, and shareholder primacy became the holy grail. Over the twenty years of what some consider to be a reign of terror, Welch assiduously pared down the company with the sole aim of boosting shareholder returns. Besides selling off or shutting down many of its core businesses, outsourcing others overseas, and acquiring profitable companies far afield from GE's original operations, he beat analysts' expectations nearly every single quarter through what Gelles calls "financial wizardry"– manipulating earnings, buying back stock, and taking on debt.

Nicknamed "Neutron Jack", Welch was well-known for his policy of systematically firing the bottom 10 percent of the workforce annually, leading to the dismissal of more than a hundred thousand employees within his first few years of being in charge. Also offensive to many was the disrespectful way in which Welch talked about the people who worked for him: " 'Shoot them,' he would say when discussing an employee he didn't like," according to Gelles. " 'They ought to be shot.'"

Chapter Fourteen - Be a Purpose-Driven Force for Good

Instead of condemnation, though, this behavior earned Welch praise and a rock-star status previously unheard of for occupants of the C-suite. Before his retirement, Welch was named "Manager of the Century" by *Fortune* magazine, and it was far from alone in heaping praise. Many business schools, Wall Street firms, business reporters, and investors embraced and promoted the idea of shareholder primacy. While history seems likely to judge this less favorably, numerous companies took the playbook Welch created as a literal instruction manual.

IDEXX was created in the midst of shareholder primacy popularity and also in the midst of a golden age of entrepreneurship in America. Along with other baby boomers and people deeply influenced by the disruptive times and idealism of the 1960s, I started my business career with considerable skepticism about shareholder primacy. I was well aware of the astounding benefits of capitalism to society but also wary of extremism versus the need for balance, moderation, and periodic reimagining of important societal institutions. This includes a concern that exceptional success can lead to complacency, stagnation, and future failure.

When the subject of shareholder primacy inevitably came up in our discussions with board members and investors, we sought to be clear that, to take GE as an example, our heroes looked more like Thomas Edison than Jack Welch. Our value proposition was based on growth and innovation by a remarkable community of inspired people, and it worked exceptionally well.

It's important to acknowledge that one aspect of shareholder primacy that appeals to some audiences is the simplicity of having a single metric of success for leading a public company. But that doesn't make it right. Since the reign of shareholder primacy began in 1970, there have been many efforts to reimagine the proper metrics for success in business to better serve society. Increasingly businesses give great consideration to benefits for other stakeholders such as employees, communities, and the environment. A variety of perspectives on this are reflected in models currently being practiced including B corporations, impact investing, citizen capitalism, socially conscious capitalism, stakeholder capitalism, or ESG, which stands for Environmental, Social, and Governance. Recently there has been a movement towards what is known as "impact accounting" that enables accounting for factors such as carbon pledges or other environmental and social liabilities not necessarily tracked in normal accounting practices. Impact accounting has been described "as an evolution of capital accounting that sets out new standardized accounting and valuation principles to account for, track, and disclose an organization's impact on all its capital sources, including natural, social, and human capital."

All of these perspectives reflect a wider and more inclusive role for capitalism, and this is appealing to me in the context of a belief that business must be a force for good in society. A guiding principle for me is that individuals and society benefit from all of us "earthlings" living lives of impact. This has been expressed in a wide variety of ways by many wise people. Rebecca Henderson had this to say in her recent book *Reimagining Capitalism in a World on Fire*: "The only way we will solve the problems that we face is if we can find a way to balance the power of the market with the power of inclusive institutions, and purpose-driven businesses committed to the health of the society could play an important role in making this happen."

In his recent book *Accountable: The Rise of Citizen Capitalism*, my friend Warren Valdmanis and his colleague Michael O'Leary provide a compelling case for the need to reform capitalism, and "save capitalism from itself." They acknowledge the enormous benefits of capitalism but also document the challenges and dangers associated with current practices and doctrines, including this excerpt: "Our most critical social and environmental challenges have been caused, in large part, by the explicit amorality of corporations. Our economy is dominated by the ideology that private vice makes for public

Chapter Fourteen - Be a Purpose-Driven Force for Good

virtue. And so our world is dominated by corporations that reflect no deeper purpose than profit." They join a growing community of thought leaders advocating for reform, calling their proposals "an unsentimental blueprint for how to build an economy that generates prosperity without peril." The need for reform is something I support as a leader in various companies, and in advocacy nonprofit organizations such as JUST Capital.

***

My views about inclusive capitalism have been largely shaped by my own experiences. Soon after graduation, I packed my belongings, jumped on my motorcycle, rode to Maine, and soon shipped out on a 130-foot steel trawler bound for the Grand Banks off Nova Scotia. I had done near-shore fishing but had never been a hired hand on a commercial vessel. This gig provided a great opportunity for experiential learning of the kind experienced by two of my literary icons, Mark Twain, and Jack London, both of whom had put in their time working on the water.

It was an intense experience. Almost as soon as we set off from Portland, a fierce storm created tempestuous conditions including ferocious waves. As the trawler climbed monster wave after monster wave and plunged into equally deep troughs, the entire crew got violently seasick. After being thrown full force from one side of the cabin to the other a few times, I learned to brace both of my hands and feet against my bunk.

Finally, after our vessel passed Sable Island, notorious for being the scene of hundreds of shipwrecks, we put out our trawling gear to fish. Trawling gear scrapes the ocean floor to capture bottom-dwelling fish including the ocean perch that we were targeting. It is an ancient fishing practice, now widely recognized to be very destructive to marine habitats. With the water still churning from the storm, we fished for five days from early morning until well past dark, operating the heavy, dangerous equipment, including giant winches and fast-moving cables. Nets teeming with thousands of pounds of orange-red ocean perch swung across the heaving deck. As fish poured from the nets onto the deck, we scrambled to get them through hatches into the ice bins below.

I piloted our vessel across the Gulf of Maine as most shipmates slept. When we finally arrived back in the Portland Harbor, my inner ear was so traumatized by the rough seas that it took several days for me to regain my balance. The first few nights at home, I fell out of bed because I was so accustomed to the violent pitching of the boat. Decades later, when I read Sebastian Junger's book *The Perfect Storm* about the *Andrea Gail's* doomed voyage, it brought back my own experience—with the fundamental difference that I lived to tell the tale.

Years earlier, my high school jobs had included working in a leather tannery for hourly wages, and in a shoe factory where I was paid by the number of pieces cut per hour from scrap leather. Like my fishing boat experience, these jobs reflected the relatively low value placed on labor in a mechanized world. I found it difficult to gain any real perspective on how my work contributed to the greater mission of the companies that employed me, and the resulting lack of purpose was demotivational.

Early in life when I viewed the corporate world as an unattractive place to work, I was also a consumer of capitalist goods and services that I could clearly see benefited my life, sometimes in remarkable ways. This disconnect fascinated me, and of course, many others in history, seeking to understand how to feel better connected, and spiritually inspired, by living an impactful life.

Today, I acknowledge that as humanity has experimented over the last two centuries with different models to maximize society's well-being, capitalism has proved to be stunningly successful, helping to

Chapter Fourteen - Be a Purpose-Driven Force for Good

raise billions of people out of poverty versus other economic theories like communism and socialism. At the same time, capitalism creates challenges such as income disparities. So while I see private enterprise as a force for good, I recognize that it requires constant stewardship to discourage outcomes that are not in our collective best interests.

JUST Capital is an example of an organization tackling this issue and for several years I have served on its Advisory Board. The mission of JUST Capital is to build an economy that works for all Americans by helping companies improve how they serve all their stakeholders – workers, customers, communities, the environment, and shareholders. Every year we rank companies based on how they serve all of their stakeholders. In partnership with CNBC, we then publicize examples of companies that best meet our criteria as JUST organizations, and those that fall short. Salesforce is an example of a company that has ranked high in our ratings, and this statement by the company's founder/CEO, Marc Benioff, illustrates why: "When we finally start focusing on stakeholder value as well as shareholder value, our companies will be more successful, our communities will be more equal, our societies will be more just, and our planet will be healthier." Mark also issued this warning: "If our quest for greater profits leaves our world worse off than before, all we will have taught our children is the power of greed."

Another important consideration in considering the most appropriate metrics for success in business is an appreciation of the vast size and power of the private sector. In the United States, the private sector represents about twenty-two trillion dollars in economic activity annually compared to less than five trillion dollars for government and philanthropic spending. This vast economic dominance of the private sector puts into perspective the challenges of unwanted consequences if it is not aimed at the right goals.

So, it's important that businesses embrace success in a way that justly benefits society including communities, workers, and the environment. Without the private sector on board, the task is too daunting. Importantly many companies make this choice because it is good for business. Patagonia is an example of a company that has gained great attention and improved its business by embracing corporate social responsibility. Yvon Chouinard, founder of Patagonia, affirmed the company's approach with this statement: "At Patagonia, making a profit is not the goal because the Zen master would say profits happen 'when you do everything else right.'"

Investors can have a significant impact on decisions about who benefits from business success. Consider the example of companies contributing to the emission of gigatons of carbon into our atmosphere, or vast amounts of plastics into our environment. Without an accounting of this expense, shareholders benefit from a cost absorbed by society. For example, if a trillion tons of carbon are emitted into the atmosphere, and trillions of pieces of plastic find their way into the air, soil, and water as a byproduct of shareholder value creation, society must determine if it is willing to tolerate this burden. On the other hand, if businesses are obliged to bear these costs it can have a very positive effect on corporate behavior.

There is growing social pressure on certain asset managers and asset classes such as university endowments and pension funds to invest more responsibly. The 2022 *Report on US Sustainable Investing Trends* shows $8.4 trillion in US sustainable investments under management, or 13 percent of all US assets under management, with a growing focus on climate change and carbon emissions as well as on fair labor practices.

As often happens with change, the growth in more responsible investing has encountered considerable resistance and derision from some sources. A backlash has emerged among some conservative politicians and activists who object to what they have branded "woke capitalism," referring to instances when the private sector takes ESG or "stakeholder" capitalism into consideration in running

Chapter Fourteen - Be a Purpose-Driven Force for Good

their businesses, and in guiding pension and investment decisions. Thoughtful debate about the aims and appropriate management of capitalism is of course entirely fitting to ensure optimal benefits to society. This includes revisiting the focus on social responsibility that Milton Friedman advocated in 1970. I side with those who welcome this debate rather than simply assaulting more responsible investing as wrong-minded. The claim that investing to benefit stakeholders beyond just shareholders results in lower returns for investors, has not been proven with compelling evidence. In fact, there is evidence to the contrary. As of December 2022, our JUST Capital index which tracks the top 100 stakeholder capital companies outperformed the Russell 1000 by more than 13% since inception. Beyond that, our JUST 100 in comparison to peers created more jobs, had better worker safety and environmental performance, paid a higher percentage of family-sustaining wages, provided more career training, and other benefits. Patagonia exemplifies stakeholder capitalism in the retail sector by protecting migrant workers, choosing suppliers with reduced environmental footprints, and offering recycled and sustainable products.

Despite resistance to "capitalism for all," there has been very encouraging progress, and this includes increased attention in the private sector to the concept of achieving a more circular economy. According to a 2023 United Nations report, the world's current "linear" economy is built on a model of extracting raw materials from nature, turning them into products, and then eventually discarding them as waste. Instead of this take-make-waste model, the circular economy mimics the living world, where all organic matter is recycled. A circular economy aims to minimize waste and promote sustainable use of natural resources through better product design, longer use, reuse, recycling, and more. The 2023 UN reported that just ~ 7% of used materials are recycled, and global material consumption continues to rise despite growing success stories as the concept of circularity is adopted by companies, countries, and communities. This improved way of doing things includes reducing and redesigning packaging to make it compostable. Rather than discarding the metals and polymers from outdated or worn-out computers, TVs, office equipment, cell phones, household appliances, and clothing, they are repurposed. The circular approach also means using renewable energy to manufacture and transport new products. The UN has identified the fashion industry as a major culprit in producing carbon emissions and a contributor to water pollution, including microplastics. I have had some direct experience with fashion companies seeking to improve their circularity.

A growing number of companies and organizations are dedicated to making a difference. On a personal level, I am inspired to support these efforts. In addition to my involvement in Modern Meadow, I am advising and investing in innovators such as Arctaris, a global impact investment firm that focuses on infrastructure projects and growth businesses in underserved communities. In 2020, we purchased Saddleback Mountain, a ski area in Maine, that had been shuttered for five years. Since then, we have developed a thirty-one-acre solar farm to generate more than twice the mountain's annual electricity usage which benefits the environment by reducing carbon emissions. Other projects I have supported include the Fish-Free-Feed, or F3 challenge, aimed at preserving threatened fish stocks by replacing the fish meal used in animal feed with more sustainable plant-based ingredients to promote ocean health.

Sustainable Harvest International (SHI) partners with small acreage farmers to adopt regenerative practices that nourish people and the planet, with the goal of removing billions of tons of carbon from the atmosphere by planting trees on deforested land and drawing down billions of tons of carbon by building up soil rich in organic matter. As an advisor to SHI, it inspires me to know that the education and empowerment programs we host with thousands of small-scale farmers can have a transformational impact on environmental degradation and rural poverty. The challenge is to scale this impact to tens of millions of small farms.

Chapter Fourteen - Be a Purpose-Driven Force for Good

"Don't judge each day by the harvest you reap but by the seeds that you plant."
- Attributed to Robert Louis Stevenson

***

There is a coda to the Jack Welch story. While I considered Welch to be an unfortunate role model for capitalism, there is often much to be learned even from those we disagree with. GE had certain performance management systems that I admired. Just as sports teams need to cultivate and support high performers, I have considered performance improvement programs to be critical to success in business.

In organizations I've led everyone gets feedback on "what" they accomplish and also "how" they accomplish things. The "what" is represented in achievements against goals set every year, often including "stretch" goals that are aspirational in nature versus more conservative goals that everyone is expected to achieve. The "how" evaluates whether team members accomplished goals in ways consistent with the core values of the organization. Critically important values for entrepreneurial companies often include innovation, teamwork, customer focus, and an ownership mindset. I believe that everyone, including the CEO, should be evaluated in this way and that the review process is most effective when it includes "360" feedback from others in the organization. Similar reviews help to improve the performance of boards of directors.

Takeaway: One of life's great opportunities and challenges for each of us, and for collective endeavors, is to determine how to best define success … how to measure success. We all need scorecards that are meaningful to us. Of course, it's important to understand societal conventions about measuring success. Yet history is full of examples where these conventions later appear wrong-minded, and progress often requires challenging convention. For each of us individually, modern neuroscience reveals the important role that spiritual inspiration plays in our well-being. Healthier and happier lives are more likely when we are spiritually inspired and fulfilled by our work. This focus on purpose and fulfillment has played an important role in my life. My decision to live a life of entrepreneurship reflects a preference for creating or co-creating purpose and impactful metrics of success rather than operating in a less inspirational framework set by others. Purpose and spiritual inspiration are powerful success factors, and they benefit from authenticity.

A January 2023 article in Forbes magazine entitled Businesses Gain When Purpose and Profit Go Hand in Hand, had this to say: "Businesses with a purpose . . . have a better chance of success in the modern world. Apart from being financially viable, such businesses can also be socially relevant for a long time. Therefore, purpose and profit are not mutually exclusive coordinates. They are symbiotic to the point where one cannot exist without the other." Similarly, the *Harvard Business Review* had this to say about purpose: "Academics argue persuasively that an executive's most important role is to be a steward of the organization's purpose. Business experts make the case that purpose is a key to exceptional performance, while psychologists describe it as the pathway to greater well-being. Doctors have even found that people with purpose in their lives are less prone to disease. Purpose is increasingly being touted as the key to navigating the complex, volatile, ambiguous world we face today."

I hope that my experience and perspective will be helpful to others in seeing the wisdom of challenging conventional thinking and seeking authentic conviction about purpose. This includes conventions such as the doctrine of shareholder primacy which defines success purely in terms of value creation for shareholders, versus other stakeholders. Capitalism has created many benefits for the world, but only in 1970 did its purpose become solely focused on shareholders. The enormous power of the private sector must be a force for good, and it's encouraging to see that this is increasingly recognized in the world. Beyond this example, my experience suggests that it's wise

Chapter Fourteen - Be a Purpose-Driven Force for Good

to beware of adopting conventional thinking versus challenging ourselves to have personal conviction about purpose, based on the impact you seek to have on the world. Be a force for good.

Chapter Fifteen
Never Abandon Optimism

"Make a dent in the universe."
– Steve Jobs

I am deeply grateful for the amazing adventures I have had over the course of my life. These include climbing some of the world's most majestic mountains, trekking extensively in Asia, Africa, and South America, and skiing some of the world's greatest landscapes. I have crossed the finish line of the Boston Marathon, completed several triathlons, and bicycled hundreds of miles across Death Valley. My life has been enriched through inspirational interactions with world leaders, remarkable artists and athletes, game-changing scientists, media celebrities, and intrepid explorers.

And on Halloween 2017, I was feted by my much-loved friend, The Divine Miss M, actress and singer Bette Midler, at the annual high-profile New York Restoration Project gala, Hulaween. Resplendent in a towering Marie Antoinette wig and eighteenth-century, lime-green gown, she stepped to the microphone at the Cathedral of St. John the Divine and introduced me to a crowd that included my family and friends: "It's my great pleasure tonight to honor a man I'm proud to call my friend: David Evans Shaw. I think of him as full of optimism for life on our precious planet. He's an explorer, a teacher, a filmmaker, a successful businessman, and a great advocate for environmental protection."

And indeed, I felt very honored–and humbled by these words.

Each of these experiences has had a great impact on me. But some of the most electric moments in my life have taken place not on mountain peaks or in fancy reception halls, but in university classrooms furnished with industrial-grade wall-to-wall gray carpeting, folding metal tables arranged in a U, uncomfortable plastic chairs, and harsh, overhead fluorescent lighting, democratic in the green pallor it lends to all who enter.

I am grateful for opportunities to offer inspiration to next-generation impact entrepreneurs to help them believe in themselves. I feel that in mentoring others I am honoring people from my own life. In addition to Bob Kinney and Ray Goldberg, another mentor, William "Bill" Pounds, was a treasured source of thoughtful support and sage wisdom, as well as a close friend and fly-fishing companion. A fighter pilot during the Korean War, Bill served as dean of MIT's Sloan School of Management and later advised the Rockefeller family. He was an expert on corporate governance and operations management, and served on boards for a wide range of organizations including IDEXX, General Mills, Putnam Investments, Sun Oil, the Boston Museum of Fine Arts, and WGBH. Working with Bill I had the opportunity to guest lecture periodically in the Sloan Fellows MBA program at MIT where I was inspired to discover that Bill's final assignment to his students was always "Make the world better."

with Bill Pounds

Chapter Fifteen - Never Abandon Optimism

The Sloan School at MIT also arranged for me to be a guest lecturer and mentor at two important universities in China: Tsinghua and Fudan. This eventually led to creating a business in China, with support from an entrepreneurial student in my classes at Fudan University.

I should also mention an important mentorship relationship with Daniel J. Terra, founder of Lawter Chemicals and the Terra Foundation for American Art, who also served as United States Ambassador at Large for Cultural Affairs in the administration of Ronald Reagan. Dan and I became close friends when we explored an investment opportunity together while I was CEO of IDEXX. More than anyone else in my life, he inspired me to appreciate art, and he shared his extraordinary knowledge of American impressionist art. Whether he stayed with us in Maine, or we traveled together to Paris, Chicago, or Washington, DC, I greatly appreciated his friendship and his enthusiasm for sharing his knowledge of business, art, and life.

It was in this spirit of mentorship, in 2021, that I launched a new hands-on, high-impact Shaw family fellowship program at three colleges: the University of Southern Maine, the University of New England, and my alma mater, the University of New Hampshire. Adapting the fellowships to their individual priorities, each university handles them a little differently. But the programs share the same values that I want this book to encourage and convey to readers: explore, learn to see, reject convention, forge your own path, remain open to serendipity, nurture your curiosity about the world, and embrace risk and challenges.

At UNH, the students we choose—mostly sophomores—don't always have the highest GPAs or the most awards in the applicant pool. They stand out by demonstrating a hunger to answer some of the same questions I grappled with at their age: how do you become your most creative and adventurous self? How do you find work that excites you? How do you contribute at a high level? How do you make a difference in the world? How do you live a big, full, and high impact life? It's a privilege to inspire students about these challenges just as I have been inspired by others, including my remarkable friend Jimmy Chin's observation that my own story is one of embracing the human potential for powerful change.

with Shaw Innovation Explorers

The Shaw Explorers program introduces these future disruptors to innovators in science and technology, sustainable businesses, art, and music—individuals who rejected the conventional path. People like acclaimed *National Geographic* marine photographer Brian Skerry, who came and spoke at the University of New Hampshire. After two years at a community college, Brian graduated from Worcester State University while working on a diving charter boat off the Rhode Island coast. He later captured the famous images of President Barack Obama snorkeling in 2016, near the Midway Atoll in the Pacific Ocean, the first time a US president was photographed underwater. Another speaker, Florence Reed, was a Peace Corps volunteer in Panama who went on to found and lead Sustainable Harvest International, a nonprofit enterprise that partners with small-acreage farmers around the world to improve environmental farming practices while alleviating rural poverty. A UNH student in the late 1980s, Flo took over the administration building to protest

CHAPTER FIFTEEN - NEVER ABANDON OPTIMISM

campus recruiting by the Central Intelligence Agency (CIA). A third speaker, Ellen Windemuth, the founder of Waterbear and executive producer of the Academy Award-winning documentary *My Octopus Teacher*, majored in history at Brown University. She talked to the Shaw Explorers about "being brave enough to hire yourself" and then having the conviction that you can do whatever job you're hiring yourself to do. Other speakers have included Marty Odlin, founder of Running Tide, a global ocean health company, Patrick Sweeney, a successful tech entrepreneur and author including *Fear is Fuel*, Andras Forgacs, founder of biomaterials pioneer Modern Meadow, and Jonathan Tower, founder and managing partner of Arctaris Impact Investors.

I try to show examples of people, including myself, who explored and struggled before they discovered what they loved. I want the Fellows to understand that adventurous exploration is a well-recognized path to discovery of purpose and avocation. Living a life of impact often calls for trail-blazing to new and inspirational destinations, rather than following well-traveled paths to familiar places. Our program seeks to support the belief that it's okay to feel restless and discontented with the status quo, in pursuing purpose that is spiritually inspiring.

Feedback from participants in this program has been outstanding including these sample testimonials: " I cannot even begin to describe the ways in which this program has changed my entire view of my future," and "this is the best thing I have ever done." The program was profiled in UNH Magazine in 2023 with the headline: Being a Shaw Innovation Explorer isn't always fun and games. The article includes a program description, examples of activities, powerful endorsements, and this recap of our goal: "to open students' minds to possibilities, but in real and tangible ways, and in a way that adds to what they may be learning during their regular academic schedules."

The UNH Shaw Innovation Explorers have come to my

home to discuss art, science, and other matters intended to develop new perspectives. As a sculptor and collector of sculpture, I enjoy experiencing these art forms with them. We have introduced them to interesting music experiences including a session at my house with a world-famous jazz saxophone player and, of course, they have played vigorous rounds of Shoegolf to help build a sense of tribe. It enriches our lives to forge these meaningful relationships with individuals or groups, young and old, and it serves as a source of hope for the future in a world where we are sometimes inundated with a constant drumbeat of disturbing news.

I love that I get to know these kids, and they get to know me. The one-on-one connections we forge remind me of what it was like to run my companies. I can feel the impact that I am having on these students. It's easy to get down about the pressing issues of our time, the endless drumbeat of worse and worse news we hear every day. But these young people, with their passion and fresh ideas, are a great inspiration and give me hope for the future.

Another reason for my hopefulness is the fact that I survived viral encephalitis and was able to resume the life I love. Our brains have remarkable healing capabilities. No longer are we shackled to the outdated thinking that the brain's structure and abilities are fixed at birth. Doctors now recognize the enormous potential of neuroplasticity—the ability of neural networks to remodel themselves through intentional practices. All of us can build an abundance of new pathways throughout our lives, particularly if we seek out new and challenging activities.

A recent cohort of UNH Shaw Innovation Explorers surprised me with a gift upon graduation from this program, and the significance of that gift is very relevant to my healing process from viral encephalitis, and overcoming other challenges. Their gift was a blue ceramic Kintsugi bowl showcasing the Japanese art of putting broken pottery pieces back together with gold "scars" to create an

Chapter Fifteen - Never Abandon Optimism

even stronger and more beautiful piece of art. Kintsugi art can serve as a metaphor for reframing hardships in life, embracing challenges, and healing ourselves with the hope of a beautiful outcome.

Underscoring the importance that I now place on brain wellness and mental fitness, I embarked in 2022 on a partnership with my friend and Manhattan neighbor, actress and mindfulness advocate Goldie Hawn. We established a collaboration to bring her MindUP preventative mental health program to Maine schools. Goldie founded the program in 2003 after the 9/11 terrorist attacks, recognizing the need to help children develop mental and emotional tools to cope with stress, anger, and other negative feelings. As Goldie puts it, "I had a call to action to create a program that would help kids learn how to self-regulate their emotions, become more resilient, and learn about how their brain works. My intention is to give them a road map out of despair and into a more positive mindset." The program is already used in many schools across the United States and internationally, and it is strongly supported by evidence-based science with direct neurological correlates for each lesson. It's a gratifying experience to work with Goldie and her team, and to see the meaningful impact we are having on the world's growing mental health crisis.

with Goldie Hawn

Wave Making : Inspired By Impact

***

In January 2021, I returned to Telluride, landing at the modern local airport more than fifty years after my memorable experience exploring the Wild West and making gazpacho or other meals in our tiny restaurant. I was there with ski buddies, eager to navigate the fresh powder of Telluride's rugged mountains. One of these skiers was my friend Mark Kozak, Executive Director of the Telluride Science and Innovation Center, and I now serve as a Special Advisor in support of our mission to advance knowledge and discovery as a think tank at the creative crossroads of physics, chemistry, energy, biomedicine, and material science. As the light faded and temperatures plunged after our day on the slopes, I walked along the lively main street of what has become a thriving ski town.

skiing in Telluride, Colorado

I reflected on my life of wave making, about the labor of love impacting consequential challenges of our times, building organizations, providing inspiration for others, and the gift of being inspired by many. It's a welcome source of meaningful accomplishment to bring good jobs, innovative technology, and strong revenues to communities I value, including the state of Maine. With the creation and growth of IDEXX, Covetrus, and other businesses, we have improved the lives of many people, and the Portland area

CHAPTER FIFTEEN - NEVER ABANDON OPTIMISM

has now become an important tech center, including animal health technologies. Another source of fulfillment has been my advocacy for genetics research, ocean stewardship, the conservation of nature, mental health, and other consequential impact programs including science innovation right in Telluride.

It has been rewarding to live a life I love and to make a difference in the world. Rock and Roll Hall of Fame guitarist Carlos Santana, expressed this sentiment beautifully: There is no greater reward than working from your heart, and making a difference in the world. It is also spiritually satisfying and motivational to have achievements recognized, for example via 6 honorary degrees. I'm grateful for remarks made in the granting of honorary doctorate degrees including these:

with Carlos Santana

For demonstrating exemplary character and contributing to the betterment of society.

For your dedication to your field and to people whose lives have been touched by your vision

For distinguishing yourself in so many ways, and propelling yourself to many new ventures, frequently leaving the stable and secure ground of success for risk, adventure, and new challenges, including planetary health and the belief that a well-run business can make the world a better place

For your intellectual, scholarly, and creative achievements

For your lifelong exploration of the social, political, and economic power of the entrepreneur. For asking the question: what does great look like, and committing to considerable initiative and risk. For your leadership in Maine, as well as nationally and globally. For your continuing investigation of the role that arts play in creating new intellectual frontiers

The role that I love most in life is the blessing of being patriarch of a family that includes three remarkable children (Benjamin, Abigail, Eliza) and twelve awesome grandchildren: Lucy, Bella, Jack, Spencer, Anika, Shaw, Hannah, Mia, Ziva, Maxwell, Sawyer, and Scarlett. I often ponder the legacy that we will leave for future generations, inheriting our accomplishments and disappointments. And I am mindful of the responsibilities captured in this wisdom attributed to Abraham Lincoln: "the best way to predict the future is to create it."

Looking up at the stars glimmering above the San Juan Mountains as I walked, exhausted, through the streets of Telluride, I felt elated about honoring my teenage vow to embrace risk, pursue adventure, and have a positive impact on the world. This "north star" has enriched my life. In an old-fashioned saloon I met friends and celebrated an epic day of skiing, a decade of surviving a deadly brain injury, a lifetime of fulfillment ... and a future full of opportunity.

CARPE MAÑANA

"Tell me, what is it you plan to do with your one wild and precious life?"

- Mary Oliver

David E. Shaw family

INDEX

1960s 227

A

AAAS, American Association for the Advancement of Science 200
Abu Dhabi 58
Acadia National Park 30
Africa 3
Agre, Peter 58
Agritech 3
Alaska 26
Albert, Prince 6
Albright, Madeleine 188
Alda, Alan 65
America's Best Leaders 158
America's cup 184
Anders, Bill 29
Anker, Conrad 123
Antarctica 2
Apollo 14
Apple 78
Arafat, Yasser 55
Arctaris Impact Investors 234
Arctic 2
Armstrong, Neil 28
Art of War 136
Aspen Ideas Festival 186
Australia 125

B

B corps 29
Babbitt, Bruce 65
Baribault, Paul 65
Bates 54
Beach bocce 89
Beach Boys 9
Beatles 150
Beethoven 150
Beluga family 223
Bermuda 176
Bernstein, Carl 64
Bhutan 63
Biodiversity 187
Biotech 221
Biotechnology 224
Bisbee 92
Black Point Group 138
BlackRock 225
Blake 26
Blue mountain coffee 44
Bluefin 191
Booker, Chakaia 92
Borman, Frank 14
Bound, Mensun 2
Branson Richard 189
Brokaw, Tom 107
Brown, Jackson 189
Brown, John Seely 64
Buddhism 60
Buffett, Warren 55

C

Campbell, Joseph 40
Canyon Ranch 127
Carnegie 191
Carson, Rachel 24
Carstensz Pyramid 71
Castro, Fidel 58
Center for Public Leadership 158
Cerf, Vinton 64
Chin, Jimmy 65
China 45
Chopra, Deepak 65
Christensen, Clayton 52
Civil War 27
Clifford, Lucille 191
Clinton, Bill 158
College of the Atlantic 211
Compass 49
Cousteau 189
Cousteau 6
Covetrus 101
Covey, Stephen 148
COVID 12
Crisp, Peter 6
Cuba 58
Curie, Marie 1
Curiosity Stream 64

D

D. Roosevelt, Franklin 1
Darwin, Charles 171
Death Valley 197
DeNiro, Robert 5
Department of Agriculture 12
Diagnostics 4
Discovery Channel 64
Drake, Peter 8

E

Earle, Sylvia 189
Earth Day 29
Edison, Thomas 226
Egypt 198
Einstein, Albert 24, 51
Ellen MacArthur Foundation 206
Emerson, Ralph Waldo 33
ESG 228
Everglades 197
Exeter 20
Explorers Club 127

F

Fiennes, Ranulph 5
Fink, Larry 225
Fleming, Alexander 218
Food and Drug Administration 12
Ford, Gerald 158
Forgacs, Andras 207
Friedman, Milton 233

G

Gabon 198
Galvin, Chris 127
Gandhi 19
Gates, Bill 205
Gelles, David 225
Genetics 151
Gergen, David 158
Gladwell, Malcolm 122

Global Philanthropists Circle 200
Gobel, George 21
Goldberg, Ray 41
Golden Claw 65
Good, Mary 55
Goodall, Jane 189
Goodwin, Doris Kearns 64
Gorilla 1
Gorilla Doctors 3
Grand Canyon 67
Great Barrier Reef 189
Greenland 198

H

Haaland, Deb 195
Hall of Fame 156
Hamilton Declaration 180
Harley Davidson 82
Hart, Mickey 111
Harvard Business School 21
Haute Route 67
Hawaii 181
Hawn, Goldie 245
Hazlitt, William 51
Heinlein, Robert 5
Helen, Keller 119
Hemingway, Ernest 10
Henderson Rebecca 228
Hendricks, John 64
Hendrix 24
Henry, Ford 99
High seas 164, 182
Hillman, Henry 135
Hockfield, Susan 7

Hoffer, Eric 213
Holdren, John 60
Homer, Winslow 115
Honduras 67
Huang, Jensen 5

I

Iceland 198
IDEXX 55
IDEXXers 81
Ikaria 162
Ikigai 49
Impact 1
Impact investing 228
India 198
Inspiration 4
Ironwood 151
IUCN, International Union for the Conservation of Nature 7

J

Jackson Laboratory 217
Jackson, Phil 195
Jamaica 44
Japan 44
Jobs, Steve 143, 99
Jomolhari 63
Jones, Jim 65
Joy, Bill 112
Joyce, James 55
JUST capital 229

K

Katmai 197
Keller, Helen 119
Kennedy 28
Khrushchev 58
Kilimanjaro 198
Kinney, Bob 48
Kintsugi 244
Knell, Gary 89

L

Lama, Dalai 61
Leadership 248
Ledecky, Katie 5
Leerink 161
Lennon, John 219
Leshner, Alan Vii
Lin, Maya 91
Liu, Edison 98
Lombardi, Vince 10
London, Jack 27
Longley 11
Longley, James 11
Lucas, George 88
Luther, Martin King 24

M

Ma, YoYo 196
Machu Picchu 198
Maine 201
Mallory, George 121
Mandela, Nelson 75
Marley, Bob 45
McChrystal, Stanley 38
McCullough, David 64

Mencken, H.L. 178
Midler, Bette 239
Miller, Lisa 117
Mills, Janet 196
MIT 106
MIT Sloan School 157
Modern Meadow 207
Monaco 6
Morocco 103
Mt Everest 121
Muir, John 24
Murray, Bill XVii
Myers 160

N

Nabokov, Vladimir 52
Nader, Ralph 37
Nappi 89
Nashua, New Hampshire 174
National Geographic Society 7
National Park Foundation 172
Nationhood Lab 164
NATO 159
Nelson, Willie 110
Netanyahu, Benjamin 55
Neuroscience 163
Ngorongoro Crater 5
NOAA 14
Nobel 219
Nobel Prize 97
Noor Queen of Jordan 189
NVIDIA 5

O

Obama 60
Ocean Elders 189
Ode to Joy 150
Odlin, Marty 243
Oliver, Mary 248
Olympic 94
Ovation 206

P

Paigen, Ken 216
Palau 70
Palmyra 188
Papahānaumokuākea 181
Paralympic 91
Pasteur, Louis 1
Patagonia 198
Pell Center 164
Penobscot 210
Peres, Shimon 55
Phelps, Michael 6
Picasso, Pablo 100
Player, Gary 219
Portland Museum of Art 92
Pounds, Bill 240
Pritzker, Penny 88
Purpose 49

R

Rabin, Yitzhak 55
Raphael, Mickey 110
Reagan, Ronald 158
Reagan, Ronald 241
Red Sox 77
Redford, Robert 88
Remengesau, Tommy 177

Rockefeller 6
Roosevelt, Franklin 1
Roosevelt, Teddy 153
Rwanda 1

S

Saddleback 234
Sages and Scientists 191
Saint-Exupéry, Antoine de 34
San Diego Zoo and Wildlife Alliance 7
Santana 247
Sargasso Sea 176
Sargasso Sea Alliance 171
Science Diplomacy 181
Scotland 198
Seaga, Edward 44
Second century stewardship 191
Service Year Alliance 38
Shackleton, Ernest 2
Shareholder primacy 225
Sharp, Phillip 106
Shaw 152
Shaw, George Bernard 152
Shepard, Alan 28
Shoe golf 65
Spielberg, Steven 88
Stakeholder Capitalism 228
Star Wars 40
Stegner, Wallace 197
Stonehenge 26
Stones, Rolling 23
Sullivan, Kathryn 14
Sustainable Harvest 200
Sweeney, Patrick 243
Synergos 127

T

Taiwan 88
Tanzi 108
Teddy Roosevelt Society 7
Telluride 246
Telluride Science Institute 246
Tennyson 26
Terra, Daniel 241
The Jackson Laboratory, JAX 7
Thompson, Nainoa 185
Thomson, Peter 186
Thorpe, Jim 2
Tibet 61
Tiger's Nest 63
Torres del Paine 198
Tory Burch 208
Tower, Jonathan 243
Twain, Mark 31
Tzu, Sun 136

U

UN Sustainable Development Goals 206
UNH 241
United Nations 177
US-Israel Science and Technology Commission 55

V

Valdmanis, Warren 228
Venrock 65
Veterinary 53
Vets First Choice 101
Vinalhaven 33
Viral encephalitis 244

W

Wabanaki 196
Walsh, Don Viii
Walton, Alice 191
Washington, George 43
Waterbear 164
Webster, Daniel 29
Weir, Bob 190
Whale 211
Wolfowitz 160
Woodruff, Bob 107
Woodstock 23

Y

Yeats 26

Z

Zion 197

Made in United States
Cleveland, OH
27 May 2025